Credentialed Dietetics Practitioners with Disabilities Get the Job Done

Credentialed Dietetics Practitioners with Disabilities Get the Job Done

Editors
Suzanne Domel Baxter, PhD, RD, LD, FADA, FAND
Cheryl Iny Harris, MPH, RD

Copyright © 2024 Suzanne Domel Baxter

All rights reserved.

No part of this book may be reproduced or used in any manner whatsoever without the prior written permission of the publisher except for the use of brief quotations in a book review.

Printed in the United States of America

First Printing, 2024

ISBN 979-8-9912993-1-2

Praise for *Credentialed Dietetics Practitioners with Disabilities Get the Job Done*

"We can all benefit from a deeper understanding of the strength and resilience required for those living with a disability in order to achieve one's goals."
—**Naomi Barbor, MS, RD, LD; Clinical Nutrition Manager, Dietetic Internship Director, Center for Human Nutrition, Cleveland Clinic**

"Thank you to editors, Suzanne Baxter and Cheryl Harris for their work in bringing this powerful book to fruition! This document provides a plethora of information and compelling autobiographies that brings to light the challenges and opportunities that individuals with disabilities face, both in their day-to-day lives and in their quest to become dietetics professionals.

We as Dietetics Professionals have been struggling for years to increase the diversity amongst professional practitioners in Nutrition and Dietetics. Danielle Sykora recognizes this with her statement, "Diversity among dietetic professionals can only lead to an improved ability to better understand, represent and serve a diverse patient population."

I read about a persistence that all those sharing their stories exercised. The energy to persist often detracted from the energy needed to live a normal life and to pursue their chosen profession. I look forward to a time when those with disabilities do not need to expend energy to simply have what able bodied people take for granted.

Some quotes by those providing insight into their lives offered compelling and convincing information for us all to consider. Jordan Griffing stated, "Navigating the world is difficult, and often made much more difficult when disabilities are also thrown in the mix. My advice for future RDs and those with disabilities regardless of occupation is to not give up. I would like to think that with projects like this book we're increasing awareness/education that makes it easier for incoming generations to follow, and maybe one day accessibility won't be something to fight for anymore and will instead be the norm."

Alarmingly, Alena Iris Basa Morales offered, "It was clear that the medical malpractice and access gaps I experienced (and continue to experience) were structurally designed to exclude me and harm me. But disability culture taught me to assert my needs, to get creative and turn my world into a place that works for me."

Cheryl Harris stated the blunt truth when she wrote, "...and this is a public service announcement for the able-bodied folks reading this—disability access isn't a special need. Making sure that co-workers, students or interns have access to a bathroom or food isn't 'special,' it's literally just the bare minimum requirement, and something that everyone should have. There's nothing special about it."

Suzanne Baxter encourages, "If you are a person with one or more disabilities and searching for a career, will you please consider the dietetics profession? It is crucial to diversify the dietetics workforce by increasing the number of credentialed dietetics practitioners with disabilities and from different races, ethnicities, and genders."

Thank you for this compelling book! I look forward to changes that allow those with disabilities to pursue their life goals in unencumbered environments."

—Ethan A. Bergman, PhD, RDN, CDN, FADA, FAND, MDiv;
Vicar, Grace Episcopal Church, Ellensburg, WA;
Emeritus Professor of Food Science and Nutrition,
Central Washington University;
2012-2013 President, Academy of Nutrition and Dietetics

"As someone who has a degree in nutrition and completed a Dietetic Internship, I found that my education lacked exposure to inclusive nutrition concepts. My understanding came primarily from personal experiences and conversations with friends with disabilities. The narratives shared by registered dietitians with disabilities in this book are empowering and illustrate the importance of self-advocacy. This book is essential reading for dietitians, healthcare professionals, and anyone interested in the intersection of nutrition and disability. It serves as both a practical guide and powerful call to action. Thank you for your commitment to inclusion!"

—Rebecca Cline, MPH,
Special Assistant to the CEO, Lakeshore Foundation

"Congratulations on the first book of its kind. This book includes a diverse and inclusive group of authors addressing disabilities in the dietetics profession by practitioners serving different communities of people with different needs. It is impressive that these dietitians are also living with disabilities. It is important for dietitians to know their audience to identify with their culture and norms. This is an excellent resource for all allied healthcare professionals. The authors expressed lived experiences and included scientific bases for the information provided. Hopefully, this book will help to recruit others living with a disability to know that there is a place for them in the profession of dietetics. Congratulations to Dr. Baxter and the 14 authors who contributed to this much needed body of work."

—**Evelyn F. Crayton, EdD, RDN, LDN, FAND;**
Professor Emerita, Auburn University;
2024 Lifetime Achievement Award and 2015-2016 President,
Academy of Nutrition and Dietetics;
Chair, Alabama Board of Examiners, Nutrition and Dietetics;
Director, Living Well Associates, LLC

"*Credentialed Dietetics Practitioners with Disabilities Get the Job Done* is a book that opens a door into the world of dietetics providing insight into the Academy of Nutrition and Dietetics, the essential volunteerism and grass roots work of the many different groups that make up the Academy, and the passion many practitioners have for their chosen career.

This book can be recommended to anyone contemplating a career in dietetics as well as for Human Resource Departments to guide them in hiring individuals with a disability and by anyone who wants to be inspired by the true and very personal stories that are shared here.

The editors are accomplished RDs who also have a disability. They offer a roadmap for anyone interested in becoming an RD to learn more about it. They clearly explain the many disability resources now available to help students achieve their goals to become credentialed and to obtain a job in the field of dietetics.

To make it real, fifteen dietetics practitioners provide autobiographies of their journey to become credentialed. As they share their stories you will see that with the right supports and a willingness to try, individuals with disabilities including those that affect vision, hearing, the immune system, and many other conditions can complete college, internships, and become gainfully employed.

These dietetics practitioners have shared their unique stories to help, inspire, and shine a light on the need to increase diversity in the field of dietetics to include individuals with a disability, seen or unseen. As you will see as you read this book, it is not easy for anyone to obtain the Registered Dietitian Credential, and even more difficult for someone with a disability to attain it.

There are chapters devoted to resources and organizations that help individuals with disabilities navigate college and careers.

Finally, this book is a volunteer fundraising project where all of the book royalties will be donated to the new Disabilities in Nutrition and Dietetics Member Interest Group to help the group share their knowledge with the dietetics workforce."

—**Jean Daniello, MS, RDN, LDN, ADCES; Nutrition Director, Regional Institute Children and Adolescents Baltimore, Maryland Department of Health; 2019-2025 Intellectual and Developmental Disabilities Resource Professional, Behavioral Health Nutrition Practice Group, Academy of Nutrition and Dietetics**

"*Credentialed Dietetics Practitioners with Disabilities Get the Job Done* highlights the expertise that dietitians with disabilities bring to their practice. As someone passionate about advancing inclusivity, I found the stories and insights in this book invaluable. The authors break down barriers and highlight practical strategies that not only serve those with disabilities but enhance the field of nutrition. This book invites readers to contribute to a truly inclusive field where all professionals can thrive."

—**Lacey Gammon, MPH, RD, LD Nutrition Coordinator, Lakeshore Foundation**

"Disabled people add value to every profession, and I am grateful for this new resource that will help to attract and support dietetics practitioners with disabilities in the United States and beyond. I encourage employers, disabled people who are interested in dietetics and nutrition as a career, and government agencies and service providers who support career development and job placement

for people with disabilities to take advantage of the knowledge and suggestions that this book provides."
—**Andy Imparato, Executive Director, Disability Rights California; Former President and CEO, American Association of People with Disabilities**

"The book *Credentialed Dietetics Practitioners with Disabilities Get the Job Done* provides extensive information about a career in nutrition and dietetics in the context of life with a disability. The importance of being a 'credentialed' practitioner is a key point. The autobiographies are invaluable as they can help individuals – both disabled and not, to understand at least in part – the challenges of embarking on a career in nutrition with physical or health challenges. A common theme is advocacy, finding your support 'team,' and perseverance. This book can help the reader find those three 'themes' for their own life. There is nothing like seeing someone else's story to realize you are not the only one. There are important resources provided early in the book and in the ending chapters. Having worked for many years with people requiring home parenteral and/or enteral nutrition support for multiple reasons, the content resonates as something I have seen – resilience, finding something deep inside – maybe that they didn't even know they had – and moving forward. This should be a must have for health care practitioners of all disciplines. Highly recommended...for all."
—**Carol Ireton-Jones, PhD, RDN, FASPEN, FAND, Nutrition Therapy Specialist, Good Nutrition for Good Living**

"This book provides a fresh perspective on disability culture and employment as seen through the experiences of credentialed dietetics practitioners with disabilities, highlighting the unique challenges and achievements in the profession. It emphasizes the need for inclusive practices and representation in nutrition, making it a must-read for anyone dedicated to advancing equity for individuals with disabilities."
— **John D. Kemp, President & CEO of Lakeshore Foundation; Author of *Disability Friendly: How to Move from Clueless to Inclusive***

"By sharing their journeys through education, internships, and professional practice, these fifteen practitioners offer powerful testimony to the capabilities of disabled professionals in dietetics. The authors' personal stories and experiences combined with practical resources, make this book essential reading for anyone committed to building a more diverse and accessible dietetics workforce."

—**Matthew Landry, PhD, RDN, DipACLM, FAND, FAHA,
Assistant Professor of Population Health and Disease Prevention,
University of California, Irvine**

"This book provides great insight into the challenges and opportunities associated with being an RDN or NDTR with disabilities. While the primary goal of the book is to attract more practitioners with disabilities so patients and clients can connect with a nutrition professional who truly understands their challenges and can provide strategies to improve their health, there are many more reasons to read this book! The principles included can help all people learn to thrive, regardless of if they have a disability, and can foster empathy so that we can all advocate for better accommodations as needed. The autobiographies provide inspiration to overcome current and future challenges and embrace their uniqueness, both for visible and invisible disabilities. I found each person's story to be fascinating, compelling, and motivating to learn more and be more aware of the environment around us."

—**Wendy Phillips, MS, RD, LD, FAND, FASPEN,
Regional Vice President, Morrison Healthcare**

"*Credentialed Dietetics Practitioners with Disabilities Get the Job Done* is an essential resource for anyone in the dietetics profession or considering it. Through candid, powerful stories from dietetics practitioners with disabilities, this book sheds light on the resilience, creativity, and determination that drive success in the field. It highlights the unique insights these practitioners bring to their work, offering an inclusive perspective that both celebrates and normalizes disability. With practical advice on navigating accommodations, overcoming barriers, and fostering disability pride, this book is a beacon of empowerment for future generations. All royalties support the Disabilities in Nutrition and Dietetics Member Interest Group, furthering the mission of accessibility, equity, and inclusion in dietetics."

Peter D. Poullos, MD,
Clinical Professor of Radiology, Gastroenterology, and Hepatology;
Founder and Co-Chair, Stanford Medicine Alliance for Disability
Inclusion and Equity (SMADIE)

"*Credentialed Dietetics Practitioners with Disabilities Get the Job Done* amazes the reader with its breadth of information about disability resources and inspiring, candid autobiographies of individuals who pursue varied career goals in dietetics in the face of often daunting odds. The stories are touching and sometimes heartbreaking tales of resilience, commitment, and dedication to improving the nutritional health of individuals and challenging accessibility issues in education and employment. The passion Dr. Baxter, Ms. Harris, and their colleagues have for these topics stems from extensive personal experience and unparallelled devotion to equity and accessibility for all. Highly recommended for dietetics professionals at all levels, educators, guidance counselors, and human resources employees to foster awareness about disability etiquette, resources, and the dedication to excellence that clearly inspired the authors and their collaborators."

—Mary Russell, MS, RDN, CD, FAND, FASPEN,
Assistant Clinical Professor (Adjunct),
Rosalind Franklin University of Medicine and Science;
Delegate to the House of Delegates for the Disabilities in Nutrition
and Dietetics Member Interest Group;
2018-2019 President, Academy of Nutrition and Dietetics

Dedication

This book is dedicated to a profession of nutrition and dietetics that is action-oriented to be inclusive, diverse, equitable, and accessible in order to better serve and support dietetics students, interns, and practitioners as well as clients and patients from all demographic categories with and without disabilities.

All royalties from this book will be donated to the Disabilities in Nutrition and Dietetics Member Interest Group to help achieve its purpose, mission, vision, and goals.

Table of Contents

Praise
Dedication
Preface
Acknowledgements

Chapter 1   1
Introduction
By Cheryl Iny Harris, MPH, RD

Chapter 2   5
The Academy of Nutrition and Dietetics (or "Academy")
By Suzanne Domel Baxter, PhD, RD, LD, FADA, FAND

Chapter 3   13
The Disabilities in Nutrition and Dietetics Member Interest Group (or "Disabilities MIG")
By Suzanne Domel Baxter, PhD, RD, LD, FADA, FAND

Chapter 4   31
Dietitians and Dietetics Technicians (or "Dietetics Practitioners"): What They Are and How to Become One
By Suzanne Domel Baxter, PhD, RD, LD, FADA, FAND

Chapter 5   41
State Vocational Rehabilitation Programs and Centers for Independent Living
By Suzanne Domel Baxter, PhD, RD, LD, FADA, FAND

Chapter 6 (Autobiography)   51
Dietitian with a Mobility Disability
By Suzanne Domel Baxter, PhD, RD, LD, FADA, FAND

Chapter 7 (Autobiography)   61
The Journey of an RD with Cerebral Palsy (or CP)
By Ryan Branson, MS, RD

Chapter 8 (Autobiography) 67
Debility, Passion, and Balance
By Catherine (Katie) Brown, MS, RD, CDN

Chapter 9 (Autobiography) 83
Driven by Vision
By Alicia Connor, MA, RDN & Chef

Chapter 10 (Autobiography) 91
Finding Dietetics Post-Spinal Cord Injury
By Liz Dunn, MS, RD, LDN

Chapter 11 (Autobiography) 97
A Registered Dietitian with Autoimmune Diseases
By Amy Epting, MA, RD, CSG, LDN

Chapter 12 (Autobiography) 105
The Evolution of a Celiac Dietitian
By Renee Euler, MS, RDN

Chapter 13 (Autobiography) 111
Inflammatory Bowel Disease (or IBD) RD
By David Gardinier, RD, LD

Chapter 14 (Autobiography) 121
Practice Resilience and Never Give Up the Goal of Becoming a Registered Dietitian
By Susan K Greener, BSN, DTR

Chapter 15 (Autobiography) 137
Chronically Fascinating
By Jordan Griffing, MS, RD, LD

Chapter 16 (Autobiography) 147
Nourishing Resilience: The Story of a Gastrointestinal (or GI) Dietitian
By Cheryl Iny Harris, MPH, RD

Chapter 17 (Autobiography)   155
How Disability Pride Catalyzed My Path to Dietetics
By Alena Iris Basa Morales, RD/RDN

Chapter 18 (Autobiography)   169
Nourished by Trust: A Blind Dietitian and her Loyal Guide Dog
By Danielle Sykora, BS, MS, RDN

Chapter 19 (Autobiography)   185
My Journey into Dietetics as A Disabled, Chronically Ill Dietitian
By Juliana Tamayo, MS, RD, LDN, CNSC

Chapter 20 (Autobiography)   197
Breaking through the Silence: My Journey to Becoming a Registered Dietitian as a deaf Individual
By Wendy Wittenbrook, MA, RD, CSP, LD, FAND

Chapter 21   211
Disability Resources
By Suzanne Domel Baxter, PhD, RD, LD, FADA, FAND

Chapter 22   245
Disability Statistics
By Suzanne Domel Baxter, PhD, RD, LD, FADA, FAND

Chapter 23   253
Concluding Remarks
By Suzanne Domel Baxter, PhD, RD, LD, FADA, FAND

About the Editors

Preface

The editors and autobiographical authors agreed to participate in this book with the knowledge that all royalties from book sales will be donated for projects (to help achieve the purpose, mission, vision, and goals) of the Disabilities in Nutrition and Dietetics Member Interest Group, or "Disabilities MIG" for short. The editors organized, edited, and self-published the book. Instead of payment, each autobiographical author and editor will receive two copies of the published book, and payment of $100 total to the Academy of Nutrition and Dietetics towards their Disabilities MIG membership annual dues. Writing and editing this book was a journey of passion, volunteer effort, and learning. Neither the Academy of Nutrition and Dietetics, nor the Disabilities MIG, provided funds to create this book.

Each autobiographical author was asked to address the following items in their chapter, and in whatever order they desired:

1. Describe your disability and accommodations used for daily life.
2. Explain why you chose a career in nutrition and dietetics.
3. If applicable, specify support you received from a state Vocational Rehabilitation Program and/or Center for Independent Living in your state.
4. Indicate where you earned your college degree(s) in nutrition and dietetics, accommodations used for college, and how you requested and obtained accommodations for college.
5. Specify where you completed your dietetic internship or equivalent, accommodations you used for it, and how you requested and obtained accommodations for it.
6. Describe the accommodations you needed to take the credentialing exam and how you requested them.
7. Explain where you have worked as a credentialed dietetics practitioner, accommodations you used for this employment, and how you requested and obtained the accommodations.
8. Describe your primary job responsibilities for each of your jobs as a credentialed dietetics practitioner.

9. Explain the methods you use to network with colleagues in the dietetics profession.
10. Indicate your volunteer and/or leadership activities in the dietetics profession.
11. Describe your disability culture concerning shopping for food, preparing food, and eating.
12. Share advice you have for future generations of dietetic practitioners with disabilities.
13. Indicate advice you have for dietetic practitioners without disabilities with whom you work and/or serve in volunteer roles and/or leadership roles.
14. Describe whether you disclose your disability, when you disclose it, and what you disclose.
15. Explain if there is anything (e.g., advice, guidelines, resources) you would do differently. If you could rewind the clock, what would you tell yourself and/or do differently as a college student, dietetics intern, or employee with disabilities? Or would you not change anything?
16. Include anything else that is relevant to your disability but not covered in a previous item.

In addition to the 15 autobiographical chapters, this book includes chapters intended to provide disability information concerning many key aspects as summarized in the following bullets:

- **Statistics:** Disability prevalence has and will continue to increase as our nation's population grows older on average and because of long COVID. If you or a member of your family do not already have a disability, you and/or a family member will more than likely experience disability at some point in the future. Chapter 22 provides key disability statistics.
- **Diversity:** Disabilities are diverse in type as well as within types. For example, the authors of autobiographical chapters 13 and 19 identified Crohn's disease as a disability, but it impacts them quite differently. Also, the authors of autobiographical chapters 9, 16, and 18 have vision impairment, but they navigate their environments quite differently.

- **Culture:** Disability culture challenges negative stereotypes and focuses on empowerment, community, and the human experience by emphasizing the strengths, creativity, and contributions of disabled people. Disability culture includes accessibility and inclusion, pride and identity, art and expression, language and representation, and activism and rights. The 15 autobiographical chapters offer insight into disability culture concerning nutrition and dietary intake including what one can eat, shopping for food, preparing food, and eating and drinking whether at home, at work, or when traveling.
- **Accommodations:** People with disabilities require various accommodations to navigate the world. The autobiographical chapters and resource chapters include details about the accommodations required to navigate college/university, internship, dietetics credentialing exam, work, and volunteer efforts.
- **Dietetics Profession:** Dietetics practitioners work in a variety of settings including hospitals and clinics, foodservice (in hospitals, school districts, colleges and universities, day-care centers, prisons, and companies), private practice businesses, community and public health, sports nutrition, the food industry, teaching/education (in colleges, universities, and internships), the military, government agencies, research, and more. Chapter 4 explains what dietetics practitioners are and do and how to become one. The 15 autobiographical chapters explain the various settings in which the authors have worked or are working as dietetics practitioners with disabilities and their key job responsibilities in each setting.
- **Resources:** Despite the numerous disability resources for disabled people as well as for educators of disabled students, preceptors of disabled interns, and/or family members, colleagues, or managers/supervisors of disabled people, awareness of these resources is limited. Chapter 5 provides an overview of state Vocational Rehabilitation Programs and Centers for Independent Living, and Chapter 21 summarizes numerous additional disability resources. By increasing

awareness of these resources, hopefully more people with disabilities will use and benefit from them.
- **Disabilities MIG:** After seven years of advocacy and volunteer efforts, the Disabilities MIG launched on June 1, 2023. The Disabilities MIG is a group within the Academy of Nutrition and Dietetics. All members of the Academy who are disabled, who work with people with disabilities, or who advocate for disability justice are encouraged to join the Disabilities MIG, whether student, active, or retired. Chapter 2 provides an overview of the Academy. Chapter 3 explains the history, purpose, vision, mission, and goals of the Disabilities MIG.

This book is intended to be a resource for readers from numerous groups including the following:
- individuals with disabilities who are exploring career options in the profession of nutrition and dietetics,
- dietetics students and interns with disabilities on their journeys to become credentialed dietetics practitioners,
- educators of students with disabilities,
- preceptors of interns with disabilities,
- staff at government agencies and service providers who support career development and job placement for people with disabilities,
- managers and supervisors of people with disabilities, and
- family members, colleagues, and friends of people with disabilities.

Thank you for your interest in disabilities and the dietetics profession, and for reading this book!

Acknowledgments

The editors are extremely grateful to the 15 autobiographical authors who shared their journeys of becoming and working as credentialed dietetics practitioners with disabilities.

The editors sincerely appreciate Joan Thomas, MS, RDN for her valuable input and help proofreading this book.

Chapter 1
Introduction

By Cheryl Iny Harris, MPH, RD

First, thank you for taking the time to read this book. We're grateful to have you with us here.

Why did we decide to write this book?

Disabilities are common; about a quarter of the US population has a disability. There are significantly fewer credentialed dietetics professionals with disabilities than expected based on the prevalence of disabilities in the general population. While that might not sound significant, often professionals living with a disability may have better insight into the daily challenges and solutions than someone less intimately familiar with these conditions.

People want health care practitioners who understand their lived experiences, who can relate to their challenges, and who have learned the tips and tricks along the way that come from daily experimentation. People with disabilities may feel more comfortable relating to a practitioner with similar life challenges and experiences, and may be more likely to follow recommendations when there is a sense of mutual understanding. And, of course, representation matters in every space.

The primary goal of this book is to attract more disabled practitioners to the profession of dietetics. We want people with disabilities to recognize that dietetics is a viable career option. We've highlighted Registered Dietitians (RDs) also known as Registered Dietitian Nutritionists (RDNs), and Dietetics Technicians, Registered (DTRs) also known as Nutrition and Dietetics Technicians, Registered (NDTRs) with a range of disabilities, and how they navigated their way through colleges/universities, exams, accommodations, internships, job interviews, and the array of formal and informal systemic barriers, ranging from structural challenges, like the inaccessible elevator, or the teachers, mentors, co-workers, etc. who might not have been fully supportive. It also includes the supports, like the supervisor who provided encouragement, short-term medical leave, flexible hours, or advocated for us in some way. Ultimately, it's the stories of how each of us found their own way to thrive. Hopefully, this will provide people with disabilities who are interested in the profession with ideas, inspiration and motivation for the path ahead. If you're considering a career in dietetics, ideally these stories will help you recognize potential opportunities and options based on the experiences of others. Also, this book includes several informational chapters to give readers some basics about the dietetics profession along with disability resources.

    A secondary goal is to help our fellow dietetics professionals to learn about us — credentialed dietetics practitioners with disabilities — our strengths, our challenges, our culture of disability, and what they can do to be better colleagues, allies, teachers, and mentors for us in every phase of our careers. Most likely it will give the opportunity to challenge the beliefs each of us hold about people with disabilities, because whether we are disabled or not, we're steeped in an ableist culture, and it's easy to underestimate our colleagues. This book's chapters on disability resources will be helpful to our colleagues without disabilities, too.

    This book was disability-driven from start to finish. The idea was envisioned by credentialed dietetics practitioners with disabilities, it was planned, funded, written, revised, published, and advertised by credentialed dietetics practitioners with disabilities. While we absolutely want all people to learn from the book, it is intended as a tool for people with disabilities to learn more about the dietetics profession. I know I learned more as I was reading the chapters, and learning from my colleagues helps me in my work with patients. While disability advocates provided support in various ways during the project, the voices in this book are the voices of credentialed dietetics professionals with disabilities, and the process centered the views and priorities of members of the disability community. Nothing about us without us.

    This book focuses on RDs/RDNs and DTRs/NDTRs with a range of disabilities. We're featuring 14 RDNs and one NDTR. Collectively, our disabilities span from visible disabilities such as cerebral palsy and quadriplegia due to spinal cord injury, to disabilities that may not be visible, such as ADHD, bipolar disorder, hearing loss, lupus, Postural Orthostatic Tachycardia Syndrome (POTS), Ehlers Danlos syndrome, blindness, impaired vision, vision loss, Sjögren's Syndrome, scleroderma, Eosinophilic Esophagitis, vestibular migraines, endometriosis, Celiac disease, Crohn's disease, and erythromelalgia. Most but not all of us became credentialed dietetic practitioners after our disabilities were acquired. Some of us are at the start of our careers; some of us are retiring.

It may be easy to presume that our collective laundry list of challenges might keep us from excelling at our jobs as credentialed dietetics practitioners. Actually, many of us work with people with disabilities similar to our own, where the knowledge gained from living with our disability has become a vital asset. Others have found ways to adapt to the challenges of disabilities and are working in settings including eating disorders, private practice, business/industry, pediatrics and clinical, sports, and culinary nutrition.

This also isn't an inspirational book that glosses over the real challenges many of us have faced along the way due to our disabilities. Many of the chapters do point out shortcomings of different institutions, and give concrete suggestions of ways our colleagues and the systems can be changed to make things more inclusive. It's a given that pain and fatigue are barriers, but the lack of accommodation of institutions often create much larger pains and barriers than any disability could possibly create. I'm hoping credentialed dietetics practitioners without disabilities give thought to ways they can be allies.

One of the things that jumped out to me as I read the chapters of the book is that for each of the authors, our disabilities impacted us and shaped how we practice dietetics. They made us more resilient, empathic, and creative. We learned how to find a way to get what we needed in systems that sometimes weren't as supportive as they might have been. I feel comfortable saying that each of us is involved with the Disabilities in Nutrition and Dietetics Member Interest Group (or Disabilities MIG), at least in part, in an effort to make the path easier for future generations of dietetics professionals with disabilities.

The statistics in a nutshell:

Disabilities are common. According to the Centers for Disease

Control and Prevention, 27% of the US adult population has a disability. Although those numbers will likely shift as definitions and demographics change, there's a particular power of representation.

Data from the Academy of Nutrition and Dietetics (Academy) indicate that around 3% of employed current dietetics practitioners reported having a disability. The survey also indicated that 2% of dietetics practitioners were not working due to their disability. This suggests both that there are barriers to working in the field of dietetics for practitioners with disabilities, and factors that make it difficult for dietetics practitioners with disabilities to get and retain meaningful work, and/or challenges obtaining the necessary accommodation(s).

Clearly, as a profession, we have a long way to go. Recent efforts to organize, such as this book, the Disabilities MIG through the Academy, educational webinars, and more are concrete steps. All revenue from this book's royalties will also be used to provide funding for projects of the Disabilities MIG to achieve its purpose, vision, mission, and goals.

And, of course, entry into the field as credentialed dietetics practitioners is just scratching the surface.

Thank you for embarking on this journey with us.

Last, but not least, I want to thank my co-editor and co-conspirator, Suzi Baxter. Very literally, this project would not have gotten off the ground without Suzi's creativity and tenacity; in so many ways, Suzi has done so much to make the Academy a more welcoming place for people with disabilities.

Chapter 2
The Academy of Nutrition and Dietetics (or "Academy")

By Suzanne Domel Baxter, PhD, RD, LD, FADA, FAND

The Academy of Nutrition and Dietetics (or simply "Academy") is the largest organization in the world of food and nutrition professionals. The Academy is committed to improving the nation's health and advancing the profession of nutrition and dietetics through research, education, and advocacy. A Board of Directors of national leaders in nutrition and health leads the Academy. The House of Delegates governs the profession of nutrition and dietetics. The Academy was founded as the American Dietetic Association in 1917 and changed its name in 2012 to the Academy of Nutrition and Dietetics.

Academy members include about 72% registered dietitians (RDs) also known as registered dietitian nutritionists (RDNs) and 2% dietetics technicians, registered (DTRs) also known as nutrition and dietetics technicians, registered (NDTRs). Other members include allied health professionals, educators, researchers and students. Over half of Academy members hold advanced academic degrees. Academy members work in a variety of settings including hospitals and long-term care facilities, public health, foodservice management, nutrition counseling, private practice, grocery stores and chains, the food industry, education systems, education of other health care professionals, the military, the government, and research. The Academy has the following campaigns:

- **National Nutrition Month**® is celebrated each March to promote healthful eating and provide practical nutrition guidance. During National Nutrition Month®, the Academy offers consumers timely, objective food and nutrition

information through numerous programs and services.
- **Registered Dietitian Nutritionist Day** is celebrated on the second Wednesday each March to recognize the contributions of RD/RDNs to the health of the public.
- **Nutrition and Dietetics Technician, Registered Day** is celebrated on the second Thursday each March to recognize the contributions of DTR/NDTRs in the delivery of safe, culturally competent, quality food and nutrition services.
- **Kids Eat Right Month®** is celebrated each August to highlight the role that everyone — from RD/RDNs to DTR/NDTRs to parents and educators — has to ensure a healthy future for children. Kids Eat Right Month® focuses on the importance of healthful eating and active lifestyles for children and families, featuring expert information from RD/RDNs and DTR/NDTRs.

The Academy's headquarters office is located at 120 South Riverside Plaza, Suite 2190, Chicago, IL 60606.

The remaining sections of this chapter summarize the many organizational units of the Academy.

Academy Foundation. The Academy Foundation is a 501(c)(3) public charity. Its mission is to fund the future of nutrition and dietetics through research and education. The Foundation is the largest grantor of scholarships in nutrition and dietetics; it also provides support for research, education, and public awareness programs.

Dietetic Practice Groups or "DPGs." The DPGs are professional-interest groups of Academy members to connect with other members within their areas of interest and/or practice. The DPGs allow their members to enhance their specialized knowledge, share practice tips, improve their job performance, and network with colleagues from around the world. Academy members pay annual dues to join one or more DPGs. The DPG dues are separate from Academy dues. The DPGs are legal groups within the Academy. Currently, the Academy has more than two dozen DPGs; their names and brief descriptions follow:
- **Behavioral Health Nutrition DPG:** Members of this DPG work with clients in areas including addictions, mental health, eating disorders, and intellectual and developmental disabilities.

- **Cardiovascular Health and Well-being DPG:** Members of this DPG are nutrition experts in promoting cardiovascular health (prevention and treatment), well-being, and physical activity.
- **Clinical Nutrition Management DPG:** Members of this DPG strive to improve the quality of nutrition care in the health industry including acute care, community services, long-term care, private practice, and government services.
- **Diabetes DPG:** Members of this DPG optimize the prevention and management of diabetes through person-centered care.
- **Dietetics in Health Care Communities DPG:** Members of this DPG provide person-centered nutritional services across the care continuum — including post-acute rehab, nursing facilities, home health, hospice, assisted living, and memory care — to promote evidence-based science and best practices in dining and clinical nutrition services.
- **Dietitians in Business and Communications DPG:** Members of this DPG have the necessary business skills to guide food and nutrition related decisions in global business and industries.
- **Dietitians in Integrative and Functional Medicine DPG:** Members of this DPG share a core philosophy that centers around a holistic, personalized approach to health and healing in order to integrate a variety of nutrition therapies including whole foods, tailored supplements, and mind-body modalities in clinical practice.
- **Dietitians in Medical Nutrition Therapy DPG:** Members of this DPG are nutrition generalists or specialists who work in a variety of settings including hospitals, long term care, assisted living, hospice outpatient clinics, dialysis clinics, industry, and corporate wellness programs.
- **Dietitians in Nutrition Support DPG:** Members of this DPG are health care practitioners who integrate the science of enteral and parenteral nutrition support to individuals in inpatient and outpatient settings.
- **Food and Culinary Professionals DPG:** Members of this DPG

are committed to developing food expertise throughout the dietetics profession by increasing food and culinary skills and knowledge among Academy members, enhancing the ability of Academy members to shape the food choices and impact the nutritional status of the public, improving the quality of life and health of the public, and expanding career opportunities for Academy members.
- **Healthy Aging DPG:** Members of this DPG are a valued source of information on healthy aging who believe the health and wellness of older adults is improved by optimal nutrition and physical activity.
- **Hunger and Environmental Nutrition DPG:** Members of this DPG optimize the nation's health by promoting access to safe, nutritious food and clean water from a secure, equitable, and sustainable food system.
- **Management in Food and Nutrition Systems DPG:** Members of this DPG are key leaders and decision makers on institutional and retail menus, raw products, equipment, and supplies as foodservice directors or in other leadership roles in food management and systems in hospitals, schools/universities, long-term care/rehabilitation/senior living, and other settings.
- **Nutrition Education for the Public DPG:** Members of this DPG promote nutrition through public education and interact with other nutrition professionals working in business and management, food industry, education, clinical dietetics, health promotion, nutrition counseling and private practice, public health and community nutrition, and communications and public relations.
- **Nutrition Educators of Health Professionals DPG:** Members of this DPG work in various settings including academic, clinical, community, research, industry, and government to educate other health professionals of all levels about nutrition.
- **Nutrition Entrepreneurs DPG:** Members of this DPG are dietetic practitioners with diverse entrepreneurial interests including authors, coaches, corporate health specialists,

private practice practitioners, and technology experts, as well as those exploring other entrepreneurial possibilities.
- **Nutrition Informatics DPG:** Members of this DPG are interested in nutrition informatics which encompasses electronic health records, standards and terminology, telehealth, patient-to-provider secure messaging, electronic discharge summaries of care, health information exchange, and more.
- **Oncology Nutrition DPG:** Members of this DPG practice oncology nutrition including research, prevention, treatment, recovery, palliative care, and hospice and work in clinical, public health, education, and research settings.
- **Pediatric Nutrition DPG:** Members of this DPG work in health care facilities, state and federal agencies, business and industry, and colleges and universities as experts and leaders in the promotion of infant, child, and adolescent nutrition.
- **Public Health/Community Nutrition DPG:** Members of this DPG apply nutrition principles and interventions in public health and community settings.
- **Renal Dietitians DPG:** Members of this DPG work in nutrition care involving the kidneys.
- **Research DPG:** Members of this DPG are nutrition and dietetic professionals who conduct, disseminate, interpret, and apply food, nutrition, and dietetic research, as well as colleagues interested in expanding their horizons about research.
- **School Nutrition Services DPG:** Members of this DPG work in school nutrition programs.
- **Sports and Human Performance Nutrition DPG:** Members of this DPG are nutrition practitioners who work with athletes and people at all levels of human performance to optimize holistic health for a lifetime by delivering content tailored for human performance in sports as well as military, tactical and performing arts, and those who are first responders.
- **Vegetarian Nutrition DPG:** Members of this DPG are experts

in plant-based nutrition.
- **Weight Management DPG:** Members of this DPG prevent and treat overweight and obesity throughout the lifecycle.
- **Women's Health DPG:** Members of this DPG promote optimal health for women throughout the lifecycle.

Member Interest Groups or "MIGs." MIGs are groups of Academy members who have common interests, issues or backgrounds other than their practice areas or geographic location. The MIGs reflect the many characteristics of the Academy's membership and the public it serves. They are crucial for helping the Academy achieve its objectives for inclusion, diversity, equity, and access. Academy members pay annual dues to join one or more MIGs. The MIG dues are separate from Academy dues or DPG dues. The MIGs are legal groups within the Academy. Currently, the Academy has eight MIGs; their names and brief descriptions follow:
- **Asian Americans and Pacific Islanders MIG:** This MIG is a community of members of the former Chinese MIG and Filipino MIG, and openly welcomes and strongly encourages those who relate with other Asian ethnicities to join, as well as those simply wanting to learn about these diverse cultures.
- **Cultures of Gender and Age MIG:** This MIG is an inclusive community of networking and promoting the exchange of perspectives across gender, age, and lived experiences via several gender- and age-based focus areas such as age related (under 30, 30-50, 50+), career stage (early career, mid-career, seasoned career, retired), students, men, and LGBTQ+.
- **Disabilities in Nutrition and Dietetics MIG:** This MIG is a community that connects Academy members who self-identify as having a disability, who work with clients/patients with disabilities, who educate members with disabilities, and/or who are interested in disabilities as related to nutrition and dietetics. For more information about this MIG, please refer to Chapter 3.
- **Global MIG:** This MIG is a community of members focused

on improving the nutritional status in regions with high burdens of malnutrition or with nutritional crises due to conflict or natural disasters, through the sharing of information, resources, and ideas among Academy members, students, governmental and non-profit aid organizations, and health workers within these countries.
- **Indians in Nutrition and Dietetics MIG:** This MIG is a community that brings together practitioners and students of Asian Indian origin or those interested in learning more about this culture via networking, quality education, professional, and leadership development.
- **Latinos and Hispanics in Dietetics and Nutrition MIG:** This MIG is a community that provides culturally appropriate nutrition resources, recipes, research, and education for those who provide nutrition care to the Latino population.
- **National Organization of Blacks in Dietetics and Nutrition MIG:** This MIG is a community for professional development and support of dietetics, optimal nutrition, and wellbeing for the public, particularly those of African descent.
- **Religion MIG:** This MIG is a resource and forum for religious diet education and community sharing because billions of people follow the tenets of a religion and dietary practices.

Affiliate Associations. The Academy has an Affiliate Association for each US state and territory. Affiliates offer education programs, networking opportunities, scholarship fundraising efforts, and more. There are about 230 district or regional associations within affiliates. Membership in one affiliate is included in Academy membership. Legally, Affiliates are separate groups from the Academy.

Commission on Dietetic Registration or "CDR." The CDR is the credentialing agency of the Academy. The CDR awards credentials to individuals at entry and specialty levels who have met its standards for competency to practice in the nutrition and dietetics profession, including successful completion of its national certification examination and recertification by continuing professional education or examination.

Accreditation Council for Education in Nutrition and Dietetics or "ACEND." The ACEND is the education accreditation unit of the Academy. It is recognized by the US Department of Education as the only accrediting agency for education programs that prepare RD/RDNs and DTR/NDTRs. The ACEND ensures that entry-level education meets quality standards via accreditation of over 600 undergraduate and graduate coordinated, didactic, dietetics technician, and supervised practice programs in nutrition and dietetics.

Nutrition and Dietetic Educators and Preceptors. The Academy has more than 1,350 educators and preceptors.

Chapter 3
The Disabilities in Nutrition and Dietetics Member Interest Group (or "Disabilities MIG")

By Suzanne Domel Baxter, PhD, RD, LD, FADA, FAND

Purpose, Vision, Mission, and Goals

The Disabilities in Nutrition and Dietetics Member Interest Group (short name "Disabilities MIG") is a group within the Academy of Nutrition and Dietetics. The Disabilities MIG is a community that connects Academy members who self-identify as having a disability, work with clients or patients with disabilities, educate members with disabilities, and/or are interested in disabilities as related to nutrition and dietetics. The Disabilities MIG delivers valuable resources; offers quality education and professional development; provides unique opportunities for leadership development, mentoring, collaborating, and networking; promotes accessibility, accommodations, and usability; encourages Inclusion, Diversity, Equity, and Access (IDEA); and fosters advocacy for individuals with disabilities as related to nutrition and dietetics. The Disabilities MIG website is www.disabilitiesmig.org.

The vision of the Disabilities MIG is a world where individuals with disabilities have accessible and inclusive nutrition guidance, nutrient-rich food to optimize health, and equitable access and inclusive opportunities to become active and fully contributing dietetic practitioners.

The mission of the Disabilities MIG is to empower members to be leaders in promoting accessible and inclusive nutrition guidance and nutrient-rich food for individuals with disabilities and to empower individuals with disabilities to achieve full access and inclusion into dietetic education programs, thrive as contributing dietetic practitioners, and serve as professional leaders.

The Disabilities MIG has the following eight goals:

1. Create a community of Academy members — students, interns, dietetic practitioners, and other nutrition and public health professionals — who have disabilities, work with patients/clients with disabilities, educate students/interns with disabilities, and/or are interested in these topics.
2. Grow the cohort of dietetic students, interns, and practitioners with disabilities.
3. Develop and share educational materials and resources concerning the connections between disabilities and nutrition, dietetics, and health.
4. Provide members with a variety of opportunities for educational, professional, and leadership development, networking, and communication.
5. Promote awareness of nutrition and dietetic resources related to accessibility, accommodations, and usability for individuals with disabilities.
6. Serve as a primary resource and content expert to the Academy; Academy groups and committees; dietetic students, interns, and practitioners; and external organizations related to nutrition guidance as well as increased understanding, awareness, and cultural humility concerning inclusion, diversity, equity, and access related to individuals with disabilities.
7. Advocate for inclusivity of individuals with disabilities within the Academy, the profession of nutrition and dietetics, food and nutrition policy and legislative agendas, nutrition research, the nation, and the world.
8. Educate and support dietetic students, interns and practitioners and the individuals with disabilities they work with about how to acquire and navigate relevant resources and accommodations regarding disabilities.

History, Volunteer Efforts, and Advocacy

The Disabilities MIG officially launched on June 1, 2023. Annual dues are $5 for students, interns, and retired members of the Academy, and $15 for active members of the Academy. Our inaugural year ended with 306 members of which 76 (25%) were students or interns.

After acquiring my disability in 2010, which led to my resignation as Research Professor late in 2016, I envisioned an official disabilities group within the Academy. It took seven years to officially launch the Disabilities MIG. This section provides a brief summary of the history, volunteer efforts, and advocacy for the Disabilities MIG from 2016 to May 31, 2023.

In 2016, Neva Cochran, MS, RDN, LD, FAND was contacted by Tracey Williams. Tracey has cerebral palsy and had graduated with a bachelor's degree in a didactic program in dietetics but was unable to match for an internship or pass the DTR/NDTR credentialing exam. Tracey was seeking mentorship to write and speak about nutrition. Neva asked me to join them in January 2017.

In October 2017, at the Academy's annual Food and Nutrition Conference and Expo — or FNCE® — Neva, Tracey, and I presented a poster about the need for data on disabilities among nutrition and dietetics professionals. The only data that the Academy had at that time was FNCE® registration data and whether attendees required any kind of special assistance. I realized that the Academy needed advocacy for disability inclusivity as well as a formal community or group for its members with disabilities.

I applied and was selected as one of four people for the Academy Diversity Leaders Program for the 2017 to 2019 cohort. To my knowledge, I was the first dietetics practitioner with a disability in that program. This program required that I complete a capstone project of my choice and identify a mentor. I identified Neva as my mentor. My capstone project had several components. One component was to write an article titled "Disabilities among Nutrition and Dietetics Professionals: Finding the Facts" that was published in the newsletter of the Research Dietetics Practice Group (DPG) in Summer 2018. A second component was to encourage the Academy to begin collecting data on disabilities among dietetics practitioners. Due to our inquiries, the Academy added disability status questions to its bi-annual

Compensation and Benefits Survey as of 2019. This was a win for our disability community, although we are still trying to get disability status questions added to the "My Profile" page on the Academy website where members self-report their race/ethnicity and gender. A third component was to write and submit an educational session proposal for FNCE® 2019. Our session titled, "Individuals with Disabilities: Essential Members of the Healthcare Team" was accepted for presentation and included video clips by several dietetic professionals with disabilities. A fourth component was to write an article titled "Enhancing Diversity and the Role of Individuals with Disabilities in the Dietetics Profession" that was published in the *Journal of the Academy of Nutrition and Dietetics* in May 2020. This article provides information on the prevalence of individuals with disabilities in the US, healthcare professions, and the dietetics profession; disability rights laws; accommodation recommendations for individuals with disabilities in various settings; online resources for etiquette strategies to interact with individuals with disabilities; professional health science associations for individuals with disabilities; and future research and inclusion needs concerning disabilities.

Next, by invitation, Neva and I wrote an article titled "Ensuring Success for RDNs and Interns with Disabilities: Clinical Managers Can Make it Work" that was published in the *Clinical Nutrition Managers DPG Newsletter* in Spring 2021. This article provides information on disability prevalence in the dietetics profession, descriptions of organizations working toward disability inclusion and the disability equality index, success stories of individuals with disabilities working in settings similar to those of clinical RDNs and dietetic interns, etiquette strategies for interacting with clinical RDNs and dietetic interns with disabilities, and perspectives from clinical nutrition managers of, and clinical RDNs with disabilities.

As the Diversity Liaison of the Research DPG, I wrote a Diversity mini grant that was funded by the Academy to create three free webinars that I planned and Neva moderated in April 2020. The first two webinars featured stories by panels of dietetics practitioners with disabilities. The third webinar had speakers from the Job Accommodation Network. Each webinar had 200 to 300 attendees and received considerable positive feedback.

In December 2020, Neva and I created a closed Facebook Group titled "Dietitians with Disabilities."

In June 2021, Neva and I submitted the formal paperwork to the Academy to form the Disabilities MIG.

In Summer and Fall 2021, the Academy conducted surveys to determine interest in creating the Disabilities MIG. The Academy requires 75 or more members to express interest in joining a proposed MIG. Results from our surveys are provided later in this chapter in the section titled "Survey Results: Interest in Creating a Disabilities MIG."

In September 2021, Neva moderated a panel session by dietetics practitioners with disabilities for a virtual symposium by the Nutrition Educators of Health Professionals DPG. The panel featured four dietetics practitioners with disabilities who worked in various settings including clinical, private practice, research and volunteer. Each panel member shared the stories of their career paths, the challenges they have faced, and the successes they have achieved.

In the June/July 2021 issue, *Today's Dietitian* published an article by Neva with brief profiles of six dietetics practitioners with disabilities to highlight their unique role in different areas of dietetics practice.

In March 2022, the Academy Board of Directors approved the creation of the Disabilities MIG. But, we first had a year of preparation to create our mission, vision, goals, and budget.

In September 2022, Neva and I presented a session titled "Enhancing IDEA in the Nutrition and Dietetics Profession by Promoting the Role of Individuals with Disabilities" for Metropolitan State University Denver's (virtual) Nutrition Diversity Conference. This session provided an overview of disabilities in the US and dietetics profession, and described the history of the new Disabilities MIG, its purposes, member benefits, member opportunities, and ways it supports the Academy's IDEA Action Plan.

Also, in October 2022 at FNCE®, we had an educational session with a panel of three dietetics practitioners with disabilities titled "Counseling for Individuals with Disabilities: Tactics from the Trenches." The panel described useful nutrition counseling strategies to promote positive behavior changes when working with individuals with mobility, hearing, or vision disabilities; discussed practical approaches for providing appropriate medical nutrition therapy to help treat and manage diseases or conditions for individuals with mobility, hearing, or vision disabilities; and explained effective nutrition counseling tactics to help decrease risk of nutrition-related chronic diseases for individuals with mobility, hearing, or vision disabilities.

Additionally, at FNCE® in October 2022, the Academy allowed the to-be-launched Disabilities MIG to have a booth at the DPG/MIG Showcase. We gave away clear face masks as an example of an accommodation for people with hearing impairment who rely on reading lips to understand what is being said. These clear face masks are also extremely helpful for healthcare practitioners and others who work with children so they can see smiling faces instead of masked faces.

In March 2023, Neva and I provided a webinar titled "Dynamic Duo: Nutrition Communicator and Researcher Team Up to Advocate for Dietetic Practitioners and Students with Disabilities" for the Research DPG. The session described how a dietetics researcher and practitioner worked together to promote inclusion, diversity, equity and access for dietetics students, interns and practitioners with disabilities; explained benefits of a researcher/practitioner collaboration in enhancing the dietetics profession; and shared strategies to create research projects between researchers and dietetic practitioners.

In April 2023, I provided a brief webinar about the Disabilities MIG for the Health Equity and Diversity Affinity Group of the Academy. This webinar summarized the Disabilities MIG history, purpose, vision, mission, goals, other key details, dues rates, and scholarship.

In the June 2023, my "Letter to the Editor" titled "Disability Culture Must Be Included in Cultural Humility Training to Promote Inclusion, Diversity, Equity, and Access (IDEA) in the Dietetics Profession" was published in the *Journal of the Academy of Nutrition and Dietetics*. This letter concerned the article titled "Evolving Beyond the World Foods Course: Creating Racially and Ethnically Inclusive Educational Spaces for Dietetics Students" published in the *Journal of the Academy of Nutrition and Dietetics* in 2022 that had overlooked disability culture and college students with disabilities.

Also, in June 2023, Cheryl Iny Harris, MPH, RD and I had our "Letter to the Editor" titled "The Diversity, Equity and Inclusion Lens is

Incomplete when Disabilities are Excluded" published in the *Journal of the Academy of Nutrition and Dietetics*. This letter concerned the article titled "Need to Incorporate Diversity, Equity, and Inclusion: Reflections from a National Initiative Measuring Fruit and Vegetable Intake" published in the *Journal of the Academy of Nutrition and Dietetics* in 2022 that had failed to mention people with disabilities.

In July 2023, I provided a webinar titled "Nutrition Education for Individuals with Disabilities: Using Cultural Humility to Promote Inclusion, Diversity, Equity, and Access" for the Public Health Nutrition Division of the Society for Nutrition Education and Behavior. This webinar briefly summarized the Americans with Disabilities Act, disability statistics, cultural competency and cultural humility and the need to include disability culture, adapted kitchen tools and utensils, digital accessibility, and the new Disabilities MIG.

In late July 2023, the Disabilities MIG was notified that the National Center on Health, Physical Activity and Disability would fund its application to the "Advancing Partnerships for Inclusive Health" grant opportunity. This one-year project included three objectives concerning leadership, advocacy, and a Disabilities MIG Affiliate Speaker Grant Program. With this funding, several members of the Disabilities MIG provided a disability presentation and exhibit at annual conferences for five Affiliates in Spring 2024. The exhibit featured adapted kitchen tools and utensils to enhance independence for people with disabilities when preparing and/or eating food.

In October 2023 at FNCE®, the Disabilities MIG had a spotlight educational session titled "Promoting Inclusion, Diversity, Equity and Access in the Dietetics Career Path for Individuals with Disabilities." This session featured a panel of three individuals with disabilities who had obtained their dietetics credentials within the previous year. The panel shared tips for individuals with disabilities to include about their disabilities for dietetic education and internship programs, suggestions for requesting accommodations for dietetic education and internship programs, and considerations for requesting accommodations for taking the credentialing exams. The Disabilities MIG also had a networking reception at FNCE® 2023 and a booth at the DPG/MIG Showcase.

Also, in October 2023 at FNCE®, two staff members from the

National Center on Health, Physical Activity and Disability provided an educational session titled "Including People with Disability in Nutrition Services and Programming." They explained the five domains of the "Guidelines, Recommendations, Adaptations, including Disability" adaptation framework as they relate to nutrition programming, community, or clinical settings; differentiated language and teaching strategies to create a welcoming and professional nutrition interaction inclusive of people with disabilities; and shared strategies and solutions to address barriers to inclusion for people with disabilities within the RD workspace. A third speaker, Liz Dunn, RD with a disability provided practical applications.

Furthermore, in October 2023 at FNCE®, Neva and I had a poster concerning accessible digital technology. The poster included a QR code with the audio recording of the poster's content.

Additionally, in late October 2023, by request, the Disabilities MIG provided detailed feedback to the Academy concerning accessibility and inclusivity for FNCE® 2023 and its mobile app. The feedback was obtained from numerous members of the Disabilities MIG and included feedback in general; feedback specific to the FNCE® venue, sessions, and hotels; and the FNCE® mobile app.

In November 2023, my "Letter to the Editor" titled "Accessible Digital Technology in Nutrition Education and Behavior Change Interventions" was published in the *Journal of Nutrition Education and Behavior*. This letter concerned the article titled "Digital Technology in Nutrition Education and Behavior Change: Opportunities and Challenges" published in June 2023 in the *Journal of Nutrition Education and Behavior* that had overlooked the need for digital technology to be accessible to people with disabilities.

Also in November 2023, several members of the Disabilities MIG and I responded to a request from the Academy Government Affairs to provide input and recommendations about whether the Academy should sign on to the Consortium for Clients with Disabilities (CCD) comments concerning HHS 504. Our response recommended that the Academy sign on to the CCD comments. We also recommended that Academy become a member of the CCD, which already includes several other professional healthcare organizations.

In December 2023, I encouraged members of the Disabilities

MIG to provide feedback to the US Census Bureau about its proposed changes to the definition of disability and how people with disabilities are counted for the American Community Survey. The proposed definition would have drastically reduced the number of people with disabilities. The disability community nationwide provided so many concerns that in February 2024, the US Census Bureau announced it was dropping the proposed changes and instead would work with the disability community to improve the disability status questions asked for the American Community Survey in the future.

Beginning in February 2024, the Policy and Advocacy Leaders of the Disabilities MIG began hosting monthly meetings to promote policy and advocacy initiatives within our MIG. These gatherings are open to all members of the Disabilities MIG and provide a valuable platform to stay informed about ongoing efforts, engage in meaningful discussions, and address any questions or concerns about policy and advocacy.

In March 2024, the Policy and Advocacy Leaders of the Disabilities MIG and I responded to a request from Academy Government Affairs concerning the US Senate Committee on Health, Education, Labor and Pensions about revising the Older Americans Act. We provided information concerning how the prevalence of disability drastically increases with age, that the provision of medically tailored meals is needed for people with disabilities, and improved and expanded transportation to senior centers for those who participate in congregate meals. The Academy included information about disabilities in its priorities submitted to this Senate Committee on March 19, 2024, concerning revisions to the Older Americans Act.

In April 2024, the Abbott Nutrition Health Institute's Power of Nutrition Podcast released a five-episode podcast titled "Accessibility in Healthcare" with Alena Morales, RDN and I as guest speakers. The podcast is available online at https://anhi.org/resources/podcasts; the titles of the five episodes follow:
1) Episode 1 – Beyond the Ramp: Disabilities in Nutrition and Dietetics Member Interest Group of the Academy of Nutrition and Dietetics – How it Started, How it's Going
2) Episode 2 – Beyond the Ramp: Building a Culture/Environment of Accessibility for Clinicians and Healthcare Students/Interns with disabilities

3) Episode 3 – Beyond the Ramp: Person-Centered Care for Clients/Patients with Disabilities in the Outpatient Setting
4) Episode 4 – Beyond the Ramp: Person-Centered Interventions for Clients/Patients with Disabilities in the Inpatient Setting
5) Episode 5 – Beyond the Ramp: Digital Accessibility.

In May 2024, three members of the Disabilities MIG and I met with ACEND about providing speakers for ACEND's Diversity, Equity, and Inclusion virtual sessions to provide disability information for directors of accredited dietetic programs and preceptors of dietetics interns. We scheduled two virtual sessions for 2025 and discussed having one session for each of the following calendar years. We encouraged ACEND to include disability information in its annual "Diversity Enrollment Trends" reports concerning dietetics students and interns.

Also, in May 2024, three members of the Disabilities MIG and I met with staff of the Commission on Dietetic Registration (CDR) to discuss five topics. The first topic concerned digital accessibility of the CDR website. The second topic concerned the process for credentialed dietetic practitioners to request assistance for recording continuing education activities on their digital activity logs. The third topic concerned including more about disabilities in the Scope and Standards of Practice as well as Focus Area articles for credentialed dietetic practitioners. The fourth topic was to inquire about the possibility of creating a Board-Certified Specialist credential, an Assess and Learn and/or a Certificate of Training concerning disabilities for credentialed dietetic practitioners. The fifth topic concerned the process for requesting accommodations for taking the exams to become credentialed dietetic practitioners.

Finally, during the seven years of volunteer efforts to launch the Disabilities MIG, I joined several groups in the Academy to advocate for IDEA in general and specifically for people with disabilities as described in the following bullets. This information is provided to encourage dietetic practitioners with disabilities to participate in various efforts of the Academy to enhance consideration of people with disabilities.

- I was selected as a member of the Evidence Analysis Library Adult Weight Management Workgroup 2020 – 2024. This

Workgroup wrote the following three articles that were published in the *Journal of the Academy of Nutrition and Dietetics*; each article mentions something about obesity or overweight in adults with disabilities.

1) Medical Nutrition Therapy Interventions Provided by Dietitians for Adult Overweight and Obesity Management: An Academy of Nutrition and Dietetics Evidence-Based Practice Guideline. *Journal of the Academy of Nutrition and Dietetics* 123 (3):520-545, 2023.
2) Weight Management Interventions Provided by a Dietitian for Adults with Overweight or Obesity: An Evidence Analysis Center Systematic Review and Meta-Analysis. *Journal of the Academy of Nutrition and Dietetics* 123 (11):1621-1661, 2023.
3) Position of the Academy of Nutrition and Dietetics: Medical Nutrition Therapy Behavioral Interventions Provided by Dietitians for Adults with Overweight or Obesity. *Journal of the Academy of Nutrition and Dietetics* 124(3):408-415, 2024.

- I was selected as a member of the Diversity and Inclusion Advisory Group 2021 and encouraged consideration of disabilities.
- I joined the Health Equity and Diversity Affinity Group as well as the Dietary Guidelines Affinity Group to encourage consideration of disabilities in both groups.
- I audited several meetings for the House of Delegates in October 2020, February 2021, May 2021, September 2021, and April 2022 to encourage disability inclusivity within the Academy and profession.
- I was selected as a member of the 2023 Farm Bill Task Force and encouraged disability inclusivity.
- I was selected as a member of the President's 2022 Strategic Advancement Group for Inclusion, Diversity, Equity and Access. I encouraged that disability be considered.

Survey Results: Interest in Creating a Disabilities MIG

Our surveys were conducted in Summer and Fall 2021; there were 176 respondents. Five statements follow about importance of the MIG and the percentage of survey respondents who strongly or somewhat agreed that it is important for the Academy to do the following to address the needs of the disability community:

1. Increase the number of member leaders in Academy leadership positions who self-report a disability: 78%
2. Educate students who self-report a disability about the Academy: 74%
3. Educate students who self-report a disability about careers in nutrition and dietetics: 84%
4. Educate all Academy members about disabilities in relation to nutrition and health: 87%
5. Develop educational materials for health professionals and consumers about disabilities in relation to nutrition and health: 85%

When asked, "If a new MIG was created for the disability community, would you join this MIG," 106 said yes, 23 said no, and 47 were unsure. The 106 "yes" responses exceeded the minimum requirement of 75 Academy members with interest to join the MIG.

For the question, "Are you interested in having access to any of the following items from the Academy related to dietitians and dietetics technicians with disabilities," respondents marked as many of the 15 items which interested them. The 15 items in order of interest of respondents follow:

- Nutrition education resources on disability topics: 76%
- Professional education webinars: 71%
- Earn continuing professional education credits: 66%
- Advocate for the disability community within the Academy: 61%
- Educational sessions at the Academy's annual conference: 59%
- Newsletter with member highlights, announcements, resources, continuing professional education and resources:

    56%
- Annual scholarship for students and interns with disabilities: 52%
- Online discussion board: 47%
- Member directory: 44%
- Social media posts: 39%
- Website: 31%
- Networking events at the Academy's annual conference: 29%
- Mentoring program: 26%
- Leadership skills: 25%
- Journal club: 13%.

For the question about interest in opportunities, respondents were to mark as many of seven opportunities that interested them. The seven opportunities in order of interest of respondents follow:

- Increase personal knowledge about various disabilities: 81%
- Develop educational resources to increase knowledge of other dietitians and health practitioners about disabilities: 51%
- Help develop various continuing professional education learning modules about working with patients and clients with disabilities: 33%
- Serve as an author, reviewer, or content advisor for articles or other media outreach: 30%
- Serve as a speaker for webinars: 22%
- Mentoring program: 22%
- Highlighted in member spotlights: 18%

The survey included several places for comments. The 176 survey respondents provided a total of 89 comments; 18 comments follow:

1. We need Certified Lactation Counselors and IBCLCs — which stands for International Board-Certified Lactation Consultants — who are fluent in American Sign Language.
2. The speaker spoke so rapidly I realized she had no idea that some of her audience might be hearing impaired. Please provide feedback during and after sessions to let speakers know whether they are speaking, or spoke, too rapidly!

3. Resources need to be closed captioned! Captions can easily be included for free in PowerPoint and other platforms.
4. As someone who's hearing impaired, I always appreciate written communications like subtitles or notes for a presentation and speakers who are more succinct because they're easier to follow.
5. For what it's worth, this form is awfully inaccessible!
6. Don't use white text on pale background for visually impaired.
7. Academy membership is very expensive for those unable to work full-time or who have high out of pocket expenses due to disabilities.
8. Many people with disabilities are unemployed and under-employed. Fees add up quickly. This can be a huge barrier to people with disabilities. Many cannot earn above poverty level or risk losing essential health care and caregiver services.
9. Experiences to engage in learning opportunities and understanding of individuals or colleagues with disabilities are key for students and current dietitians to build a broad base for career choices and build empathy, curiosity and understanding for working with diverse populations.
10. Advocates for people with disabilities are needed both for them and to inform the rest of us.
11. I think this is a great idea. I do not identify as a person with disabilities but do provide services to those with disabilities. This includes patients and having students in my classes.
12. Having been asked to speak to groups about or for people with disabilities, and not finding much information, more is needed.
13. I'm a person with legal blindness/low vision RD with resources and insight to share. I'm looking forward to this group!
14. This MIG is crucial to advancing IDEA (inclusion, diversity, equity, and access) in the profession.
15. Include neurodiversity and invisible disability (e.g., autoimmune diseases, depression, anxiety, and other

mental health diagnoses).
16. Involve dietitians in the Leadership Education in Neurodevelopmental and Related Disabilities (LEND) training program, funded by the Maternal and Child Health Bureau.
17. I work for the National Center on Health, Physical Activity and Disability, a resource for information serving persons with physical, sensory and cognitive disability across the lifespan. I am very much interested in developing continuing education opportunities for dietitians to learn more about nutrition for disability.
18. I am a student with multiple disabilities, and it's been a very defeating experience to make myself a competitive candidate for internships. Due to the nature of my limitations, I have only been able to go to school. I can't keep up with students who work, go to school, and volunteer all at the same time. I look like a terrible candidate on paper. The short personal statement portion of the internship application doesn't allow me to fully explain the situation. Due to fatigue, I need a part-time internship. I feel I can't be fully honest about my limitations without it working against me. I don't feel I can even be honest with professors at school about my situation. I can be a REALLY great dietitian and contribute so much, but I need someone to give me the opportunity to complete the internship. I really hope this MIG moves forward. I've felt so alone and ashamed. This can help educate others and help them see that individuals with disabilities are capable. The fact that this MIG is being considered is very encouraging.

Disabilities MIG Scholarship: The LaVerne and Edwin Domel Memorial Scholarship

The Disabilities MIG has an endowed scholarship titled "The LaVerne and Edwin Domel Memorial Scholarship" established in Spring 2021 via the Academy Foundation. One scholarship is provided annually for a member of the Disabilities MIG who is a dietetic student or intern with one or more disabilities, or lived experiences with one or more disabilities, to pursue an education or internship in nutrition and dietetics. This scholarship was made possible by a large inheritance to me from my mother. The following paragraph provides background about my parents and family.

My mother, LaVerne Helen Hobratsch Domel, passed from this life on August 12, 2020, in Fort Worth, Texas, at age 83, from COVID pneumonia complicated by Alzheimer's disease. LaVerne was born on September 10, 1936, in Walburg, Texas, the youngest of five children. My father, Edwin A. Domel, passed from this life unexpectedly on December 25, 1970, in Walburg, Texas at age 41, from a cerebral aneurysm. Ed was born on September 16, 1929, in Walburg, Texas as an only child. Zion Lutheran Church in Walburg was where LaVerne and Ed were baptized and confirmed, where they attended private church school for grades one to eight, where they married, and where they are buried. LaVerne graduated in 1954 from Georgetown High School, where she was very active. Ed graduated from Jarrell High School, where he was a star football player. Ed served his country in the army during the Korean war. LaVerne and Ed were high school sweethearts and married on June 19, 1955. The young couple initially remained in Georgetown, where their first child, Lori, was born. They then moved to Richardson, Texas, where they had me as their second child, and third child, Neal. LaVerne and Ed were two of the founding members of Messiah Lutheran Church in Richardson. After Ed was called to his eternal home on Christmas Day 1970, LaVerne, widowed at age 34 with three children, ages 13, 12, and 7, went on to raise them as a single parent and sent them all to college. Lori earned a law degree and Neal and I each earned PhDs. LaVerne later graduated with her own bachelor's degree at age 62. LaVerne and Ed had many passions and a keen sense of loyalty to their family, church, and community. Both loved traveling, visiting family, and bowling. LaVerne loved hobbies like genealogy, square-dancing, water aerobics, gardening, and causes such as protecting the environment through recycling and composting. Both were active volunteers in the church and in the community.

 *My parents on their wedding day with two flower girls and two ring bearers.*

 *My family with my parents, paternal grandparents, older sister, and baby brother.*

Editors: Suzanne Domel Baxter and Cheryl Iny Harris

Chapter 4
Dietitians and Dietetics Technicians (or "Dietetics Practitioners"): What They Are and How to Become One

By Suzanne Domel Baxter, PhD, RD, LD, FADA, FAND

Introduction

The formal names for dietitian are "Registered Dietitian" (abbreviated as "RD") and "Registered Dietitian Nutritionist" (abbreviated as "RDN"). The formal names for dietetics technician are "Dietetics Technician, Registered" (abbreviated as "DTR") and "Nutrition and Dietetics Technician, Registered" (abbreviated as "NDTR"). These four titles — "registered dietitian" and "registered dietitian nutritionist" as well as "dietetics technician, registered" and "nutrition and dietetics technician, registered" — are all legally protected titles. This means that these titles and credentials can only be used by dietetics practitioners who have completed specific educational requirements and passed a national exam, and who continue to learn throughout their careers. Dietitians and dietetics technicians are referred to collectively as "credentialed dietetics practitioners" or simply "dietetics practitioners."

There is no specific, standardized meaning for "nutritionist." Anyone can call themselves a nutritionist. Nutrition and health recommendations by unqualified individuals can harm people in general, and especially people with medically complex nutrition conditions. Check for credentials to make sure that people who call themselves "dietitian," "nutritionist," or a similar term (e.g., nutrition therapist, nutrition coach) are qualified nutrition experts.

A credential is a professional qualification to let the public know that the practitioner is a trained expert. Examples of other credentialed health care practitioners include MD for doctors or physicians and RN for registered nurses. In nutrition and dietetics, the credentials for trained experts are RD or RDN and DTR or NDTR. Usually when someone says "dietitian," they are referring to an RD or RDN. Similarly, when someone says, "dietetics technician," they are referring to a DTR or NDTR. The Accreditation Council for Education in Nutrition and Dietetics (or ACEND) is the accrediting agency for education programs that prepare students to become RD/RDNs and DTR/NDTRs. The ACEND makes sure that students who are preparing for careers as RD/RDNs and as DTR/NDTRs get the education they need to become eligible to take the national RD/RDN exam or the national DTR/NDTR exam. The Commission on Dietetic Registration (or CDR) is the credentialing agency for RD/RDNs and DTR/NDTRs. In addition to RD/RDN credentialing, many states have regulatory laws that require RD/RDNs to be licensed.

What is a Registered Dietitian (RD) / Registered Dietitian Nutritionist (RDN)?

An RD/RDN is a food and nutrition expert who has earned a minimum of a graduate degree from an accredited dietetics program, completed a supervised practice requirement, and passed a national RD/RDN exam, and who continues to earn professional development credits throughout their career. There also are specialty credentials for RD/RDNs in areas of gerontological nutrition, sports dietetics, pediatric nutrition, renal nutrition, and oncology nutrition who are board-certified by CDR. There are diverse and flexible career options for RD/RDNs because they can do the following:
- perform medical nutrition therapy as part of the health care team in health care facilities such as medical centers, hospitals, and clinics.
- manage foodservice operations in various settings including hospitals, school districts, colleges and universities, long-

term care facilities, memory care facilities, day-care centers, prisons, and corporations to oversee menu creation, food purchasing, food preparation, food safety, and foodservice staff management.
- have their own private practice businesses and provide consultations for individuals, food companies, foodservice, restaurants, and corporate wellness programs.
- work in community and public health settings to teach, monitor, and advise the public in programs such as the Extension Service, Supplemental Nutrition Assistance Program (or Food Stamps), and the Women, Infants, and Children Program (or WIC) to improve dietary intake and the quality of life via nutritious eating habits.
- work in sports/performance nutrition to educate athletes, police forces, firefighters, and members of the military about the connections between food, hydration, fitness, and performance so they can excel at their activities and fulfill their duties in the field.
- work in communications, consumer affairs, public relations, advocacy, grocery stores, marketing, or product development for food and nutrition-related businesses and industries.
- work at colleges, universities, and medical centers to teach dietetics students and health care practitioners such as physicians and nurses about food, nutrition, and dietetics.
- work for government agencies including the US Department of Agriculture, National Institute of Food and Agriculture, and Department of Health and Human Services.
- conduct research for colleges, universities, hospitals, and food and pharmaceutical companies to investigate aspects of nutrition and dietetics, answer critical nutrition questions, and identify alternative foods or nutrition recommendations.

Editors: Suzanne Domel Baxter and Cheryl Iny Harris

What is a Dietetics Technician, Registered (DTR) / Nutrition and Dietetics Technician, Registered (NDTR)?

A DTR/NDTR is someone trained in food and nutrition who has earned at least a two-year associate's degree from an accredited DTR/NDTR program, completed 450 hours of supervised practice experience, and passed a national DTR/NDTR exam, and stays up to date in nutrition and dietetics via continuing education throughout their career. A DTR/NDTR works as a team member in partnership and under the supervision of RD/RDNs in a variety of settings as an integral part of healthcare and/or foodservice management teams. There are diverse and flexible career options for DTR/NDTRs because they can:

- screen patients and clients, gather data, and perform other tasks to assist RD/RDNs in providing medical nutrition therapy in hospitals, clinics, extended care facilities, nursing homes, memory care centers, retirement centers, hospices, home health care programs and research facilities.
- plan menus, purchase food, prepare food, manage employees, and maintain budgets for foodservice operations in school districts, colleges, universities, day-care centers, prisons, restaurants, health care facilities, corporations and hospitals.
- assist RD/RDNs to implement and present classes to the public for the WIC Program, public health agencies, Meals on Wheels, retirement centers, and other community health programs.
- help educate clients about the connection between food, fitness and health in health clubs, weight management clinics, and community wellness centers.
- oversee foodservice sanitation and food safety in food companies, contract food management companies, food vending, and food distribution operations.

How Does an Individual Become an RD/RDN?

The following bullets explain the steps to becoming an RD/RDN:

- Step One is to earn a minimum of a graduate degree from an accredited college or university recognized by the US Department of Education or foreign equivalent, and coursework through a dietetics program accredited by ACEND. Coursework includes food and nutrition sciences, biochemistry, physiology, microbiology, anatomy, chemistry, foodservice systems, business, pharmacology, culinary arts, behavioral sciences, economics, computer science, sociology, and communications. A master's degree is required to become eligible to take the national RD/RDN exam. Some accredited dietetics programs include a master's degree, whereas some students complete their undergraduate in dietetics and then earn a master's degree in another field such as public health, business, or communications.
- Step Two is to complete at least 1,000 hours of supervised practice to gain real-world experience and apply knowledge learned in the classroom to the field in various work settings.
- Step Three is to pass a national exam for RD/RDNs. After you complete the degrees and supervised practice, you are "RD/RDN eligible" to take the national exam for RD/RDNs to become credentialed.
- Step Four is to meet requirements to practice in your state. Many states have regulatory laws (i.e., licensure) for dietetics practitioners. All states accept the RD/RDN credential for state licensure purposes.
- Step Five is to maintain the RD/RDN credentials by completing continuing professional education requirements throughout your career.

An online directory of accredited dietetics programs can be found by searching on "Program Directory – eatrightpro" that allows you to search by state and program type. The following bullets summarize the three kinds of accredited dietetics education programs which each offer a distinct experience and route to becoming RD/RDN eligible.

- **Coordinated Programs (or CP).** The CP route combines didactic classroom learning with supervised practice experiences into a single program. Students who graduate from the CP route meet both the graduate degree and supervised practice eligibility requirements to take the national RD/RDN exam. The CP route can take less calendar time and thus be less expensive. However, the days will be long (e.g., eight hours), full, and busy. For example, didactic classroom learning may occur on Mondays, Wednesdays, and Fridays whereas supervised practice experiences may occur on Tuesdays and Thursdays.

- **Didactic Programs in Dietetics (or DPD) + Dietetics Internships (or DI).** The DPD + DI route consists of two education programs. First, an accredited DPD is completed with classroom coursework. Next, an accredited DI is completed with supervised practice in real work settings. One must either complete a master's degree before entering a DI program or during the DI program, concurrently with supervised practice. Most students who take the DPD + DI route apply for a DI position through a competitive online matching process. However, some DPDs have placement agreements with DIs to make sure their graduates secure DI positions. So, if considering the DPD + DI route, ask whether the DPD includes "pre-select matching" for a DI. Note, most DIs charge tuition and often require relocating to another city or state. There are "Distance DIs" which avoid relocating because one identifies preceptors in their area who are willing to provide supervised practice opportunities. Students who graduate from the DPD + DI route and have completed a master's degree meet both the degree and supervised practice eligibility requirements to take the national RD/RDN exam. Although most DPDs offer bachelor's degrees, some DPDs satisfy the minimum graduate degree requirement. The DI programs will either require interns to complete a master's degree prior to entering the DI program, offer a master's degree as part of their program, or require interns to complete a master's degree of their choosing while they complete the DI.

- **Future Education Model Graduate Program (or FEMGP) in**

Nutrition and Dietetics. The FEMGP route is a single accredited program that includes graduate-level coursework and supervised experiential learning. Graduation from the FEMGP route satisfies both the degree and supervised practice eligibility requirements to take the national RD/RDN exam. A word of caution: Be sure to differentiate between accredited FEMGPs and other regular master's or doctorate programs which may not include the specific coursework or supervised practice required for RD/RDN eligibility. For example, there are advanced degrees in disciplines that existing RD/RDNs might pursue to complement their credential but those degrees are not accredited by ACEND for graduates to meet the eligibility requirements to take the national RD/RDN exam.

Individuals who already have a bachelor's and/or master's degree that is not in nutrition and dietetics and are interested in becoming an RD/RDN should have their college transcript evaluated by the director of the ACEND-accredited dietetics program that they wish to attend. The program director will review the person's previous academic preparation and identify courses that will need to be completed to meet the educational and supervised practice/experiential learning requirements to be eligible to take the national RD/RDN exam.

How Does an Individual Become a DTR/NDTR?

The following bullets explain the steps to becoming a DTR/NDTR:

- Step One is to earn at least an associate's degree and complete a dietetics technician program accredited by ACEND. These programs include 450 hours of supervised practice experience in various community programs, health care and foodservice facilities. Or earn at least a bachelor's degree by completing a dietetics program accredited by ACEND.
- Step Two is to pass a national exam for DTR/NDTRs. After

the educational requirements are completed, one can schedule to take the national DTR/NDTR exam to become credentialed as a nutrition and dietetics technician, registered.
- Step Three is to maintain the DTR/NDTR credentials by completing continuing professional education requirements throughout your career.

An online directory of accredited dietetics technician programs can be found by searching on "Program Directory – eatrightpro." Note, there are far fewer dietetics technicians programs than there are dietetics programs. The following bullets summarize the three kinds of accredited dietetics technician programs which each offer a distinct experience and route to becoming DTR/NDTR eligible:
- **Dietetics Technician Programs** offer associate's degree level coursework and at least 450 hours of supervised practice required for eligibility to take the national DTR/NDTR exam.
- **Didactic Programs in Dietetics Programs** offer bachelor's and graduate level dietitian coursework.
- **Coordinated Programs in Dietetics** offer bachelor's and graduate level dietitian coursework.

Salaries and Job Outlook

For RD/RDNs, the median full-time annual salary is $72,000 according to the 2021 Compensation & Benefits Survey of the Dietetics Profession. Salaries for RD/RDNs vary by region of the country, employment settings, scope of responsibility, and supply of RD/RDNs. Salaries for RD/RDNs increase with experience. Many RD/RDNs earn incomes that exceed $90,000, particularly RD/RDNs in business, management, education, and research.

For DTR/NDTRs, the median annualized salary is $49,900 according to the 2021 Compensation & Benefits Survey of the Dietetics Profession. Salaries for DTR/NDTRs vary by region of the country, employment settings, scope of responsibility, and supply of DTR/NDTRs. Salaries for DTR/NDTRs increase with experience. The greatest reported income for DTR/NDTRs was $75,000 for Director of Food and Nutrition Services.

The job outlook for dietetics practitioners is positive. The US Bureau of Labor Statistics expects employment of dietetics practitioners to grow faster than the average for all occupations. Several factors contributing to this growth include increasing awareness of and emphasis on the role of food and nutrition to prevent and treat diseases, a growing and aging US population, management of chronic diseases (e.g., diabetes, obesity, heart disease), expansion of healthcare settings, and corporate and public health initiatives.

Financial Aid and Scholarships

The Academy of Nutrition and Dietetics Foundation offers scholarships for eligible dietetics students. Students must be members of the Academy of Nutrition and Dietetics to apply for a Foundation scholarship. Students planning to become DTR/NDTRs must be enrolled in their first year of study in an ACEND-accredited dietetics technician program to be eligible to apply for a Foundation scholarship to use in their second year of study. Students planning to become RD/RDNs must be enrolled in their junior year in an ACEND-accredited dietetics program to be eligible to apply for a Foundation scholarship. The Foundation also has scholarships for students in ACEND-accredited dietetics internships and graduate studies. The Foundation has a scholarship specifically for students/interns who are members of the Disabilities in Nutrition and Dietetics Member Interest Group; please refer to Chapter 3 about this scholarship.

State Vocational Rehabilitation Programs and Centers for Independent Living are two primary resources for students/interns with disabilities to help with college expenses; please refer to Chapter 5 about these two resources. In addition, there are numerous scholarships for students with disabilities to attend college; Chapter 21 has a section on financial aid and scholarships.

Editors: Suzanne Domel Baxter and Cheryl Iny Harris

Chapter 5
State Vocational Rehabilitation Programs and Centers for Independent Living

By Suzanne Domel Baxter, PhD, RD, LD, FADA, FAND

Introduction

This chapter summarizes two key resources for people with disabilities — state Vocational Rehabilitation (or "VR") programs and Centers for Independent Living (or "CILs"). Awareness of these two key resources can be extremely beneficial for people with disabilities including current and future dietetics practitioners with disabilities. Awareness of these two key resources is useful, too, for people without disabilities including dietetic practitioners without disabilities because they may work, serve, teach, precept, and/or be related to people with disabilities as colleagues, clients, patients, students, interns, and/or family members.

State Vocational Rehabilitation (or VR) Programs

State Vocational Rehabilitation (or VR) programs support people who have disabilities and the desire to work to help them to prepare for, obtain, and/or retain employment. State VR programs are federally funded but are usually administered by state agencies; thus, the eligibility requirements, services offered, amount of time needed to obtain services, and/or the specific name of the program may vary from one state to another. Each state VR program has offices located throughout the state to support people with disabilities to help them get jobs and live independently. Some states have a separate state VR program for people with vision impairment and/or blindness. For a person to receive services from a state VR program, they need to make an appointment with the program and be assessed to demonstrate that they have a physical, sensory, mental, or an invisible disability that poses a substantial barrier to employment, that they want to be employed, and that they can benefit from services of state VR programs to be employed. State VR programs often collaborate with CILs in the specific state as well as disability services offices at colleges or universities.

To identify the specific name of the state VR program in your state, search online for "Vocational Rehabilitation Services [name of your state]." For example, this search will identify the name of the state VR program in South Carolina as "South Carolina Vocational Rehabilitation Department" and in California as "California Department of Rehabilitation." Then, search for the offices on this website to identify the location of the VR office closest to your location to make an appointment with a VR counselor. The VR counselor will assess the specific situation (including ability to do the job, desire to do the job, the feasibility of being employed in the job) and determine the services available.

Individuals may request out-of-state services from state VR programs on occasion. Recently the US Department of Education's Rehabilitation Services Administration released a guidance document (dated August 4, 2024) detailing how state VR programs should respond to out-of-state service requests. The guidance indicates that if a recipient of a state VR program is seeking services that fall within the needs identified in their individualized plan for employment, the state VR program should accommodate an out-of-state option if no comparable in-state option exists.

State VR programs might offer numerous services for people with disabilities to support their career goals. For example, consider individuals with spinal cord injuries (or SCIs) and/or vision impairment who want to become dietetics practitioners. The state VR program services would be tailored to meet the specific needs of the individual to make sure they have the support and resources necessary to achieve their career goals of being a dietetics practitioner despite the challenges posed by their SCI and/or vision impairment. Specific examples of these tailored services from state VR program follow:

- **Assessment, Career Counseling, and Planning:** The state VR program typically begins by assessing the individual's abilities, interests, and dietetics practitioner employment goals. Then, the individual and a VR Counselor collaborate to create an Individualized Plan for Employment that addresses the SCI and/or vision impairment to outline the steps to become a dietetics practitioner. This plan would include identifying educational requirements and necessary accommodations or services.
- **Educational Support:** The state VR program might provide financial support for tuition, books, and other educational expenses needed to complete the required college degree(s) and number of supervised practice hours to become a dietetics practitioner. For the person with vision impairment, the state VR program might help with the conversion of textbooks and course materials into accessible formats (e.g., braille, large print, audio) to make sure the person can fully participate in their coursework for dietetics practitioners. The state VR program could arrange for specialized tutoring services (e.g., tutors skilled in working with students with these disabilities) if needed that accommodate the mobility challenges and/or the vision impairment.
- **Assistive Technology and Equipment:** The state VR program could help with adaptive computer technology needed by the person with a SCI by providing specialized software or hardware, such as voice-activated software, adaptive keyboards, and/or other tools to facilitate using a computer and/or mouse. For the person with vision impairment, the state VR program might provide screen reader software (e.g., Job Access With Speech or JAWS; ZoomText) to help the person to read and navigate digital content on computers. If the person uses braille, the state VR program might provide a refreshable braille display or braille note-taker to assist with academic as well as dietetics practitioner professional

work. For a person with both limited mobility and vision impairment, the state VR program might provide software that allows for voice commands and dictation. For the educational program's lab work, the state VR program might provide or arrange for accessible lab equipment (e.g., talking scales, tactile measuring tools). The state VR program might help to obtain specialized mobility aids (e.g., power wheelchair) and/or vision aids (e.g., white cane, service dog) required by the individual to navigate the campus or workplace. The state VR program might ensure that educational materials for dietetics practitioners are available in accessible formats (e.g., digital or large print).

- **Physical and Occupational Therapy:** If needed by the person with a SCI, the state VR program might coordinate and/or fund ongoing physical therapy and/or occupational therapy to maintain or improve the individual's physical abilities to make sure they can perform the physical demands of dietetics practitioner employment. Also, the state VR program might provide specialized training to help the person with mobility and/or vision challenges to navigate the educational and work environment for a dietetics practitioner safely and independently.
- **Workplace Modifications:** The state VR program might arrange for an ergonomic assessment of dietetics practitioner workstations and/or help to provide customized workstations (e.g., adjustable desks, accessible kitchen tools) to accommodate the mobility and/or vision impairments. For the person with vision impairment, the state VR program might help modify kitchen equipment or tools to include tactile markers and/or auditory signals to enable the person to work safely and efficiently as a dietetics practitioner.
- **Internship and Job Placement Assistance:** The state VR program could help find and secure supervised practice experiences required to become a dietetics practitioner, and make sure that the sites are accessible and that necessary accommodations are provided as needed by the individual

with mobility and/or vision impairment.
- **Job Search Support:** The state VR program might assist with the job search for dietetics practitioners, including support writing a resume, preparing for interviews with accommodations, arranging for accessible interview sites, and connecting with employers who value diversity and inclusivity in the workforce.
- **Transportation Assistance:** The state VR program might provide or coordinate accessible transportation services (e.g., accessible vehicles, paratransit services, travel training to use public transportation) to make sure the individual can travel to and from school, supervised practice locations, and work for dietetics practitioners. Also, the state VR program might provide financial assistance to purchase assistive devices that support independent travel (e.g., GPS devices for people with vision impairment or that identify routes with ramps).
- **Credentialing and Licensure Support:** The state VR program might offer resources to prepare for the Commission on Dietetic Registration (CDR) exam required to become a dietetics practitioner including accessible study materials and preparation courses tailored to a person with mobility and/or vision impairment, to pay the fee to take the exam, and to coordinate the necessary accommodations to take the exam (e.g., extended time, private testing room with adaptive technology, screen reader). If applicable, the state VR program might offer resources to pay the fee to be licensed as a dietetics practitioner in the specific state.
- **Post-Employment Services:** After dietetics practitioner employment is secured, the state VR program might continue to provide support (e.g., additional training or equipment, workplace modifications, and/or assistive technology upgrades) to make sure the individual can perform and maintain their job effectively as a dietetics practitioner. Also, the state VR program might connect the individual with mentors and/or peer support groups, especially those with similar disabilities, to offer guidance

and encouragement in their new role as a dietetics practitioner.
- **Business Services:** Some state VR programs work with employers to provide information about hiring people with disabilities, offering tax incentives, and creating accessible workplaces.

This book includes several autobiographies of individuals who have received support from their state VR program for their journey to become and work as credentialed dietetic practitioners with disabilities. Readers are encouraged to check for details in Chapter 7 by Ryan Branson, Chapter 9 by Alicia Connor, Chapter 10 by Liz Dunn, Chapter 17 by Alena Morales, Chapter 18 by Danielle Sykora, and Chapter 20 by Wendy Wittenbrook.

Centers for Independent Living (or CILs)

Centers for Independent Living (or CILs) are community-based, non-profit, advocacy organizations operated by and for people with disabilities. The CILs have a crucial role in helping individuals with disabilities live more independently and participate fully in their communities. There are CILs located throughout the US. The CILs are usually funded by federal, state, and local sources, along with private donations. The CILs philosophy is rooted in the belief that people with disabilities should have the same rights, choices, and opportunities as anyone else. The CILs focus on empowerment, self-determination, and inclusion. At least 51% of the staff and board members of a CIL must be people with disabilities; this ensures that the services and programs offered by CILs are guided by the perspectives and needs of the people with disabilities who they serve. The CILs often collaborate closely with state VR programs to enhance the ability of both organizations to empower people with disabilities to achieve greater independence, particularly in areas related to employment, education, and community living. The following bullets highlight the five core services of CILs.
- **Information and Referral:** CILs provide information about disability services and resources for people with disabilities.
- **Independent Living Skills Training:** CILs teach skills (e.g., cooking, budgeting, using public transportation) to people

with disabilities to promote their independence.
- **Peer Counseling:** CILs offer support from people who have personal experience with disability.
- **Advocacy:** CILs work to change policies and systems that impact people with disabilities at both the individual and systemic level.
- **Transition Services to Community Life:** CILs help people with disabilities move from institutional settings to independent living, and help young people with disabilities transition from school to adulthood.

There are several options to find the CIL located near you. One option is the "National Council on Independent Living" website which has a directory of CILs across the US. A second option is the "Statewide Independent Living Council" website; to find this website for your state, search online for "[name of your state] Centers for Independent Living." A third option is the "Independent Living Research Utilization" website which has a comprehensive directory of CILs in which you can search by state or zip code to find the CIL nearest to you. A fourth option is to contact your local disability advocacy organizations which can direct you to the nearest CIL.

To illustrate the CILs within a state, let's consider South Carolina which has five CIL offices. Each CIL office serves different South Carolina counties as indicated in the following numbered bullets:
1. "Able South Carolina – Upstate" serves 10 counties,
2. "Able South Carolina – Midlands" serves 13 counties,
3. "Walton Options – North Augusta" serves four counties,
4. "Walton Options – Lowcountry" serves six counties, and
5. "Accessibility" serves five counties.

The CILs can offer various forms of assistance for people with disabilities. For example, consider people with SCI, vision impairment, and/or hearing impairment who want to study dietetics and become dietetics practitioners. They might receive the following various forms of assistance from CILs:
- **Adaptive Technology and Accessible Study Materials:** CILs can provide people with disabilities with information and training on adaptive technologies (e.g., screen readers, magnification tools, speech-to-text software) to make

studying and working as dietetics practitioners more accessible. Also, CILs can help connect people with disabilities with resources that provide dietetics textbooks and study materials for dietetics practitioners in accessible formats (e.g., Braille, large print, audio).

- **Education and Training:** CILs may offer career counseling services to assist people with disabilities in understanding the requirements, identifying educational pathways, and developing plans to become dietetics practitioners. CILs can help people with disabilities to advocate for necessary accommodations (e.g., extra time when taking exams, accessible lab equipment, sign language interpreters) during education and training to become dietetics practitioners.
- **Employment Services:** CILs can assist people with disabilities with job placement as dietetics practitioners and identify potential employers who are inclusive and supportive of employees with disabilities. Also, CILs can guide dietetics practitioners with disabilities in requesting reasonable accommodations (e.g., ergonomic equipment for those with mobility impairments, magnification or braille aids for those with vision impairments, communication aids for those with hearing impairments) in the workplace.
- **Peer Support and Mentoring:** CILs often facilitate peer mentoring programs so people with disabilities can connect with others with disabilities who have successfully become dietetics practitioners. Also, CILs may offer support groups for people with similar disabilities who are becoming or are employed as dietetics practitioners with disabilities to share experiences, strategies, and encouragement.
- **Advocacy and Legal Support:** CILs can advocate on behalf of people with disabilities to ensure they have equal access to education to become dietetics practitioners, employment opportunities for dietetics practitioners, and accommodations for dietetics practitioners. Also, CILs can provide information on the legal rights of people with disabilities who are becoming or working as dietetics practitioners, such as the Americans with Disabilities Act,

and help with any challenges related to discrimination or accessibility.
- **Life Skills and Independence Training:** CILs can provide training for people with disabilities to help them manage personal care as well as professional responsibilities as dietetics practitioners. Also, CILs can help to identify accessible transportation options or training in using public transportation to attend dietetics classes or commuting to work as dietetics practitioners.
- **Community and Networking:** CILs are often connected with other community organizations, professionals, and resources for people with disabilities to provide additional support, mentorship, or networking opportunities in the field of dietetics.

Summary

State VR programs and CILS provide a variety of numerous potential services for people with disabilities. Understanding these potential services can be key to meeting both educational and employment goals for individuals with disabilities.

Chapter 6 (Autobiography) Dietitian with a Mobility Disability

By Suzanne Domel Baxter, PhD, RD, LD, FADA, FAND

Suzanne ("Suzi") Domel Baxter

Deciding on a Career

I am the middle of three children, with a sister two years older and a brother five years younger than me. One Christmas when I was in early elementary school, I received an Easy Bake Oven with several mixes of items to bake. I went through those mixes in just a few days! I soon graduated to the oven and stove in the kitchen to create desserts of all kinds. I made pralines one year, entered them in the state fair, and won a ribbon! When I was in sixth grade, my father died unexpectedly so my mother had to go to work to support our family. I began to cook meals for our family to help her. After I got my driver's license, I enjoyed shopping for groceries for our family.

When I was a senior in high school, I did not want to go to college. But my mother encouraged me not to waste my brain. I let her decide where I should go to college. She selected Valparaiso University in Indiana. That was culture shock for me because I was born and raised in a suburb of Dallas, Texas. For my first semester in college, I had a home economics class, several music classes because I played the violin, a chemistry class, and a religion class. I was very homesick and also developed some health problems. I begged my mother to let me stay at home for the spring semester and attend a local community college.

For an assignment for one of my community college classes, I had to spend 40 hours shadowing someone working in a job that was of interest to me. I talked with my mother and decided that because of my interest in food, I should either become a chef or a registered dietitian. My mother knew a registered dietitian at our church, and encouraged me to talk with her. Her work in a hospital did not appeal to me, but she told me that dietitians also work in many other places such as schools. I contacted the school district where I had attended elementary, junior high, and high school and they connected me with the dietitian. For my 40-hour assignment, she explained what a typical workday was for her, and I helped her with a health fair she was planning for the foodservice employees of the school district. I attended the health fair and enjoyed learning about foodservice. I decided to become a dietitian.

Degrees in Nutrition and Dietetics

After I decided to become a dietitian, I searched for a dietetics program near my home so I could come home on weekends. I identified two universities within an hour of home and visited both. One was going to close its home economics program soon. The other was Texas Christian University (or TCU) in Fort Worth, Texas.

I began attending TCU as a sophomore and took summer classes at the local community college. I attended the coordinated undergraduate dietetics program at TCU for my junior and senior year. Those were busy years because we had classroom instruction on Mondays, Wednesdays, and Fridays from 8am to 5pm, and then we had our practicum courses on Tuesdays and Thursdays at various sites in and around Fort Worth. I was at a different location for each of the four semesters of my practicum. For example, I spent one semester with the dietitian at the public health department in the Women, Infants, and Children program; one semester with two clinical dietitians at an osteopathic hospital; and one semester with the dietitian who managed foodservice for a small school district for a suburb outside of Fort

Worth. Sometimes I envied my sorority sisters who had hours each day without classes. My long days and long hours were worth it because I was eligible to take the registration exam to become a registered dietitian immediately after graduation at the end of my senior year.

After working for five years as a registered dietitian in various settings, I decided to attend graduate school at Texas Woman's University in Denton, Texas. Each semester, I worked as a graduate assistant. I was a teaching assistant one semester, and a research coordinator one summer. For most of the semesters, I worked in the Nutrition Counseling Center in the Department of Nutrition and Food Sciences and provided nutrition counseling for college students, adults, and children. For my master's thesis, I collaborated with the Dallas Public Health Department to create and teach a weight control program for low-income Black women. For my dissertation, I continued to collaborate with the Dallas Public Health Department to create a weight control program for low-income Hispanic women, pilot test it in several locations, and conduct small-scale studies of the weight control program for Black women in several locations.

Where I Worked as a Registered Dietitian

For my first job, I worked one year in Galveston, Texas at a residential school for children with cerebral palsy and other disabilities. The staff included nurses, physical therapists, occupational therapists, speech pathologists, psychologists, music therapists, and special education teachers. I wrote the general menus, created special menus for children who needed to lose or gain weight, supervised the foodservice staff, conducted dietary assessments on children when they enrolled in the school, taught nutrition education to the children, and worked with the rest of the staff. I had not had any classes concerning disabilities in college, so I learned what I could about disabilities from the rest of the staff.

For my second job, I worked one year in Galveston, Texas at a general outpatient clinic for adults at the University of Texas Medical Branch. The clinic patients were primarily low income. Instead of having patients see me only one time after being referred by a doctor, I initiated a system to schedule follow up appointments. Many patients lived an hour or more away from and rode shuttles for their clinic appointments, so my follow up appointments were scheduled whenever they returned to the clinic again for their next medical appointment. I created and used my own nutrition education handouts.

For my third job, I worked one year as the training and quality control foodservice supervisor in Grand Prairie, Texas. It had a central warehouse where all food items were delivered and stored, and a truck and crew that delivered items to each of the schools weekly. I spent half of my time visiting each of the elementary, middle, and high schools in the district during breakfast and lunch and completed sanitation checklists. My supervisor would only allow the school cafeterias to receive the food items needed for a week at a time. So, I spent the other half of my time splitting and repacking food items into smaller units. The central warehouse had a tiny test kitchen where I spent a few days to revise recipes to decrease the amount of sugar, salt, and fat.

For my fourth job, I worked for two years at the Fort Worth Public Health Department as the supervisor of the Women, Infants, and Children program. This is where I had spent one semester for a practicum during college, and the dietitian was the same person. I visited the clinics to observe the staff teaching nutrition education classes and issuing food vouchers to clients. I helped create our monthly nutrition education materials. I tracked pre- and post-test scores from the nutrition education classes. The dietitian who supervised me had recently gone back to school and graduated with her master's degree. She said it changed her life and encouraged me to attend graduate school.

After attending graduate school and earning my master's and doctoral degrees in nutrition, I completed a two-year postdoctoral fellowship in pediatric nutrition research at the Medical College of Georgia. I helped evaluate a nutrition education program to encourage elementary school children to eat more fruits and vegetables.

I became a faculty member and worked at the Medical College of Georgia for ten years. I was Principal Investigator for several competitive grants from the National Institutes of Health. My research primarily concerned the accuracy of children's self-reports of diet. Data collection occurred in numerous elementary schools in a local school district where my staff observed children eating meals, and then interviewed children to obtain dietary recalls. I traveled a lot to attend conferences where I presented my research. I published results of my research in peer-reviewed journals.

I was a faculty member for 13.5 years at the University of South Carolina in Columbia. I continued my research concerning the accuracy of children's self-reports of diet, and expanded it to include childhood obesity and participation in school meals. Data collection occurred in many elementary schools in several local school districts. I continued traveling to present my research, and publishing results of my research.

My Disability and Accommodations

I acquired my disability while at the peak of my career as a faculty member at the University of South Carolina. I noticed episodic burning pain in my hands and feet. I was diagnosed with erythromelalgia, or "Burning Feet Syndrome" in 2010. The diagnosis took two years to confirm — because it is so rare — many appointments with physicians and unusual medical tests, and two trips to the Mayo Clinic in Rochester, Minnesota. Erythromelalgia is a rare neurovascular, peripheral disease characterized by episodic painful extremities often precipitated by exertion or heat. Erythromelalgia can be primary — which means it occurs spontaneously — or secondary due to neurological or autoimmune diseases or cancer. My erythromelalgia is primary so it is not related to another condition. There is no known cure and no specific medical treatment or drugs that work for each person with erythromelalgia. It is not fatal but is life-changing because major lifestyle modifications are needed to minimize pain episodes. My pain episodes are triggered by exposure to loud environments, riding in cars and planes, exertion, heat, walking, standing, and anything that puts pressure on the palms of my hands or soles of my feet. I no longer drive a car and avoid riding in a car except when necessary. I am usually barefooted. The only shoes I can wear are open-toed flip flops. I elevate my legs and feet whenever possible to reduce swelling in my feet and ankles. In bed, I use a "canopy" over my feet to keep the covers from touching and allow air to circulate. In addition to erythromelalgia, I have frequent headaches and kidney stones.

My career as a research professor was almost at its peak when my disability was diagnosed. My job was to write grants and obtain extramural funding to conduct research and pay for the majority of my salary and fringe plus all salary and fringe of staff who I hired and supervised. I often traveled to a total of five conferences annually — state, national, or international — to present research results, and to Washington, DC, three times annually to review and score research grants submitted to the National Institutes of Health. I was always writing, submitting, and revising research manuscripts for publication. I worked 50-65 hours per week.

When my disability hit, I had to make drastic work and lifestyle changes to decrease pain episodes. I worked for six years after my diagnosis by spreading my workweek over all seven days, telecommuting from home most of the time, and arranging rides when I had to go into the office. To decrease pain episodes caused by walking too much, I used a power wheelchair or a power scooter at the office. However, it eventually got to the point that I had made all lifestyle accommodations possible, but the episodes of pain continued to interfere with my ability to concentrate and work. I had to resign at the end of 2016 due to my disability. Much of this was because I could not sleep due to pain, and/or sleep on a regular schedule.

My first power scooter had three wheels and my current power scooter has four wheels; both scooters come apart and fit into the trunk of a car. Using my power wheelchair meant I needed to be driven in a van with a lift. Both my scooter and wheelchair require me to use ramps to access doors to buildings. My office was in a building with a ramp to the front door but there was only one space for handicap parking. The parking garage had a ramp to a coffee shop in the building, but the coffee shop closed daily at 2pm. There was only one accessible parking space by the ramp to the building's front door. There was one ramp in the loading dock, but it was much too steep for wheelchairs or scooters. I asked the university to designate more accessible parking spaces close to the front door. They did, but on the narrow and busy street in front of the building, and there was no ramp from the street to the sidewalk! Inside the building, the door to the ladies restroom was very heavy; often, I had to ask someone to open it for me. It was difficult for me to reach the buttons to request an elevator because the keypads were blocked by large trashcans. It was challenging to attend meetings in other buildings on campus because I had to find the ramps. Some buildings had ramps that were only accessible from the parking garage.

I realized how unaware I had been of ramps until I needed them because I was in a wheelchair or on a scooter! In airports, I am frustrated by the limited number of handicap stalls in restrooms, and by having to wait to use them because people without disabilities are using them to change clothes or even to read books!

Networking with Colleagues

I rely on email, discussion boards, text, cell phone, and virtual meetings to network with colleagues in the profession. I occasionally travel to state or national conferences when my husband can travel with me for help. Travel exhausts me so I schedule one or two extra days to rest before the conference sessions begin.

Volunteer and/or Leadership Activities

Before I acquired my disability, I reviewed grants for the National Institutes of Health. I volunteered with the South Carolina affiliate to help raise funds. I reviewed scholarship applications for the Foundation of the Academy of Nutrition and Dietetics. I was President of the South Carolina Affiliate when my disability was diagnosed.

My disability requires me to avoid exerting myself too much. Virtual volunteer activities are easier for me with my disability than in-person activities. I have days when I cannot do any volunteer activities, and days when I can do some. Some of my leadership roles since acquiring my disability include groups within the Academy of Nutrition and Dietetics. For example, I co-founded the Disabilities in Nutrition and Dietetics Member Interest Group — or Disabilities MIG — was its inaugural Chair, and am now its past Chair; Chapter 3 includes my volunteer and leadership activities concerning the Disabilities MIG. I was Treasurer and Diversity Liaison for the Research Dietetic Practice Group. I was Membership Chair and Treasurer for the Cultures of Gender and Age Member Interest Group. I am a member of the National Organization of Blacks in Dietetics and Nutrition Member Interest Group. For 15 years before and after acquiring my disability, I was a member of the Board of Editors of the *Journal of the American Dietetic Association/Journal of the Academy of Nutrition and Dietetics*. In Spring 2024, I became a volunteer for Disability Rights South Carolina for its

Advisory Council and Voting Coalition. In October 2024, I self-published a children's book titled *"When I Grow Up, I Can Be a Dietitian"* that is available on Amazon. The book is beautifully illustrated by a dietitian and features ten children from diverse backgrounds including race, gender, and disability who each want to become a dietitian and work in ten different settings. I am donating all royalties from the children's book to three efforts to help diversify the dietetics workforce; one of the three efforts is the Disabilities MIG. I am co-editor for this book with Cheryl Harris, and have truly enjoyed our collaboration. I am a believer and know there is purpose for my disability.

My Disability Culture for Shopping, Preparing, and Eating Food

Before my acquired disability, I loved to shop for food, cook, and bake. But the pain from erythromelalgia forced me to stop most of that. Now, we order groceries online and have them delivered to our home, or my husband goes shopping for food. He usually picks up meals for us to eat at home. Sometimes he prepares our meals at home. The extent of my meal preparation now consists of microwaved oatmeal with cranberries or whole-grain gingerbread or pumpkin bread with Greek vanilla yogurt for breakfast, a salad with Romaine lettuce, pecans, dried cranberries, and shredded Parmesan cheese for lunch, and sometimes crockpots of 15 bean soup or split pea soup for supper! Whenever I ate pizza before my disability, I would cut it up into pieces and eat it with a fork. Since I acquired my disability, I just pick up the piece of pizza and bite into it. When I eat dry cereal now, I put it into a plastic glass without milk and pour the cereal into my mouth because that is easier for me than using a spoon. It is easier for me to eat soup from a mug without a spoon, too.

Advice Concerning Dietetic Practitioners with Disabilities

I was hesitant to disclose much about my disability to the university. In hindsight, I wish I had disclosed more because it could have helped with accommodations. For example, I think they would have provided an accessible parking spot in the parking lot close to the ramp to access the front door, and relocated the large trash cans that obstructed access to elevator keypads.

Amy Joye, a dietitian on my research team, had a medical tragedy that left her in a semi-comatose state for years. She was relatively young when it happened. I initiated a fund-raising effort with her family and created the endowed "Amy Joye Memorial Research Award" via the Academy Foundation. Amy had enrolled in long-term disability insurance through our employer. So, the next time our employer had open enrollment for insurance, I enrolled in long-term disability. I encourage people to obtain long-term disability insurance. There was a tremendous amount of paperwork, but it was worth it. My long-term disability, along with social security disability, paid almost 70% of my salary for approximately seven years after I had to resign and until I turned 65.

After I acquired my disability, I turned into a sponge to learn whatever I could about disabilities. Disability culture, digital accessibility, and the Web Content Accessibility Guidelines are especially interesting to me. I continue to take online classes about digital accessibility that are available for free for people with disabilities from several companies such as Deque and WebAIM.

I encourage people with disabilities, and people who work with or serve clients or patients with disabilities, to refer to Chapter 4 about state Vocational Rehabilitation Programs and Centers for Independent Living, and to Chapter 21 about disability resources for valuable information concerning disability.

Chapter 7 (Autobiography) The Journey of an RD with Cerebral Palsy (or CP)

By Ryan Branson, MS, RD

Ryan Branson

My name is Ryan Branson, and I am a registered dietitian specializing in the treatment of eating disorders. I chose a career in nutrition and dietetics because I have always loved science, and educating and helping people to live their best life possible, of which nutrition and health is an ongoing component. I chose to pursue a path specifically within the realm of eating disorders because I have seen first-hand how devastating eating disorders are, how they completely consume the lives of those suffering, and feel passionate towards providing care and hope to individuals, working along-side them to help in getting their lives back, and to know that recovery is possible.

My disability is spastic cerebral palsy (or CP). I was born 3 months premature, and only weighed one pound at birth. The impacts from CP can vary widely from one individual to another; for me, CP primarily affects my walking, and I use both a walker and mobility scooter to assist me. Living with CP has definitely had its challenges, but I have never been one to let obstacles that I encounter in life hinder me, including with education aspirations, and in daily life. I have lived on my own since undergraduate, and this has further encouraged me to be an advocate for myself, and in navigating the tasks of daily life. This includes shopping, and I have come to really appreciate grocery delivery. Of course, delivery can be very expensive, and may not be an option for everyone. Personally, I like to make quick type meals in crockpots and appreciate pre-cut produce due to having difficulty cutting/chopping ingredients related to spasticity in my hands from the CP. Recognizing that purchasing pre-made/cut items is often much more expensive (you pay for convenience), when working with individuals with disabilities, it is important to consider how shopping for, preparing, and eating food may look different.

I earned a master's degree in nutrition and dietetics from University of Illinois at Chicago (or UIC), and a second master's degree specifically in eating disorders and clinical nutrition from University College London (or UCL) in the United Kingdom. In college, the Department of Rehabilitation's Vocational Rehabilitation Program (a program that assists individuals with disabilities in attaining careers and living independently) was a very valuable resource, helping me to obtain a successful education through financial assistance with tuition and housing fees. Other accommodations included accessibility with campus and campus housing; I requested this through the Disability Services department on UIC campus, and they were always very helpful in making sure that the accommodations that I required were put into place to best support me. I recommend everyone in need of accommodations for college reach out to the Disability Services department on their campus as soon as possible (even before you officially start — do it early); they are there to support and assist you, and the more open, specific, and honest you can be with what your individual needs and accommodations are, the better they will be able to help you.

As someone who had never lived or studied abroad before, I wasn't sure of how the accommodation process would differ in the United Kingdom, and in the city of London specifically. However, I have never been someone to let anything foreign or unknown get in my way, and I have always made a promise to myself that I will never back down on something I really want to do or accomplish just because the CP might throw a few extra bumps in the road. I have been through and accomplished a lot in my life, and I was not about to let CP (or anything else for that matter) get in the way of my academic dream to pursue this one-of-a-kind master's program to better myself and my professional future. Fortunately, in the end, there was not much difference in the accommodation process. The main barrier was that some areas/aspects of the campus (including the size of elevators) were not as accessible as you would find in the US, given the historical elements of London. However, I have to say that everyone at the UCL Disability Services office (and staff in my specific program) were very supportive and helpful with moving locations of lecture halls if needed for accessibility. In the end, this all speaks to the importance of advocating for yourself and your needs, and being open and honest about how you can be best supported. If you don't communicate, how can people help and support you? It can seem daunting at first, but trust me, the more you speak up and advocate for yourself the easier it becomes, and the more you are helping yourself make navigating life easier.

I completed my dietetic internships at a variety of locations, since I was in a Coordinated Program. All of my internship locations were handicap accessible, and preceptors were super supportive in making sure that any reasonable accommodations that I needed, to be as successful as possible in my rotations, were honored. I started the conversations early with my preceptors, even before I knew that the location was 100% confirmed, because I knew it would be so important to make sure that accommodations required would be possible; I did not want to wait until the last minute and potentially add more stress for myself. It is so important to have the conversations with your preceptors early so that you can ensure that the location will work for you, and that any accommodations will be put in place, starting on day one. Advocating for yourself is so important because no one knows you like you do, including what works best for you, so please do not feel afraid to "lay it all out" from the very beginning. Let them do what they are there for — to support you — but they can only do that if you communicate openly and honestly about how.

After successfully completing the Coordinated Program, I prepared for the registration exam — the final step before being able to finally call myself a dietitian and begin to practice! For exam accommodations, I reached out to the Commission on Dietetic Registration (or CDR) early while still preparing to take the exam, and requested exam accommodations that included an accessible test-taking area, and additional time for completing the exam. Just like when preparing for my internships, I coordinated my accommodations early on, and was very open and honest about my needs; the CDR was very helpful with making sure that my exam experience was accommodated as much as possible, which I appreciated to not add additional stress from preparing and sitting for the exam itself.

Following the successful passing of the registration exam on the first go-around, I have been working as a dietitian in the specialized area of eating disorders in treatment center facilities for several years now. When I was applying for positions, I was always open and transparent from the initial interviews about the CP, and the need for reasonable accommodations, including an accessible workplace with an elevator if the building has multiple levels. Key duties in my role as a dietitian specializing in the treatment of eating disorders include: assessing patients for nutritional risk, and creating individualized meal plans tailored to best support each patient in their recovery journey; conducting individual weekly sessions with patients (and patients' families) to discuss and assess progress of nutritional goals, current eating disorder behaviors and thoughts, and implemented interventions; creating, organizing and leading weekly nutrition education groups discussing Intuitive Eating and challenging eating disorder thoughts and behaviors; providing support to patients during meal and snack times, including restaurant and snack exposures; and kitchen maintenance of the facility, including ordering and maintaining of supplies.

In addition to my profession as a dietitian in the eating disorders field, I have been involved in many volunteer opportunities, including serving as an Ambassador to the late United Kingdom based charity Men Get Eating Disorders Too (or MGEDT). I was also a participant in a documentary about male eating disorders to help bring increased awareness, and continue breaking down barriers and stigma around mental health and males opening up, to feel more comfortable seeking help. Additionally, I have also participated in interviews to bring additional awareness to male eating disorders, and conducted two different research studies; one focused on college-aged students' awareness of male eating disorders, and the other focused on the experiences within eating disorder treatment centers for male patients, and identifying areas of change needed within treatment to help males feel as comfortable as possible with sharing their stories. Given that males are often out-numbered by females in treatment, one finding from the latter study was that male patients being able to have gender-specific group opportunities with other males to talk about male-specific areas of shame or struggle, can be extremely helpful with feeling more comfortable opening up.

For future generations of dietetic practitioners with disabilities, I recommend continuing to speak up and advocate for yourself and your needs. No one will fight for you as much as yourself, and you know yourself and your own needs best, so it is very important to be your own best advocate. We need more dietetic practitioners in the field; bringing increased diversity, and showing how a disability does not have to define you or dictate what you can or cannot accomplish in life, including with your profession and the differences you can play a role in making.

Editors: Suzanne Domel Baxter and Cheryl Iny Harris

Chapter 8 (Autobiography) Debility, Passion, and Balance

By Catherine (Katie) Brown, MS, RD, CDN

Catherine (Katie) Brown

Introduction

My name is Catherine (Katie) Brown and I became a registered dietitian in 2015. I've lived in Buffalo since 2014. I am originally from San Diego, CA, which is where I met my amazing husband, Ryan. We have two adorable dogs, Jade and Ramone. I love to advocate for causes I care about, garden, play board games, and swim. I currently have six invisible disabilities.

My disabilities include several mental health conditions; anxiety, bipolar depression, ADHD, and insomnia. I also have an autoimmune disease, it doesn't have a formal name, but it can be called incomplete lupus, undifferentiated connective tissue disease (UCTD), also known as a collagen disorder. For this writing I will refer to it as UCTD. I have scoliosis which runs in my family. This means I get more spine and neck pain and my spine is prone to become arthritic more quickly. I was born blind in one eye. I will talk more about these later.

I have been a dietitian since 2015 and started a private practice in 2021. In addition to my work, I have been an active volunteer throughout my career. I have been involved in the New York State Academy of Nutrition and Dietetics (NYSAND) since 2020. This has included District President, Delegate, Career Guidance, and several committees in NYSAND. I stepped in as interim Public Policy Coordinator and Nutrition Services Reimbursement Specialist for part of 2024. I am currently President of NYSAND which is a commitment through June 2025. I'm passionate about the field of dietetics. Everyone should have equal access to a dietitian, and I want dietitians to feel appreciated and supported in their profession.

Dietitians play a crucial role in the health of the population but it doesn't always feel that way. Insurance companies have limited nutrition coverage even for conditions like malnutrition. Historically our profession was prevalent in the foodservice industry and many hospital staff continue to see dietitians as a "lunch lady" rather than a part of the medical team. I have seen great progress in these areas since becoming a dietitian and hope to contribute to the modernization of the profession.

The Early Years

I have always been disabled. I was born blind in my right eye. The eye specialists think my eye started to form in the womb and then stopped part way through. No one really knows the cause. It's rare for this to occur only to one eye. Specialists thought since it was only one side, I might have something wrong with my brain like cancer. When I was an infant I had surgery to check my brain and everything appeared fine! The real cause continues to be a mystery. In addition, I don't have an optic nerve on the right side. That means even if a cool robotic eye is developed in the future, my brain would be unable to accept it. I am lucky that I was born this way because my brain was able to adapt early on. Depth perception or a normal field of vision are foreign to me, however I am able to estimate depth better than most people with only one eye. Another cool thing is that I notice how sound changes when something is near my right ear. It's a way my brain adapted to not having vision on that side. Around age 20, I learned how some deaf children can use echolocation to detect items as small as a watermelon. It's not the same as seeing but it helps to avoid walking into walls on my right side as much (still occurs frequently). People always ask me what it's like being blind in one eye. It is hard for some people to understand what it means to see nothing. Imagine having an eye tattooed on the back of your neck. What would you see through it? Nothing.

At one week old, my mom was told that I would never be allowed to fly a plane or drive a bus. I'm not sure I would want to do either but it's odd growing up knowing there are some jobs that are out of reach. Sports are a big challenge as it's difficult to track the ball in space. On the flip side, I am good at art because I do not have to convert 3D images to 2D since all I see is 2D.

As I got older, my blind eye shrunk (it's called phthisis bulbi if you want to learn more) and eventually I was given a fake eye at age 11. It helped me look like everyone else, but it was uncomfortable and did not correct my vision nor provide depth perception. If I had a choice, I don't think I would have gotten it. I never saw a need to make myself look like everyone else, the way I looked is just how I was born. But now that I have a fake eye, it's challenging to go back because it stretched out my tissues, so I have accepted it as a part of my life. Unfortunately, vision wasn't my only challenge in life.

Starting in first grade, I struggled to learn how to read. I spent a lot of time with tutors and in summer school so I wouldn't need to be held back. Eventually, it was determined my issue with reading was a combination of ADHD and reading with one eye. I had an eye tracking issue that made me struggle to follow lines of text. My learning disability and blindness led me to be often picked on as a child. I turned to binge eating and became overweight, which added fuel to the bullying. I became withdrawn, depressed, and did not have many friends as a child. As I went on medication for ADHD and learned how to read with one eye, things improved. I went to a specialty art high school where I finally had a solid set of friends and flourished. I love artists because their uniqueness is celebrated instead of ridiculed. People at my school wore all different outfits, from capes to funny hats, to Halloween costumes year-round. I didn't feel so different or alone in that environment and this is a lesson I take with me today.

Choosing Dietetics

When I graduated from high school, I thought art was my path since I had spent so much time practicing fine art. Yet the more I thought about it, the more I realized that I didn't like the idea of doing art for money or other people's desires. In addition, I have always felt called to help others since I was a child and art did not feel like it fit that longing.

In my final semester as a high school senior, I took physics and that is when I realized I really liked science. Being a woman with disabilities, I had never been encouraged to explore science. As I contemplated my future career, I considered how I was always reading and watching things about nutrition. In high school, I was briefly no longer overweight due to a combination of ADHD meds, anxiety causing nausea, and increased exercise. The more I learned about food, the more things didn't add up. The amount of conflicting information in the world of nutrition was crazy, and I wanted to be the one to understand. I wanted to be able to watch something like *The Biggest Loser* and know if what they were saying was true. Then I wanted to use that information to guide others so they didn't end up confused about nutrition like I was.

College

When I applied to college, I applied to art programs, yet as it approached time to actually go, I became more certain I wanted to be a nutritionist (I didn't know what a dietitian was at the time). Since I had specifically applied to art programs, I needed to go to community college to complete my general education classes before applying to a nutrition/dietetics program at a university.

Community college in San Diego was fine. I neither registered with the Disability Services Office nor requested any accommodations. I did not struggle much with my learning disability, but I started having chronic pain and severe fatigue. I struggled to stay awake for more than six hours at a time and had no appetite. I became underweight. I went to my doctor and was diagnosed with vitamin D deficiency, which was treated, but I still never felt well. I was tired, achy, and became sick frequently. I managed to stay in school, but couldn't work a job and keep up with my schoolwork at the same time. I transferred to a prominent public institution in the Midwest to continue my undergraduate education, with passable grades from community college. This is where things got harder.

This school had "weed out" classes and put a strong emphasis on curved grading. It appeared that the university didn't want everyone to succeed, and students were pitted against each other. Yes, the program aimed to create self-sufficient graduates, but at what cost? Adding to my stress, the dietetic program strongly encouraged a minimum GPA of 3.4 to qualify for a dietetic internship program. At the time, only half of all applicants were accepted. I was terrified that all my undergraduate work and financial investment would be in vain if I didn't secure an internship. I experienced an incredibly unhealthy amount of anxiety during this time, which contributed to me feeling sick all the time. I was also struggling with depression, and binge eating during this period.

I had one professor who would not budge on anything. It was Anatomy Physiology with a class size of 725 students! We had lectures twice a week which consisted of a PowerPoint presentation. We were expected to go home after the lecture and memorize everything in the PowerPoint slide deck. The professor wanted the average grade to be a B-. We had a motivated class of students who needed good grades for their advanced programs (dental, medical, pharmacy, nursing etc.). When we kept having a higher average on the test than desired by the professor, the test was made harder. The textbook for this class was over 1,000 pages, and it is the only textbook I actually read cover to cover throughout my entire college career. People say you need to focus on what's important, but in this class everything was important. I struggled to memorize the mountains of information I needed to know. In addition, the cadavers gave me so much anxiety that it was hard for me to learn and think. I tried to get my tests changed to other methods so I did not have to see the cadavers, but they refused — even after I got my therapist involved. Getting through those two semesters was by far the hardest of my schooling.

While in undergrad, I registered with the disability

department. My only accommodations offered were taking tests in a different environment and double test times. I did not find those accommodations helpful. I could think quickly, but I struggled to keep up with assignments and the amount of information I needed to memorize. Having a learning disability combined with the persistent feeling of having a chronic flu, made it really challenging. I honestly should have reduced my class load but I couldn't afford to pay for more semesters. My family was not supportive of slowing down, I was taught to push through and I did. I was close to many nutrition professors, and some gave me extensions on projects and papers when I was struggling. This was not official, but they saw that I was trying. In one class, I bombed a test due to just feeling so crappy one day, but luckily, my professor adjusted my grade because I did so well on everything else.

Research shows lectures and testing are an ineffective way to teach, yet so many of the "best" schools teach that way. A study published in 2014 in the *Proceedings of the National Academy of Sciences* titled, "Active Learning Increases Student Performance in Science, Engineering, and Mathematics" showed that active learning reduces failure rates by 55%. Active learning is when students are involved in the learning rather than observing such as in lectures. While the conclusions from studies on whether active learning improves mental health are mixed, I personally find it beneficial because I retain more information and have to spend less time studying (Cooper KM, Downing VR & Brownell SE. *International Journal of STEM Education* 5, 23; 2018).

I'm all for accommodations in the learning environment, but I think the environment at these types of schools is toxic for anyone. Many students were mentally struggling. By the end of the semester many students reported experiencing burn out. Are having "weed out" classes really more important than mental health and well-being?

I don't think any accommodations would have made my experience better. The sink or swim mentality is unhealthy for everyone. If I had the information I do now when I was considering schools, I would have gone to a different undergraduate program. Not because of the nutrition department but the chemistry and science departments were brutal. When picking a school, it's important to look at the teaching styles, retention rates as well as graduation rates. If many people are not completing the programs, then it's probably not a healthy environment. If there's an option, I would do the undergraduate program a bit slower, maybe over five or six years instead of four. Also, if attending a school locally you can live at home and save money. Going to community college did save money, and was a more supportive environment. I was so concerned with getting my degree from a good school; however, my focus should have been on what was best for my health instead. There are many ways to be successful, and going to the best school isn't worth compromising your well-being.

    I attended the University of Buffalo (or UB) for my master's and dietetic internship. They wanted everyone to do well in the classes. They supported all the students, and it was no longer a competitive environment. The homework assignments and projects were provided to help students learn the material. They also had less test-based grading, and lots of practical projects and activities. When we did have tests, they were often written and I found I do better explaining a concept than trying to select a multiple-choice answer. It also allows for partial credit when you understand some of a concept but maybe struggle with one part. I learned so much more at UB, and was significantly less stressed than in my undergraduate program. I remember my public health course would introduce a topic each week and we would write about how that topic related to or interacted with our chosen profession. I learned so much in that class and I don't think we ever had to take a test.

    For my dietetic internship I attended a variety of rotations in places like hospitals, nursing homes, commercial kitchens, daycare, and wellness organizations. I usually spent 24 hours per week in rotations with the other days for classes, assignments, and studying. I was very busy and exhausted but I enjoyed seeing all the different areas where dietitians worked and I liked the active learning. I spent significantly less time studying and learned more.

    My program had three semesters of internship rotations. In the fall, I did clinical studies which included a general hospital, pediatric hospital, dialysis center, and kidney transplant program. Spring was foodservice, community nutrition, and management. In the summer, I did additional community rotations and taught cooking classes at a private school. The internship rotations were exhausting and caused frequent illnesses and exhaustion. I spent all my free time doing schoolwork or sleeping. My husband paid all the bills, did all the housework, and cooked meals for me.

In the first semester of the dietetic internship, I caught all the germs going around the hospital, and it was a bad flu season. At one point, I had strep and the flu simultaneously. I was so tired I couldn't stay awake or think. Even when I wasn't sick, I had a hard time thinking and staying organized. I occasionally turned things in late. My internship directors were very kind and gave me a lot of flexibility. If it weren't for my kind internship directors and my husband I would not have completed my dietetic internship.

It's hard when you don't just have one thing wrong with you, but a collection of ailments that all interact to make you significantly more disabled. It's even more challenging when there is no underlying diagnosis for what's wrong. I didn't know I had an autoimmune disease until five years after graduating from the master's program, so how could I ask for specific accommodations? I personally struggled with wondering if this was all in my head or stress related. Some of my doctors also implied that many of my symptoms may have been psychological. How could I feel this sick all the time?

During the last semester of my master's program, I worked part-time as a diet technician at a local hospital. Working at a trauma center was my dream job but due to my learning disabilities and fatigue, I couldn't keep up with charting. There was nowhere for me to work that was quiet. I realized there was no way I would be able to do a registered dietitian (or RD) workload in a hospital.

I took the RD exam and passed without any accommodations on my first try. I didn't find it challenging, I took a study course and did practice exams. I only needed a 70% to pass. The test has since been made more challenging so I would take advice from someone who took the most recent test.

Work after Graduation

I ended up working in a nursing home as my first official RD job. It was not a good place to work for anyone. There was really high turnover and chronic understaffing. I never received proper training, and struggled to even understand all the parts of my job. I also got mixed messages from the administration about how I should be doing my job. I never bothered to ask for accommodations, I just wanted proper staffing and training. For almost eight months, I was the only dietitian trying to perform the workload of two positions. I became really behind and burned out. The administration did not prioritize hiring another RD, which was frustrating. When we finally had adequate staffing, I struggled to get caught up because things got so behind and I was so burned out. I am good at nutrition, but writing long assessments is something that I am very slow at, especially on the old computers provided by the nursing home. I tried to advocate for better technology, but they wouldn't spend $200 on a computer. I was stuck on a nine-year-old notebook with a tiny screen. Clinical jobs require extensive charting which wasn't something I could handle well.

While working at the nursing home, I started having more medical issues, and was struggling to even come into work. Eventually, I quit. I decided to take some time to work on my health issues, which I attributed to stress. I quickly realized what was wrong with me was not stress related. I was having severe joint pain and digestive issues. I continued to go to doctor appointments, but it was no help. One told me my symptoms were because of my bipolar disorder and that I should just focus on that. The pain continued to increase, then I became stiff. I finally realized that it could not be in my head when I couldn't keep up with an 85-year-old woman in my water aerobics class who had just gotten a hip replacement. I was 28 at the time.

A Diagnosis

I had a friend with an autoimmune disease who said I should get tested for one. In 2020, I finally decided to go to a rheumatologist. I was worried they would have no answers for me, but they were so patient and told me they would get to the bottom of things. After blood tests and X-rays, I was diagnosed with Undifferentiated Connective Tissue Disease (or UCTD).

Connective tissues are what hold your body together and include joints, tendons, ligaments, muscles, and skin. In an autoimmune disease your immune system attacks healthy tissue thinking it's an infection. Acute flare ups come and go. Depending on how active my autoimmune disease is dictates my level of pain and disability. Sometimes my hands are stiff, and I struggle to use the computer or grip things. Other days, my hips really hurt and it's hard to sleep. I get tingling in my extremities and sometimes my feet feel cold even though they are warm. When my inflammation is high it causes brain fog, mood changes, and fatigue. In addition, I have to worry about my autoimmune disease affecting my organs, eyesight, blood vessels, and brain. I spend a lot of time getting checkups and blood tests done.

When I was diagnosed, my CRP (a measurement of inflammation) was 20. The goal is to have it below eight. I was prescribed methotrexate to hopefully bring it down. Methotrexate is a chemotherapy drug that works by limiting your cells' ability to divide. The goal is to weaken your immune system, so it cannot attack your body. Despite being on the lowest dose of methotrexate, I started having complications after only a couple weeks. I experienced numbness in my legs, and severe muscle weakness that made it hard for me to walk short distances or roll over in bed. I was scared I would never fully recover my strength and sensation. Tests later showed damage to my liver. Movement was making me weaker instead of stronger and I had to budget my strength for things like going to the bathroom.

My husband helped care for me, and hired a person to come and help me at home because I could not even stand long enough to make a sandwich or get myself water. My liver enzymes failed to improve even though I was off the medication for several months. My muscle weakness progressed even after stopping the medication. I did not get normal sensations back in my muscles for 12 months. I got ultrasounds and MRIs of my liver, which eventually healed. While I was recovering from methotrexate's side effects, I continued to have my original autoimmune disease symptoms and chronic pain.

Finally, nine months after taking methotrexate, I was prescribed sulfasalazine. It worked! Unfortunately, there was a severe shortage due to COVID-19, so taking it reliably was challenging. It helped, but not having it consistently was stressful.

While working to regain strength, I slowly began my private practice.

I would say the hardest thing about my disabilities is the unpredictability. I will have months where I feel almost normal, and I take on new projects and hobbies. Then I will fall back into feeling really tired with relentless brain fog for a few months. It makes my work output really unpredictable and inconsistent, which is difficult. My recommendation is to be very careful where you work and be open to leaving if it's not a good fit.

Getting on Track

Four years later I have minimal autoimmune symptoms most of the time. I still experience flare ups of my disease but they usually subside after a couple of days instead of months as they did before.

I have been working in my private practice since 2021. I create my own schedule which has allowed me to adapt to my health needs. In 2024, I partnered with a telehealth startup with the goal of building a telehealth platform of dietitians for complicated patients like me. I love helping people overcome or deal with their mental and physical struggles so they can feel better and improve their lives. I know what it feels like to believe there is no hope, and that no one truly understands what you are going through, and to finally find someone who cares about you and can offer solutions that work. Creating a group practice of dietitians provides patients with more insurance coverage. This allows our unique patients to see a dietitian who is trained in their complex condition and not worry about paying large out of pocket expenses like I did. We have a collaborative approach with other medical disciplines to maximize outcomes. I am excited to see how this company evolves over time as well as all the people impacted in a positive way.

Thoughts and Reflections

Below are some of my opinions and thoughts based on my experiences as a disabled person seeking care and as a RD with disabilities. I hope you find my insights useful.

My View on Functional Medicine and Being an Ethical Practitioner

  I first tried to control my autoimmune disease with lifestyle interventions. Since I was unsuccessful on my own, I saw some integrative and functional practitioners who my friend said had helped her. I was told my issues were related to lifestyle and gut health. They claimed if I could fix my shortfalls, I would stop being ill. I was desperate, and spent thousands of dollars on nutrition, supplements, and chiropractic care. When I didn't get better, I was told it was my fault, or I just needed to do it for longer. Trying to follow a complicated diet while feeling awful every day was really hard, so I got expensive pre-made meals. When my autoimmune disease did not improve, I was interrogated about what "I" must have done wrong to make that happen. It was very much MY fault that I wasn't getting better. I was expected to never deviate from the health plan which included never taking any painkillers including ibuprofen. I was told it could take 2-3 years for me to see if the interventions were successful. I was suffering and being expected to continue to be in pain for 2-3 years to see if it worked was cruel.

  Looking back, it makes me livid. I could have seen specialists covered by insurance, but I was told those covered by insurance don't do functional medicine. Appointments with Functional Medicine providers can be covered by insurance if they choose to enroll. Testing and supplements may not be covered. I have found several functional providers (including myself) since then who do take my insurance and helped me recover. I became very distrustful of the medical field, and saw that I was being taken advantage of financially. Integrative and Functional Medicine/Nutrition does have a place, but people shouldn't avoid conventional medicine either. Alternative medicine health care providers should not be scaring their patients out of seeking traditional medical care. Those suffering should use all the tools available to get better. Providers should also be considering quality of life and how realistic their interventions are. Maybe a new and complex diet would help alleviate some symptoms, but if it is too difficult or expensive for the patient to follow then it may not be practical or feasible.

I see dietitians pushing fresh food and complex home cooked meals. That isn't doable for everyone and it's impossible to expect that. Reasons people may struggle to home cook can include disabilities, lack of time, energy, cooking skills, kitchen equipment, or finances to do it. Why should people feel guilty? We created a society where people are disabled and sick and medical care is sometimes unreachable. Many jobs don't provide adequate paid sick time, vacation or breaks, and then we shame people for not taking responsibility for their health. We don't expect someone with the flu to cook, so why do we expect someone with a chronic health condition to cook?

Even if something can be treated with a diet, if the person is unable or unwilling to follow it, we need to be able to accept their choices and adapt our interventions. This is especially common in mental health conditions where motivation may be minimal. Providers should avoid shame or judgment, while offering realistic solutions. Adults have autonomy and we need to respect their decisions and preferences.

It's important as dietitians that we do not financially prey on those who are desperate. I know we all need to make a living, but these are real people who are struggling. Providers should not promote false hope, or blame the patient for being sick. I recommend at least trying to accept insurance. It's unfair that in America, people have to go bankrupt to get the medical care they need. I refuse to be a part of the problem, and accept over 15 insurance plans in my practice. I am also helping build a telehealth dietetics company that would provide high-quality nutrition care (including functional medicine) to those with complex disorders, all covered by insurance. I advocate for increased medical nutrition therapy coverage through insurance plans, Medicare, and Medicaid. Some patients are offered pro bono sessions if in dire need without coverage.

Workplace Advice

While in undergrad, I was invited to a disabilities conference in Chicago. It was really interesting. One thing I will always remember is one of the talks said frequently, accommodations given to someone with a disability can actually support those without the disability as well. For example, closed captioning can be good for those with language processing issues, as well as for those hard of hearing or for whom English is not their first language. Quiet work environments can benefit many people, not just those with ADHD. I want disabled people to have accommodations, but I think in general, we need to set up learning and working environments based on what works for humans biologically. A lot of jobs treat humans as robots, which we are not. These systems affect all of us, but it affects those with disabilities more.

"Everyone is a genius. But if you judge a fish by its ability to climb a tree, it will live its whole life believing that it is stupid." — author unknown.

One thing that is important to me is being able to plan my own schedule, so I have time for self-care and to go see doctors. I work part-time, and that is something I can successfully manage. If I needed to financially support myself, though, I probably would go into something else — like developing software, because those jobs can be very flexible and much more accommodating. My husband works in software development, so I have seen the possibilities for effective workplace accommodations in this field through my husband. Many have unlimited vacation and you can work from home. It's also easy to find a programming job with medical benefits. Healthcare is just a really hard field for anyone to work in, and with a disability it is extra challenging but not impossible.

If you absolutely want to go into inpatient as a dietitian with disabilities, I recommend looking for a state or government job. I lack first-hand experience with these jobs but have been told that they tend to be less stressful, pay more, and have good benefits. They may also be better about providing accommodations from what I understand.

Disabilities and Poverty

My story has a positive ending mostly because I have always had people supporting me financially. My parents, grandma, and husband helped pay my college tuition and living expenses. My husband also supported me through my autoimmune disease and recovery from methotrexate. He provided health insurance, paid for medical care out of pocket, and covered our living expenses.

If I were on disability, I wouldn't have been able to afford the treatments and care I needed to get better. Even now, my husband pays for a personal trainer and chiropractor so I can maintain my mobility and minimize pain. He does most of the work around the house, and we get pre-made meals and hire a housekeeper. I would not be able to work or volunteer without his support. I am so grateful for my situation but I am aware others may not have the same level of support.

Being on social security disability in America is mandated poverty. You can't have any significant savings. How are you supposed to save up for a deposit for an apartment, or to buy a car? Frequently, my disabled patients run out of food stamps and money for food. If they tried to eat a Mediterranean or anti-inflammatory diet, they wouldn't be able to do all the cooking and shopping plus would run out of food stamps faster. Some try to work to have some extra income, but they can only earn a tiny amount before they lose their insurance coverage. I work with a lot of people with disabilities, and it makes me so upset with society and how we treat those who are disabled. If we provided better care, so people could take care of themselves and get better, then maybe they could go off of disability. Many people need disability for the insurance, which has affordable copays. Even the best jobs have insurance with copays and deductibles. My care routinely costs over $4,000 per year for copays and non-covered medical care and I am on one of the best plans. Most with disabilities have to pick between having almost no money to survive, but health insurance coverage, or a job with money but poor insurance that doesn't cover their needs.

Disability and Trauma

Something that's often overlooked is that disability and trauma have a close relationship. Developing a disability and receiving a disability diagnosis is traumatic. If you were born with one, then the way people treated you was likely traumatic. It's hard to live in a world not made for those with disabilities and not experience trauma. Having PTSD is a type of disability, which compounds the other disabilities many of us have. People with disabilities also tend to have less money, and chronic poverty can be traumatic. I personally believe that to support individuals with disabilities you must also be trauma informed.

Life with a Disability

Living with autoimmune diseases has profoundly changed me. The unpredictability of my conditions means I never know how long I will be able to do the things I love, such as walking, working, or volunteering. This uncertainty has led me to prioritize what truly matters and strive to leave a meaningful impact on others. I've learned that what matters most is how I feel and view myself. Instead of focusing on looking or acting a certain way, I prioritize my health and comfort. I stay extra days when I travel out of town to conferences so I have time to rest. I wear ridiculous hats and shirts outside to reduce my sun exposure. I take breaks in the middle of my workday to lay down for a while. I don't let my limitations stop me from following my dreams, but I plan around what my body needs. Often, that means shorter workdays, and lots of scheduled self-care time. Although this approach can feel awkward at times, it allows me to continue engaging in activities that are important to me.

Choosing to prioritize self-care over following your dreams can be heartbreaking, but it doesn't signify weakness or failure. Putting my body and health first has allowed me to find a balance, enabling me to do what I love while taking care of myself. This took lots of practice and trial and error. You can do anything if you have enough drive and people around you to provide support.

Chapter 9 (Autobiography)
Driven by Vision

By Alicia Connor, MA, RDN, & Chef

Alicia Connor

Our culture relies heavily on visual cues to gather information and it's therefore common for people to make assumptions about a person's abilities (and disabilities) based on appearance. These assumptions are often unconscious and can lead to inaccurate conclusions.

My vision loss began gradually when I was 16, revealing itself slowly and subtly over time. I have hypoplasia of the optic nerve, which, in my case, I inherited from my mother and grandfather. I am now low vision and legally blind, both near- and far-sighted, which cannot be corrected with lenses. Upon meeting me, you might not register my vision loss right away. I do some things differently, but my visual impairment may not always be obvious to the casual observer.

Life, for me, is more about the "how" to participate than "if." It's a matter of figuring out how to do it. The key to doing so lies in the powerful tool of asking questions, paving the way for my independence. By asking the right questions, I discover what truly works for me, which can surprise others. Some people wince or show concern when they learn that I ride a bicycle, but my comfort level participating in that activity is unique to me. The way I adapt to different experiences and daily activities might seem unfamiliar to some, but they allow me to navigate life and solve problems independently and with support.

I have primarily worked as a dietitian for nine years, providing nutrition counseling with medical nutrition therapy in an outpatient clinic. Common counseling topics include meal planning, recipe modification, ingredient sourcing, how to embed exercise into busy schedules, mindset coaching to support weight loss, and proper hydration. I began this work part-time and increased to full-time, working four ten-hour days per week.

In addition, I am a group facilitator for a medically monitored weight loss program. I also run a private practice, focusing on personalized nutrition counseling and meal planning. My work also extends to workplace wellness. In 2020, I expanded my business by founding an online program to help members create meal planning systems for a lifestyle approach to wellness that is sustainable.

Like many others, my work before the pandemic was entirely in-person. Since March 2020, I have been working from home rather than the office. While I personally prefer working from home, each environment has its pros and cons. In person, about 25% of my work involved using a computer for tasks like charting, emails, and correspondence, while the remaining 75% consisted of group or one-on-one appointments. This was much easier on my eyes due to less screen time. Virtual work, on the other hand, is about 90% computer-based, including virtual appointments, charting, emails, and additional administrative and organizational tasks that weren't necessary in person.

For me, breaking down tasks into manageable steps requires the right equipment, human support, and adequate time. Whether I'm working on administrative tasks, counseling clients, managing my business, speaking, or attending a lecture, every situation requires different accommodations and approaches. There is no one-size-fits-all solution for me; each situation requires a nuanced approach. For example, reading a synopsis of a theatrical production beforehand would allow me to better enjoy the visual experience with context. In my practice, I have my clients fill out a comprehensive intake form prior to our first consultation. When participating in webinars or conferences, I request presentation slides in advance so I can read them during the session. I prefer printed slides with one slide per page, allowing me to avoid navigating a device during a presentation, whether online or in person. I often use my iPhone to take pictures of names or emails; then I delete the pictures when the tasks are done.

As a speaker, my approach varies between in-person and online events. For in-person presentations, I create two separate slide decks: one for the audience and one for myself. I tailor my personal slide deck by using larger print. Then, I print my slide deck and organize it in a three-ring binder, with one slide per page, accompanied by handwritten notes or sticky notes. A well-lit stage enhances my ability to read my prepared materials. I request support for someone to advance the slides for me.

Before presenting at a conference, I went to get water from a standalone water dispenser. This type of water dispenser was uncommon. I picked up a cup and tried to fill it, but there was no lever to dispense the water. There was nobody around to ask for help, and I thought to myself "Oh well, I guess I'm not getting any water." Then, I noticed a sign with small text above the dispenser. I took a picture and zoomed in to read the instructions, which indicated that the dispenser was operated with a foot pedal. I was able to use the foot pedal and fill my cup with water. However, if the water dispenser's sign was a large print, high-contrasting colored arrow pointing to the foot pedal, this problem would not have presented itself. So that day, I began my presentation with, "This world was not built for people with disabilities," and shared this story with the audience, providing a real-time example of my topic.

In my daily life, I rely on several accommodations. Currently, I use a 4x dome magnifier for spot reading things with small text, like my credit card. I keep one at my computer station, another inside the entrance of my apartment, and often carry one with me when using ride-sharing apps that are not currently accessible. To use inaccessible apps, I either take a screenshot to read the information, such as my destination's address, or use the magnifier on the go. The most common device I use is my smartphone. When shopping, I often take pictures of labels or price tags with my phone and then magnify the picture. My computer station includes an external monitor, mouse, large print keyboard, and full screen magnifier on my computer.

For transportation, besides walking, riding my bike, and public transportation, I prefer taxis, especially from airports, because rideshare pickups at airports can be hard to find in unfamiliar settings. When leaving home, however, I'm more likely to order a rideshare because my quiet street has fewer moving cars which makes it easier for me to locate the vehicle. When I fly, I use several accommodations. When booking my flight online, I usually indicate my disability. If there is assigned seating on the flight I ask for help locating my seat. If I am in an unfamiliar airport or running late, I ask for assistance getting to my gate or finding the baggage carousel.

At home, I've adapted my oven dial by marking the 350-degree temperature with red electric tape. For writing, I prefer using thick, bold ink pens in black or dark blue because the high contrast and wider text is easier for me to read.

These accommodations and strategies illustrate the adjustments I make to navigate daily life and maintain independence. Each person has different needs, and what works for one person may not work for another, even among individuals with vision impairment.

As a highly tactile and visual person, I prefer to engage with the world by seeing, hearing, touching, feeling, breathing, and even tasting, my experiences. Seeing people's faces when they talk is important to me because it helps me understand their expressions and emotions. For example, in a social setting like a party, my ideal distance for a conversation is about an arm's length.

Despite having a vision impairment, I am predominantly visual. In my role as a nutrition counselor, whether in person or through telehealth, I rely heavily on visual cues to gauge my patients' reactions to the conversation and my recommendations. If I notice a client is uninterested based on their facial expression, I can quickly modify my approach.

My journey into the field of dietetics stemmed from my initial career as a chef and working in foodservice. As my vision continued to decline, I recognized the need for a different profession. Working in professional kitchens is physically demanding, and — coupled with my vision loss — I knew it wasn't a sustainable career.

My aspirations extended beyond preparing delicious food; I wanted to educate others on how to cook meals that were both tasty and nutritious. Health has always been a priority for me. Growing up, my mom instilled a health-conscious mindset. She cooked predominantly from scratch with fresh ingredients. However, during my high school years, she struggled with depression and cooked less frequently. During this time, I worked two jobs in the summer, one of which was a physically demanding landscaping job. It was up to me to provide myself with nourishing meals to fuel me through the days of hard work. These experiences played an important role in my discovery of the power of healthy food and the vital skill of cooking.

Given my background and interests, a career as a Registered Dietitian Nutritionist (or RDN) was a perfect fit by combining my culinary expertise with my passion for health and nutrition. This career allows me to make a meaningful impact on people's lives while also focusing on my own health.

To help fund my education and career transition, I sought financial assistance through Social Security Disability Insurance. When I applied, I didn't just cite my legal blindness; I also included my back issues as part of the justification for seeking career change training and education. Also, I contacted the California Department of Rehabilitation. I was connected with a counselor who, after an assessment, suggested several tools tailored to my specific needs, including a computer with a larger monitor, a large print keyboard, assistive software that magnifies and enhances computer screen displays, and various other magnifying tools. Some tools, like magnifying lenses, proved less helpful. This was all before I had a smartphone.

I began my back-to-school adventure to pursue a bachelor's degree in dietetics at the age of 27. Initially, I took one class at a community college, then gradually increased to three classes. This was the most sustainable course load to balance my studies and work. I spent four years at a community college before transferring to San Francisco State University, where I completed my undergraduate degree in dietetics over the course of three years. It took me 10 years total to complete my undergraduate and master's degrees.

For the time I was going to community college and San Francisco State for my undergraduate degree, I received a California Promise Grant, so I didn't need to pay for tuition. As a person with a disability, I also received a free public transportation pass. The California Department of Rehabilitation also reimbursed me for my textbooks. For the dietetic internship, the California Department of Rehabilitation paid the tuition.

While attending community college, I relied on accommodations provided by the college's Disability Services & Programs for Students Center. I met with a counselor before each semester to determine the necessary accommodations. I was consistently granted double time for exams which were provided in large print, typically 36-point font on 11- by 13-inch paper. For two chemistry classes, I used a "Clarity Classmate" device, which was similar to a camera with a monitor. This device was stored in the professor's office where I would have to retrieve it before each class and set it up. It was bulky and took up an entire desk, but it allowed me to see chalkboard writing from a distance.

At San Francisco State University, I met with counselors from the Disability Resource Center to determine necessary accommodations. The "Clarity Classmate" was not available so I had to adapt. For example, during the semester when taking organic chemistry, the class was held in a stadium seating lecture hall with desktops attached to chairs. I used a monocular to view presented slides and I had paper copies of the slides in a larger format. Unfortunately, this note-taking method caused nerve pain in my arm and required pain medication. I sought help from the Disability Resource Center, and for other semesters was provided with a student note-taker when necessary. The note-taker's diagrams were essential for biochemistry. I coordinated with instructors for the required paperwork to ensure they were aware of my accommodations, such as double time and large print for exams.

As a graduate student, the Disability Resource Center provided accommodations to assist with typing my thesis, including a student scribe. I greatly benefited from a variety of helpful accommodations throughout my path of higher education. There was a lack of proactive assistance in the system, leaving me to continually advocate for myself to ensure I had the necessary resources to succeed. Ideally, it would help if there were training for instructors about challenges experienced by students with disabilities and how to better provide support.

For my dietetic internship, I was placed in rotations where public transportation was available, even if it meant long commutes. For a rotation in a long-term care facility, I was provided with a laptop and requested screen magnification software due to compatibility issues with the electronic medical records system and the small laptop screen hindered productivity and usability. Although the preceptor and team initially agreed to read handwritten notes for me, there were challenges with consistency and availability which led to my concerns about completing chart notes. Eventually, the chart notes were completed on a desktop computer using screen magnification.

To request accommodations for taking the RDN exam, I made sure to visit the testing center in advance to discuss my needs, including double time and screen magnification software. These accommodations provided me with the support I needed to take the exam and pass it on the first attempt.

In my employment as an RDN, the California Department of Rehabilitation has provided technology updates like new laptops and smartphones. I utilize accommodations to facilitate teaching and clinical work. At San Francisco State University, where I taught a foodservice management course, I requested ZoomText software for both classroom presentations and office work. I found a student to advance my lecture slides because my hands were occupied with the printed slides and binder. In clinical settings, I transitioned from using ZoomText to the Windows Screen Magnifier, a Windows accessibility tool that enlarges the display. This tool is more user-friendly for me, especially when paired with the large monitor.

I prioritize networking for maintaining relationships with colleagues, former interns, and members of the Disabilities in Nutrition and Dietetics Member Interest Group. I attend events like the Food and Nutrition Conference and Expo of the Academy of Nutrition and Dietetics.

In my personal life, my approach to shopping, meal preparation, and eating reflects my background as a chef with a focus on efficiency and healthy eating. I stock up on groceries during larger grocery runs and utilize transportation services or delivery. My cooking methods include roasting, making soups and stews, creating versatile salads, and freezing individual meals aligned with my preferences for health and practicality. Other than marking my oven dial with red tape, I do not require many adaptations in the kitchen. I still have my knife skills and all my fingers!

I encourage future generations of dietetic practitioners with disabilities to communicate, seek help when needed, and not be discouraged by the unknown. I encourage dietetic practitioners without disabilities to avoid making assumptions, prioritize individual needs instead of a "one size fits all" mentality, and maintain a welcoming environment.

Regarding disability disclosure, I believe in sharing information as needed and as one feels comfortable to ensure access to required accommodations. As mentioned previously, I continue to be supported by the California Department of Rehabilitation as needed which provides me with updates in technology.

I recognize the profound value of advocating for necessary accommodations. In the past, I have paid out of pocket rather than requesting accommodations, such as a larger monitor, webcam, and large-print keyboard. Some employers are less than enthusiastic about making accommodations due to cost and it can feel easier to handle it myself.

Addressing the unique needs of individuals with disabilities requires a personalized approach that recognizes and respects differences. People with disabilities can fully participate by understanding and providing necessary accommodations for each individual and the specific situation.

As an RDN, I get to believe in others when they struggle to believe in themselves. Everyone needs some validation and elevation from time to time. I also get to empower people to empower themselves. I'm fond of the notion that we are all in partnership with our body and in a long-term relationship with ourselves until death do us part. As for me, I love this work because I get to help others while also improving myself. The issue of whether or not to participate in life isn't even considered, it's simply a matter of figuring out how.

Chapter 10 (Autobiography) Finding Dietetics Post-Spinal Cord Injury

By Liz Dunn, MS, RD, LDN

Liz Dunn

My journey into nutrition and dietetics began following my traumatic spinal cord injury (or SCI) when I was a little less than halfway through my junior year of college. Adjusting to life as a quadriplegic and wheelchair user was quite the journey, but I always knew I wanted to return to school. Prior to becoming disabled, I always had an interest in wellness, exercise, and nutrition. However, I was not aware of what a Registered Dietitian (or RD) was or what they did. During my hospital stay and subsequent rehabilitation stay, I was introduced to several RDs.

After speaking with these RDs in more detail about the profession, as well as being on the receiving end of nutrition care, I ultimately decided that when I returned to college I would study nutrition and dietetics. Prior to my injury, I was enrolled in a pre-pharmacy program. After speaking with my advisor in depth about me being able to continue in that profession, we decided it might not be best given my lack of hand function. Looking back, I believe there may have been a way for me to continue, but several things about nutrition and dietetics intrigued me. I loved the food first approach to the profession. The thought of working with people to help prevent issues, rather than treat them, was also important to me. Also, as someone new to the SCI world, I was learning about nutrition to prevent pressure injuries, hydration to prevent urinary tract infections, and so on. In addition, I had already completed two years of basic science courses including biology, chemistry, microbiology, organic chemistry, and many of those were also required for nutrition and dietetics. This made my transfer to the undergraduate program at University of Pittsburgh rather seamless.

Prior to beginning as a junior at University of Pittsburgh, I did take a few online courses that were required of me. This was good though, as it helped me transition back into school after two years off while I focused on rehabilitation. The online courses were easier for me to take as I did not have to worry about factors such as wheelchair accessible transportation, classroom set up, accessible desks, etc. This allowed me to focus on the coursework itself and not the added stressors of new environments.

Once I arrived on campus to attend classes full-time, I worked with the university's Office of Disability Resources and Services. They assisted me in setting up accommodations such as an accessible desk in my classrooms, extended time for exams when needed, alternative testing formats as many courses used scantron forms which were very difficult for me to fill out, and additional accommodations as needed. The process for accommodations was simple, as they supplied a letter of my needs with documentation to provide to my instructors.

During my undergraduate education, I also received funding through the Pennsylvania Office of Vocational Rehabilitation to assist with tuition. They also worked with me to provide me with a new laptop, speech-to-text software, as well as other employment related services such as driver's training with adaptive equipment and car modifications.

Following the completion of my undergraduate degree, I applied to and was accepted into the University of Pittsburgh's Coordinated

Master's in Nutrition and Dietetics. This program included all required internship hours as well. I received a full scholarship from the Craig H Neilsen Foundation which provides scholarships to selected colleges, universities, and community colleges for students with SCIs to pursue higher education. These scholarships cover tuition and fees for undergraduate or graduate students and include supplemental financial support for eligible students.

The process of requesting accommodations for my graduate degree was similar to my undergraduate degree, with a few more additions. I worked closely with my instructors and preceptors to come up with a plan allowing me to meet all of my competencies, even if it meant completing them in a slightly different way. Because my injury affected my hand function, there were some tasks I could not complete. One that stands out in my mind is portions of the nutrition focused physical exam. For this, I ended up having to verbally describe how to perform the aspects of the exam I was not able to do, such as palpating organs or muscles and taking blood pressure.

There were a few other accommodations I used throughout my internship, such as completing my foodservice rotation in a smaller long term care facility, instead of the large hospital I was originally assigned to. I also completed all of my charting for clinical rotations on a touch screen tablet because the regular computers were not accessible to me due to my limited hand function. Overall, I did not need too many disability accommodations throughout my education. As long as the locations I was required to go to were accessible, and I had access to restrooms, I could do almost everything else as-is.

That being said, towards the end of my final year I was struggling with fatigue and minor medical problems due to coursework and internship hours totaling over 40 hours a week. I did obtain permission from my program to cut down to four-day weeks, which subsequently extended my education by about a month to still complete the required hours.

Upon graduation and completion of all my competencies, I was eligible to sit for the registration exam. Thankfully, I had had previous experience in requesting accommodations for exams like this, as the GRE (Graduate Records Examinations) was required for my graduate program. The only accommodations I requested for the registration exam were extended time, and frequent and extended breaks. The exam was multi choice and I was able to use the standard keyboard and mouse as long as I had additional time. Any accommodations are requested through the test administrator, by submitting documentation such as a doctor's note. Approved accommodations were listed on my test confirmation.

Since becoming credentialed, I have worked with two different universities as part of their intern programs with the sports nutrition department. I assisted with running fueling stations, creating educational resources for athletes, and educational program development. I've also presented to dietetic student groups, as well as professionals at conferences. More recently I have had writing opportunities about disability and nutrition as well. In addition, I am also employed part-time outside of the nutrition and dietetics field. I work as a data coordinator on a longitudinal research study for people with SCIs. This position allows me a lot of flexibility when it comes to working when I am able to, and does not require me to be in an office frequently. Plus, I love being able to interact with the participants and also serve as a peer mentor when appropriate. Research is incredibly important and I was fortunate to find this position.

Much of the work that I have done is computer based, so I do not require many accommodations. I do prefer opportunities that are remote as it is easier for me to work from home. That is not always the case though, so when I am in person I need to be in environments that are wheelchair accessible and do not require any lifting or complex hands-on tasks. These requests have been through my supervisor who assists me in my needs. The process for requesting accommodations depends both on job requirements, as well as the place of employment. I tend to seek out opportunities that require little accommodation for me to perform my work.

Many of my experiences have been the result of networking such as participating in Dietetics Practice Group (DPG) volunteer work as a student, connections I made during my education at my university, or even reaching out to other RDs working in my area of interest. I have always made it a priority to meet others in the profession both locally, at national conferences, and even via social media.

A good way to begin networking is as a student, because groups are often looking for volunteers. Some volunteer hours I did were required by my program, but I did several things as a student simply out of interest for both helping others as well as learning new skills. There were many local events, such as providing nutrition education resources at community events and working with local food pantries. I also volunteered to assist with newsletter writing for a DPG as a student.

I have also continued to volunteer as well. I've presented multiple times on the basics of nutrition for SCI, as well as accessibility in the kitchen, and discussed tips and tricks for food preparation and options that are easier to cook. I also signed up to be involved in the leadership team for the Disabilities in Nutrition and Dietetics Member Interest Group of the Academy of Nutrition and Dietetics. Each of these opportunities have been a wonderful way to network with others both within the profession and with those in related professions. It is because of these volunteer positions that I have been able to gain more opportunities, both paid and unpaid. Networking is an important thing to keep in mind as you enter and continue with the profession.

Other advice I have for future dietetic practitioners with disabilities is to research the education required to be credentialed. Not all programs are alike; although they do have to meet the same competencies, many areas of the programs themselves can differ. It is important to look into the programs, reach out to program coordinators and set up a meeting or call to discuss the program, and even post on social media groups or within related support groups to find current or former students of specific programs. You can do many of these with or without disclosing your disability as well.

The more information you can get on a program the better. Certain programs will allow for different education tracks depending on your interests as well. I'd also recommend shadowing other dietetic professionals in a few different specialties to get an idea of what area of dietetics you may be interested in.

Completing the education requirements to become a RD can be difficult for anyone, and it's especially difficult for those of us with disabilities who must navigate additional challenges such as setting up accommodations as well as potential biases and stereotypes of others. I believe the more people learn about disabilities, the more inclusive the profession will be. I wish I had a resource such as this collection of disabled RDs experiences prior to going through my education to become an RD. At the time I did not know of any other quadriplegics that had gone through the prerequisites and internship required to become an RD. This is one of the many reasons that I continue to share about my journey. Everyone may follow a different path, but having the resources available to learn from others that have been through something similar can be incredibly helpful.

Chapter 11 (Autobiography) A Registered Dietitian with Autoimmune Diseases

By Amy Epting, MA, RD, CSG, LDN

Amy Epting

My knowledge of nutrition and healthy eating came way before I graduated college and my internship. Growing up as an overweight child, I was always on some kind of diet program. I felt a lot of pressure to keep my weight at a normal level all through my late childhood and teen years because I showed quarter horses at a high level of competition. This led to my interest in wanting to help others with weight problems and that is how I entered the field of dietetics. However, the autoimmune diseases and other health problems I experience did not come along until I was in my early 30s.

Upon graduation of high school, I attended the Pennsylvania State University and majored in applied nutritional sciences. I also took psychology courses because that interested me. I was a volunteer for the Women, Infants, and Children (or WIC) Program, a teaching assistant for an introductory nutrition class, and assisted one of my professors with a research project using data from the National Health and Examination Survey II at the time. In the summers, I worked as a dietary aid prepping the salad bar and washing dishes in a drug and alcohol rehabilitation facility that was in contract with Sodexo at the time for foodservice. Upon graduation, I applied to Sodexo's part-time dietetic internship in Allentown, Pennsylvania. While I was in my internship part-time, I also worked part-time at WIC in inner city Reading, Pennsylvania. WIC provides federal grants to states for supplemental foods, health care referrals, and nutrition education for low-income pregnant, breastfeeding, and non-breastfeeding postpartum women, and to infants and children up to age five years who are found to be at nutritional risk. At WIC, I would keep track of infant's and children's weight, height, and diet. I would then interview the mother and child (if the child was able to talk) and I would find deficiencies in their diet and I would give them a check for what they needed. There is a list of foods that are allowed to be bought with WIC vouchers. The foods provided through the WIC Program are designed to supplement participants' diets with specific nutrients. WIC-authorized foods include infant cereal, baby foods, iron-fortified adult cereal, fruits and vegetables, vitamin C-rich fruit or vegetable juice, eggs, milk, cheese, yogurt, soy-based beverages, tofu, peanut butter, dried and canned beans/peas, canned fish, whole wheat bread and other whole-grain options. For women who do not fully breastfeed, iron-fortified infant formula is provided for their infants. Special infant formulas and medical foods may also be provided if medically indicated. In addition, nutrition education is provided to WIC participants.

    After my internship, I passed the registered dietitian (RD) exam immediately and landed my first job as a Clinical Dietitian in a 650-bed nursing home in Nazareth, PA. I worked there with my Clinical Nutrition Manager and one other dietitian. I began taking care of six floors with 40 residents on each floor. It was fast-paced and difficult learning how to deal with complaints from residents and nurses every day, and learning how to conform to a thorough and efficient way of monitoring and documenting. At that time, it was 2006, and electronic health records had still not been adopted by this facility so I wrote all my notes and assessments plus care plans. I completed admission assessments, readmission assessments, quarterly notes about how the resident's nutritional status was doing overall, and weight loss or weight gain notes and what my intervention was or if I was not putting any in place. I also was part of the wound care team with the wound care nurse and the manager of the nursing unit. We would look at the residents with skin sores weekly and put interventions in place if needed. We would follow them until about two weeks after the wound had healed. I continued my interventions (if I had one in place) until about 2-3 weeks after the wound was healed. I learned a lot working there for two years and became great friends with my Clinical Nutrition Manager and the other RD I worked with. We helped each other and truly were a team. To this day, we are all still close friends. I hated moving on and leaving there, but I needed a job closer to home because I was now married.

I enjoyed working with older adults and found the long-term care environment enjoyable, yet challenging. For the next few years, I worked for Genesis Healthcare as the only RD in a facility of 240 residents and one day a week I was asked to travel to other facilities to provide coverage or assistance. This was good experience for me because it allowed me to work in many different nursing homes, meet and talk with a lot of different people, and learn how to adapt quickly and communicate with new people and situations. During this time, I was blessed with two wonderful children, Adam who is now age 15 years, and Aubrey who is now age 12 years. I took some time off of work when they were very little because I wanted to concentrate on raising my children. Overall, I worked with older adults in long term care for about 15 years. I am also Board Certified in Gerontological Nutrition.

When my daughter started school, I went back to work to another nursing home, Kutztown Manor. It is a 240-bed facility. I was responsible for new admission assessments, readmission assessments, significant change assessments, quarterly notes, and weight change notes. Each week I would meet with the Director of Nursing and the Unit Manager and we would review each resident's weight for any trending losses or gains or large weight losses or gains with them and to help maintain or gain weight. We would all strategize the intervention to stop the weight loss and agree upon interventions for any weight changes. For example, fortified foods may be given. Fortified foods are regular foods such as mashed potatoes, pudding, cookies, or oatmeal. Butter, whole milk, cream, or gravy may be added to these foods to increase the number of calories and protein per bite. Double portions of a resident's food(s) and commercial supplements (for example, a high-calorie, high-protein milkshake or juice-based drink) could be given, too. I was also part of the wound care team, which made rounds once per week to check on residents who had sores on their skin. If the resident was not getting enough calories and protein in their diet, I would order double portions of their favorite high protein foods, fortified foods, a commercial supplement, or protein liquid or powder if extra protein was needed. Each long-term care facility I worked at used Point Click Care for electronic health charting which monitors weights and a lot of other health information on the residents. I made it a habit to run a weight report weekly for each resident. I also ran meal and supplement intake reports for each resident. I called families and informed them if their friend or family member had any weight changes and what my intervention was going to be. I would ask them for their input, too. I believe it is important for the RD to make themselves known to a resident's family and to have a positive, ongoing relationship with them outside of the care plan meeting or care conference. I believe RDs need to make themselves known as important members of the health care team because I think sometimes, RDs are overlooked.

  About a year or two after my daughter was born, I began having pain symptoms of my autoimmune diseases. It began as shooting pain in my legs and extreme fatigue. I also started to get sick a lot. It seemed as if I was in the hospital with pneumonia every month. The worst time was when I developed a horrible lung infection which consisted of the pneumonia virus and the methicillin-resistant Staphylococcus aureus (also known as MRSA) bacteria. The infection caused one lung to fill with fluid and the infection tunneled into my chest cavity and into my blood stream. I ended up getting sepsis. My husband was working third shift at the time and when he came home, he found me on the floor unconscious. He picked me up and took me to the hospital where my blood pressure was extremely low and my oxygen level was low. I had a breathing tube along with a feeding tube and was in the intensive care unit intubated and unconscious for 10 days. After this happened, I began seeing a different doctor who referred me to the Allergy and

Immunology Clinic at The Pennsylvania State University Hershey Medical Center. The doctor I began seeing there tested my immunoglobulin levels because I kept getting pneumonia. They found I was deficient in Immunoglobulin G. I now have been doing weekly infusions of Immunoglobulin G. Thankfully, I no longer get sick as much.

I also began seeing a rheumatologist who suspected Sjogren's Syndrome because I was exhibiting symptoms such as dry mouth and eyes, and every woman on my father's side of my family had Sjogren's Syndrome. In addition to dry mouth and eyes, I would get ulcers in my mouth that were very painful and made it difficult to eat. I could relate to my residents! The worst part of Sjogren's Syndrome is that suffering from dry mouth aids the production of cavities. I went to the dentist about a year after I was diagnosed and I had a cavity between every single tooth. It was a nightmare getting them all fixed. One tooth needed a root canal and another was in such bad shape I had it pulled. My dentist told me that this would keep happening despite some dental interventions I could take. He recommended that I get all my teeth pulled and get veneers or false teeth. At the time I was 42 and there was no way I was going to wear false teeth! My rheumatologist gave me Salagen which produces saliva. So, I still have my regular teeth and get the cavities filled. I am also on Plaquenil to prevent the disease from progressing.

My doctors also did blood tests on me to detect other possible autoimmune diseases. My symptoms and the blood test showed that I have lupus. My blood test also indicated possible scleroderma. My rheumatologist tested me for fibromyalgia because I said I was so tired all of the time. According to Dr. Shashanka Chillapuram, "Fibromyalgia is a chronic widespread musculoskeletal disorder where the patient experiences pain and tenderness throughout the body. For the disease diagnosis, the American College of Rheumatology has come up with clinical criteria where the patient has a history of widespread pain lasting for more than three months and finding 'tender points' — there are 18 designated possible tender points." I experience fatigue every day and muscle soreness, but thankfully my family helps me out with housework.

In addition to medical ways of controlling my symptoms, I also follow an anti-inflammatory diet to control symptoms. I eat mostly lean meats that include chicken, salmon, turkey, nuts, seeds, and healthy fats (extra virgin olive oil or coconut oil). I also use herbs and spices for flavor or Mrs. Dash. Some good ones for inflammation are ginger, turmeric, garlic, and Mrs. Dash. Sometimes I will make smoothies and include flaxseeds or chia seeds. I also have nuts such as walnuts, almonds, pecans, and hazelnuts for a snack or in a salad. Fat-free yogurt with flaxseeds or chia seeds is also a good snack. I avoid high salt, sugary, processed foods, alcohol, red meat, soda, fried food, butter, and margarine. I get most of my fat through extra virgin olive oil and coconut oil when cooking. In addition, salmon provides omega-3 fatty acids.

My last job in long-term care was with Health Care Services Group. My responsibilities at this facility were completing admission assessments, readmission assessments, significant change assessments, quarterly notes, and weight loss or gain notes. I also intervened if there was a weight loss or gain with either food or supplements for weight loss and smaller portions usually for weight gain. If I observed someone having difficulty chewing or swallowing, I referred them to the Speech Therapist. If their cognition was still intact, I provided them with weight loss or gain education. **I was also part of the wound care team, which made rounds once per week to check on residents who had sores on their skin. If the resident was not getting enough calories and protein in their diet, I would order double portions of their favorite high protein foods, fortified foods, a commercial supplement, or protein liquid or powder if the resident was not eating well or they had high protein needs.** Once a week I would attend care plan meetings which involved updating the team about a group of residents chosen quarterly and also usually updating the family. My manager was unhappy with my attendance and made me go on family and medical leave act (or FMLA) because I used all of my vacation and sick days early in the year. In addition, my lower back began to hurt really badly. So, I went to a chiropractor who did tests on me and diagnosed Degenerative Disc Disease in my spine and arthritis in my sacroiliac joints and both hips. The bottom three discs of my lower back are crunched together and the other discs in my spine are wearing away. I experience a lot of pain with this, mostly in my lower back, buttocks, and down my legs. I see a pain management doctor who gives me steroid shots in the area of pain and I also take pain medicine and a muscle relaxant. When I was working my last job, I had trouble sitting and standing for long periods. I asked my lead RD if I could go home and do my charting after I talked to everyone, collected all of their recent information for my notes, and put interventions in place for them if needed. She allowed me to do that a few times but the administrator started to get upset that I wasn't in the building all day so that was cut short. So, after I exhausted my FMLA, I stopped working there. I wasn't able to do it anymore.

I started my own business a few months after that and I did that for almost two years. I saw patients through telehealth or by phone, whichever they preferred. I decided not to keep the business going because I did not offer insurance and everyone wanted to see someone who provided insurance. It was good experience running a business on my own and the clients I had were happy with the results they achieved.

I am now trying to get Social Security Disability benefits, but have been denied five times to date. My lawyer is now pushing to go to court for a hearing. In the meantime, I am looking for a remote RD job and I plan to continue volunteering with the Disabilities in Nutrition and Dietetics Member Interest Group (or Disabilities MIG for short). I love our group and I hope to join in more in the future and take on different roles. Right now, I am the Nominating Committee Chair-Elect. Last year, I was the Sponsorship Coordinator.

My advice for RDs and other foodservice professionals who work with RDs with disabilities is to try to understand their situation and ask them if they need any help with anything and accommodate their needs if they need something to get their job done comfortably. This also applies to administrators and Directors of Nursing. Managers must be flexible when someone is having a bad day (meaning a bad health day). They need to listen to their employee and understand it is not their fault and they cannot control flare-ups or other health-related issues. Along with their employee, the manager should have a group meeting with the administrator Director of Nursing, and the head of Human Resources to discuss the problem and come up with a solution that works for everyone on the team.

That is my story and I hope to continue working with the Disabilities MIG and in the future perform different roles to spread nutrition education to both disabled dietetic students and disabled people in the community. I also believe in the rights of people with disabilities and I hope to advocate to make that better and to draw attention to the community about disabilities.

If I could go back in time, I would not change anything. I love my profession and I am good at what I do. I genuinely care about people and I love helping them become healthier. If you're a student or intern with a disability, don't let anything stop you from becoming an RD if that is your true passion. If you need accommodations because of your disability, do not be afraid to speak up and make your needs known. No matter what you want to do in life, just go for it. Do not let your disability hold you back. We all get one life so make the most of it! However, I believe that people with disabilities who have much pain and other difficulties that interfere with productivity should have a discussion with their employers and ask them what accommodations can be made for work to be a more pleasurable experience and more productive.

Chapter 12 (Autobiography)
The Evolution of a Celiac Dietitian

By Renee Euler, MS, RDN

Renee Euler

Celiac disease is an autoimmune disease that affects the normal digestion process. Consuming gluten from wheat, barley, and/or rye damages the small intestine and prevents the absorption of nutrients from food. Gluten is a protein that is found in many foods like bread, pasta, cakes, cookies, and many packaged foods. The only treatment available is a life-long gluten-free diet. It is estimated that about 1% of the world's population has celiac disease, although many are undiagnosed.

I was diagnosed with celiac disease in 1995, just as I was preparing to return to The Ohio State University for my sophomore year. I had just been admitted to the Landscape Architecture program and was looking forward to digging into the core classes in my major. I was planning to live in the dorms again and had a standard meal plan. Having spent my freshman year in the same dorm, I knew the attached dining hall didn't have many options for a gluten-free diet. However, we called the Dining Services department, but they would not allow me to cancel my meal plan contract, saying that it was a requirement for students living in the dorms though they were not able to offer any guidance on how to access safe, gluten-free meals in the dining hall.

Luckily, we did have refrigerators and microwaves in our dorm rooms, so I prepared to make it work by bringing plenty of quick foods that could be made using the tools available to me like Minute rice, rice crackers, canned chicken, peanut butter, canned Progresso chicken and rice soup, canned Dinty Moore beef stew, cheese, salsa, corn Chex, and the only readily available bread to me, Ener-G brand white rice bread that tasted like Styrofoam. I also brought my own toaster, despite it being against safety rules, so that I could make peanut butter toast in my room each morning. At that time, the only gluten-free breads available did not taste good unless they were toasted, so if you were going to eat any gluten-free bread, you needed a dedicated gluten-free toaster for toasting. Luckily, our Resident Assistant had a romantic interest in my roommate and overlooked this safety violation. I was also lucky to have a car on campus, so I was able to go to the grocery store and restock my supplies as needed. I would go to the dining hall for meals to socialize with friends and would stick to things that "looked" gluten free, or things on the salad bar that looked "safe" without inquiring about their gluten-free status as the staff did not understand my questions. For example, I would choose meats that did not have breading or sauce on them, baked or roasted potatoes, plain vegetables, and plain fruit. We were allowed to take one piece of whole fruit out of the dining hall with us, so I always took a piece, just so I had more options if I got hungry later. At the salad bar, I avoided the obvious gluten containing things like croutons and chow-mein noodles and stuck to containers of salad toppings that were visually not impacted by cross-contact from gluten-containing foods and ingredients. And I stuck to using oil and vinegar for my dressing as some salad dressings may contain gluten. I also ate many bowls of soft serve ice cream that year, which made my ice cream loving soul happy. Thankfully, I survived that year without too much trouble. I am sure I was getting gluten in my diet but at the time my symptoms had pretty much resolved, and I had not been given any recommendations for follow-up with my gastroenterologist – "just eat gluten-free," nor was I ever offered a consultation with a Registered Dietitian.

It troubles me that nearly thirty years later, people newly diagnosed with celiac disease are not commonly referred to a celiac-specialist RD to receive instruction on a gluten-free diet unless they are diagnosed at a celiac specialty clinic. Of course, celiac-specialist dietitians are not available in all areas, but referral to a celiac-specialist dietitian is recommended in the latest clinical care guidelines for people with celiac disease.

Implementing a gluten-free diet can be challenging due to the many details and widespread misinformation, which can cause anxiety and affect the social and emotional well-being of those with celiac disease. A celiac-specialist dietitian can help patients understand and focus on the important details as well as help reduce their anxiety about the gluten-free diet. I feel that many people's transitions to a lifelong gluten-free lifestyle would be less challenging if they were able to meet with a celiac-specialist dietitian at diagnosis. In this digital world we live in, I think that every person with celiac disease can and should have a relationship with a celiac-specialist dietitian. As you will soon read, it is one of the main reasons why I became a celiac-specialist dietitian.

And so, in an ideal world I would have been referred to a celiac-specialist dietitian at diagnosis, and they would have been able to help me navigate the foodservice situation at the university dining hall, as well as help me figure out what a nutrient dense gluten-free diet looked like and how to implement it as a college student.

At diagnosis, I was told that I had a "mild case" and "could probably cheat on the diet periodically since she isn't losing weight." The gastroenterologist put this in my chart notes, which I have a copy of, and my current gastroenterologist and I have had many a good laugh over this, reflecting on where we were then and where we are today in understanding celiac disease.

My mother and grandmother were very helpful during this time. My mom reached out to a local support group and talked to the leader many times in that first year as I was trying to navigate this new lifestyle. It is hard to believe there was a time before the internet, but the internet was in its infancy at the time, so we relied on a few library books and cookbooks, photocopied handouts from the support group, and member-created recipe collections. My mom and grandmother started experimenting with baking bread and recreating family holiday treats for me while I navigated campus life. I connected with the national Celiac List-Serv and attended the annual Nationwide Children's Celiac Disease conference, which took place there in Columbus, Ohio not far from campus. This conference has been held annually since 1988 and is organized by Registered Dietitian Mary Kay Sharrett, a long-time voice in the celiac disease community. Looking back, I think those initial connections early in my gluten-free life showed me the importance of connecting with others with celiac disease, or any chronic disease. Mary Kay was the first dietitian I ever met but it still never occurred to me that I might be able to have a consultation with a dietitian with knowledge of the gluten-free diet. She worked (and still does) at the Nationwide Children's Hospital, and I was a college student, receiving my care from an adult gastroenterologist, not a pediatric gastroenterology center. Ironically, Mary Kay and I now work together for the Dietitians in Medical Nutrition Therapy Dietetics Practice Group (or DMNT DPG) of the Academy of Nutrition and Dietetics.

I completed my degree in Landscape Architecture and practiced in the field for almost 15 years in Ohio, Chicago, and New Mexico. While living in Chicago, I became involved with the Chicago-area chapter of the Celiac Sprue Association, taking on leadership roles including editing the newsletter and planning the annual "Making Tracks for Celiacs" walk to benefit celiac disease research. I was also a volunteer board member for the newly formed University of Chicago Celiac Disease Center.

Unfortunately, my husband was laid off from his job the year before the Great Recession and we had to move to New Mexico in the fall of 2007 for a new position for him. I was lucky to find a job in my profession as the architecture-engineering-construction industry was already starting to feel the effects of the developing recession. Over the next couple years, during the recession, I was able to hold on to my job, but every time another group of my colleagues was laid off, I would go home and add to my list of "what do I do if I get laid off" ideas. I had already been feeling like I wanted to move on to something new, but the big question was what comes next.

Prior to 1995 when I was diagnosed with celiac disease, I ate food without much thought. My diagnosis, as well as connecting with my husband who eats a lacto-ovo vegetarian diet, made me much more aware of food and it became a significant part of my everyday life. In addition, I found that I enjoyed being a leader in the celiac disease community. And so, one of those ideas on my what-if-I-am-laid-off list was: investigate a career in nutrition. It took a while, but I found the courage to speak to the Chair of the Nutrition department at the University of New Mexico (or UNM). Shortly thereafter I took the plunge and left my old profession to go back to school with the goal of helping people with celiac disease as a Registered Dietitian.

I received my bachelor's degree and master's degree from UNM. I also completed my dietetic internship through UNM. While in grad school, I also discovered that I liked teaching nutrition. I worked as a clinical dietitian in a local hospital for a couple of years before leaving to teach nutrition at the local community college and open a small private practice focusing on gastrointestinal conditions.

While I acknowledge and educate my own clients that accommodations for celiac disease are covered under the Americans with Disabilities Act (or ADA), I myself have never requested accommodations in my education or workplace. Being diagnosed in 1995, shortly after the ADA was enacted in 1990, it wasn't well-known that celiac disease was covered. But I am not hesitant to disclose my condition and needs to others. For better or worse, if you know me, you know that celiac disease is a part of who I am, and even more so now as a gastrointestinal (or GI) specialist dietitian. I am not hesitant to request what I need or bring my own food wherever I need it, so I have never felt the need to request accommodation.

I have a motto: "Have food, will travel" which comes in handy when driving in the rural Southwest where sometimes even gas stations are few and far between. (This isn't to say that sometimes I don't get frustrated with my gluten-free options when out and about.) I have a "go-bag" that is always pre-packed with plastic utensils, napkins, and a sharp knife so that I am ready for any adventure. For road trips, I add a small cooler with cheese, yogurt, baby carrots, fruit, chocolate, and maybe a homemade quinoa salad of some sort, if I have had advance notice of the excursion. Then an assortment of gluten-free crackers, gluten-free pretzels, popcorn, nuts, peanut butter, and gummy bears, of course, – are packed in a reuseable grocery bag, and we're on our way, ready to eat while driving, or at a rest stop along the way. If I am flying, I will create a smaller version of this and pack it into a gallon size plastic zip top bag so that it passes through the security checkpoint easily.

As a second-career dietitian, I had the benefit of having already developed workplace skills and experiences for my new career. I believe this provided me with a level of confidence that allowed me to seek out connections within the field early in my career. Also, I recognized that there was no one in my local area doing what I wanted to do – be a celiac-specialist dietitian – so I knew I had to connect with others beyond my local area. I became a member of the Dietitians in Gluten Intolerance Disorders (DIGID) subunit of the DMNT DPG within the Academy of Nutrition and Dietetics while I was still an undergraduate student. Just before I finished my undergraduate education, a leader in the subunit asked if I would be willing to write a continuing education article for their quarterly newsletter on celiac disease. Hesitantly I said yes, thinking, wow, surely there are people more qualified than I, since I wasn't an RD yet. I am very thankful for the opportunity because it led to being appointed the Vice Chair of the subunit the next year. And the Chair and I then expanded the subunit to include all gastrointestinal disorders and renamed it the Dietitians in Gluten and Gastrointestinal Disorders while maintaining the same acronym, DIGID. The connections I have made as a leader in both DIGID and DMNT DPG since 2016 have helped create the dietitian I am today. Those roles and connections led me to plan and coordinate the first two DIGID Digestive Diseases Nutrition Series virtual conferences, as well as become the co-liaison for the partnership between the Academy and the American Gastroenterological Association, among other opportunities. I maintain these connections by meeting up with my GI-dietitian colleagues at conferences every year.

I am sure many readers have had their life's journeys dictated by a diagnosis or disability. For me, my disease moved my life in a positive direction, and I have allowed it to define who I am, which has led me to where I am today. And for that I am thankful. I also want to acknowledge that I have been incredibly privileged to have the opportunity to go back to school to study nutrition when I already had a degree and a successful career. Additionally, not everyone will feel comfortable leveraging their disability in the way I have, and that is okay too. As you move through your career you will find many dietitians whose passion stems from personal experience, whether that is a disability or not. I encourage those who feel comfortable doing so to embrace their disability in creating the career and life they desire.

Chapter 13 (Autobiography) Inflammatory Bowel Disease (or IBD) RD

By David Gardinier, RD, LD

David Gardinier

Florida in the summertime — the air is thick, hot and altogether unpleasant. The sun beats down on the land without mercy or yield, and air conditioning becomes a basic necessity for survival. As I entered my black car in the midst of another summer in central Florida, I knew something was wrong. Instead of reaching for the knob to turn on the A/C, I reached over to the knob on the other side of the dashboard and cranked up the heat. The cold I felt couldn't be natural, it couldn't be normal, and I thought to myself "what is wrong with me."

That question would be answered almost eight months later just after my first colonoscopy at the ripe old age of 18. I had a chronic, inflammatory condition affecting the gastrointestinal tract known as Crohn's disease, a type of inflammatory bowel disease (or IBD). I'd like to think I took the diagnosis in stride. Instead of feeling bummed out or wallowing in self-pity I was glad I had a diagnosis and happy to start a medication that would help. I remember thinking to myself that I was thankful it was me who was diagnosed and not another member of my family. The medication I started, Humira, quickly began working and a few months later I was back to being a normal teenager. I graduated high school, and soon after left for a Christian summer wilderness camp. We spent time hiking and building a cabin — hauling logs, chopping wood, and nailing together the foundation. I didn't feel disabled at all, in fact I felt like I was in the best shape of my life.

That fall I shipped off to college, excited to start a new chapter in my life. I was looking forward to finding a new community and branching out on my own for the first time, though I wasn't quite sure what I wanted to major in. Like many incoming freshmen, the thought of deciding what to do for the rest of life at the age of 18 was a terrifying prospect. I decided on industrial engineering, a nice safe option. The job market looked pretty good, and I knew any engineering job would be enough to pay the bills. My first semester went well. I ended up pledging a Christian fraternity and meeting friends that will be standing beside me as groomsmen at my wedding later this year. I excelled academically, and I found out that I have a passion for ultimate frisbee. Throughout it all, the only reminder of my disease was the brief visit every two weeks to the campus nurse to get my medication administered.

Winter break, my mother gifted me a book called *Breaking the Vicious Cycle* by Elaine Gottschall. The cover of the book draws you in. A border of plant-based foods surrounds the title, and under that sits the words "intestinal health through diet." This idea may not be very novel today, but at the time there wasn't as much press about the role of diet in gut health. In high school I had a passing interest in nutrition and diet as a tool to help me lift more in the gym, but I hadn't considered the possibility of a connection between the food I put in my mouth and the chronic disease in my gut. I decided to give the book a read, and it changed my life.

Breaking the Vicious Cycle covers a diet called the specific carbohydrate diet. The author claims this diet can help a variety of chronic illnesses, from Crohn's disease to diverticulitis, to cystic fibrosis, to autism. Following the diet involves a reduction in a variety of processed foods, as well as multiple grains, starches, and sugars. These dietary changes are theorized to improve gut health through changing the intestinal microbiome. It felt like I was reading a book ahead of its time. My doctors never discussed the relationship between diet and my chronic illness, and I felt as though this could be the missing piece that would "cure" me of this disease forever.

I bet you can tell where this is going. I went off of my medication in January of 2017 (without telling my doctor) in favor of starting the specific carbohydrate diet. Reading *Breaking the Vicious Cycle* sparked a passion for nutrition, and so I also ended up changing my major to dietetics upon returning to college for the spring semester. At first it appeared that my diet was actually working. I continued to be symptom free for the next two months and stayed highly active playing intramural sports. One day, however, I noticed a small lump on the lower right side of my stomach. I ignored it, as one does when young and ignorant, until it began to grow in size and became painful to the touch. When it got to be about the size of a golf ball, I finally decided it might be a decent idea to have a doctor take a look at it.

It turns out, going on the specific carbohydrate diet and off all medications did not control my disease. The doctors found that all of the inflammation that was well controlled on my prior medication had returned, and that the golf ball sized lump protruding outward from my stomach was an intestinal abscess. The following few months I would consider the toughest period of my life. I underwent drainage of the abscess, limped across the finish line for the spring semester, and ended up getting surgery to remove part of my bowel and give me a temporary ileostomy. A temporary ileostomy is where the surgeon takes part of the last portion of the small intestine, the ileum, and brings it out through the wall of the abdomen. This allows the contents leaving the small bowel to exit into a bag attached to the abdomen, and prevents the contents from entering the colon. It is helpful for allowing the colon to heal without having food passing through it all the time.

After a summer recovering from surgery, I began my sophomore semester of college. Despite many hurdles from my chronic disease, I still had not registered with my college's disability resource center. So far all of my professors had been very understanding, and at that point I had never really had a need for any well-defined accommodations. My fall semester went by smoothly, and with the ileostomy I was in the best shape of my life. I've spoken with many people over the years who have valid concerns about being able to stay active with an ileostomy, but in my experience I was able to hike, rock climb, swim, weight lift, and play intramural basketball and football without any trouble at all. I did end up buying an ostomy shield to protect my ileostomy from any contact while playing sports.

Having an ileostomy in college is a strange experience. I knew that the ileostomy was there, and I could hear, and feel every little time it functioned. On the other hand, it wasn't very easy to notice from an outside perspective. The ileostomy bag was pretty easy to hide under my clothes, so I looked like any other college kid. One thing I did have to plan around was bathroom access. I learned fairly quickly the bathrooms on campus that were single person occupancy since this made me feel more comfortable emptying the ostomy bag into the toilet. Overall having the ileostomy created this dynamic where I felt like I had a secret that nobody else knew about, a piece of my identity that nobody else could see.

I finally started taking classes related to nutrition my sophomore semester of college. I knew that nutrition was still my passion, as I would go to class and be actively interested in every little detail the professor lectured on. Homework for those classes didn't feel like work, and this reinforced that I had finally found a major that could lead to a career I would enjoy. Unfortunately, spring of 2018 I began to feel worse with my ileostomy and developed diversion proctitis. Once again I limped across the finish line with my spring classes and underwent another major surgery, this time to reverse my ileostomy and reconnect my bowels.

I spent the summer of 2018 trying to recover, but it was a rocky road and by the time the Fall semester of my junior year rolled around I was still very sick. I decided to sign up for classes anyways, but within the first few weeks I ended up withdrawing from my classes and moving back in with my parents. This challenged me as a person, and I was always the type of guy who was very independent and could handle any challenge thrown my way. For me withdrawing from classes made me feel like a failure, and like I wasn't good enough to make it through college. It was the first time where my disease really limited me from doing what I wanted to do.

After months of suffering, my health finally turned around December of 2018 after I was hospitalized for a severe flare up of my Crohn's disease. While I was admitted, I met a new doctor who switched my medications and I began to feel better. I took the spring semester of 2019 off and continued to recover during that time. My one setback during that recovery was a reaction to an iron infusion, which ended up resulting in multiple food sensitivities that I continue to deal with to this day. After that iron infusion I began getting hives to a variety of different foods, and I started to have to be much more careful with my diet. It was frustrating as somebody so interested in nutrition to have to limit my diet, especially when it came to limiting healthy foods.

In summer of 2019 I finally returned to college, and I also signed up for the disability resource center. After having to withdraw from classes due to my health I wanted to make sure that I wouldn't be penalized negatively for having to do that again in the future if needed. I was given some accommodations that included a separate area to take tests and the ability to leave class or testing facilities to use the restroom if needed. I ended up sending these accommodations to each of my professors at the start of each semester, but thankfully never ended up needing them.

The remainder of my time in college I was overall healthy. The last two years of college for me were wonderful, and I really enjoyed having most of my schedule be nutrition classes. I learned about nutrition and metabolism, was taught how to conduct a nutrition focused physical exam, and developed an understanding of how nutrition could impact multiple chronic illnesses. Throughout it all I was still hooked on learning about how what people eat could affect their health.

Looking back at my time in college, it is easy to see how it was both a time of difficulties and challenges as well as growth. One aspect of my journey in college that helped me stay resilient and continue to have hope even in the darkest times is my faith. I attended Greenhouse church during my time at the University of Florida, and that community helped me to grow in my relationship with God and trust him even when times were difficult or when I felt little hope for the future. In a similar and more personal way, the friends in my Christian fraternity also supported me. They never treated me differently for having a chronic illness, and were more than supportive when I needed to be careful with my diet or have any special accommodations due to my illness. A few examples I remember of how they supported me include letting me bring separate food to our retreats, allowing me to break dress code by not wearing a belt when I had an ileostomy, and surprising me with a packet of nutritional shakes I was drinking to help maintain my weight. Without the support of my friends and my relationship with Jesus, college would have been a much more difficult journey.

Toward the end of my final semester in 2020, I got the news I had been accepted to my number one choice for the dietetic internship program at VCU Health in Richmond, Virginia. I was very excited to begin my hands-on training to become a dietitian and learn from dietitians who have been practicing for a long time. I was also looking forward to the change of scenery. I had been living in Florida for the past 10+ years in my life, and moving to an area where I could explore something new had been a priority.

Moving is always difficult with a chronic illness. I had a good relationship with my doctor in Florida, and credit him for my recovery from the severe flare up I had in 2018. It is hard to leave behind somebody you trust and start over building a patient-provider relationship all over again. Luckily, I was able to find a wonderful new provider in Richmond, and he and his nurse practitioner took good care of me during my time at VCU Health.

I didn't get any formal accommodations for my disability in my dietetic internship, but similar to how I managed in college I informed my internship director as well as all of the preceptors I worked with about my disability. They were all very understanding and supportive, and were perfectly fine giving me a morning off to attend doctors' appointments or get imaging done. Once or twice during my internship I asked to go home early for the day due to having abdominal pain, and the preceptors were always okay with that. VCU Health made it easy to have a disability and be able to accomplish my goal of learning how to become a capable dietitian.

One of the parts of the internship I couldn't take advantage of was the free lunch and coffee we were given as interns. Due to my diet being so restricted and the ongoing food sensitivities I gained after the iron infusion, I was unable to find anything I could eat at the cafeteria or drink the coffee. This wasn't anything new to me, but some days it did bring me down slightly to see everyone else enjoying delicious, healthy food while I was stuck eating the same thing over and over again.

During my internship, one of my goals was to gain as much experience in the field of gastrointestinal (or GI) dietetics as I possibly could. This was another area where I felt very supported at VCU Health, as they tailored my internship to place me with preceptors who covered the GI population. I was also able to select a few specialty rotations, and so I also rotated in a private practice specializing in GI and the outpatient pediatric GI clinic twice. I was hoping that in gaining this experience as a dietetics intern, I would be able to find a job as a GI dietitian right away after passing the RD exam.

About two weeks after completing my dietetic internship I signed up to take the RD exam. Since I had been feeling well overall, I didn't end up requesting or needing any accommodations at the time. The exam went smoothly overall, and at the end I got the news: I had passed and was officially a registered dietitian.

I took a few weeks around the holidays to rest and relax, then started applying to jobs at the start of 2023. At the beginning I kept my applications focused on positions for GI roles, and I was lucky enough to get a few interviews. I've always been very open about my condition, so when the question would come up asking "why are you interested in this role" I would tell the interviewers a little background about my own condition and how it influenced me to want to help others with GI diseases. Interviewers were always very receptive, and it would often open up the floor for them to share the more personal reasons they might have gotten into dietetics. I was never met with any inappropriate questions, but my thought was that if somebody reacted poorly or started asking about my ability to work in the interview it would be a good indicator I wouldn't want to work at that organization anyhow. Part of the interview process was for me to evaluate the organization to see if they would be a good fit for my disability, and I am glad to be able to say that the organizations I had the opportunity to interview at passed.

I was surprised to end up with a few different GI related job offers after only a month of job searching, but I held out hope for an offer from the Cleveland Clinic. They had an opening for an IBD dietitian position, which was my long-term career goal I was dreaming of when I changed my major to dietetics years prior. When I got the call that I had been offered the job I was over the moon. The fact that I had no prior job experience but got the specialized position made me feel like God had his hand in the process and was guiding me to Cleveland. I accepted the position, and started preparing to move to a new city for the second time in two years.

During onboarding, I disclosed my disability to the company, my manager, and my lead. I was met with a lot of support, and it was encouraging to know that the people in charge of me cared about not only my success at work, but also my overall health and wellbeing. I quickly found out working a job was different from both college and the dietetic internship. One big change was the level of responsibility. In this new position I not only was responsible for myself, but also for creating a world class experience for my patients. That level of responsibility led to difficulty on days when my Crohn's disease was flaring up, because now not only would my flare up impact me but it would impact the experience I was able to give my patients. This led to me following a very strict diet in order to limit my symptoms during the workweek so that I could give my patients the best experience possible.

It is a weird feeling following a restrictive diet as a dietitian. On one hand I've found out that for my disease it is an absolute must, but on the other hand I often tell patients to focus on trying to get a wide variety of foods whenever possible in their own diets. There is a disconnect between being able to "practice what I preach" and "do what is right for my body." As a dietitian I know variety and balance are important parts of a healthy diet, but I have tried adding in food after food after food only to be met with worsened GI symptoms each time. There is certainly a mental toll that occurs when you talk about food all day despite having a poor relationship with it yourself.

Despite my restrictive diet, I ended up having a flare up of my disease about a year and a half after starting my job. During that time, I had to take time off to get imaging or see my doctors on a few occasions. After the 3rd or so time I called off, my manager suggested I apply for the Family and Medical Leave Act (or FMLA), which is a law that entitles eligible employees to take unpaid leave for certain medical conditions. The leave is protected, which means that I have the right to return to the same job I had prior to taking the leave.

This was a great suggestion, and after some paperwork from my doctor's office I could now take leave for flare-ups that would not count against the limited number of yearly call-offs we get at work. Ever since getting approved for FMLA I feel like I have a safety net in case something goes horribly wrong, and that provides me a sense of peace and comfort. I value and enjoy my career as an IBD dietitian, so it is nice to know that I can take time off if needed for my illness and come back to my same position. I wish I had signed up for FMLA before needing it, but better late than never! I will have to get the forms filled out yearly, but it is a small price to pay for peace of mind.

Currently, I am able to complete my job without any significant day-to-day limitations. My disease is fairly well controlled with medication, and I have the safety net of FMLA if needed for future flare ups. The major limitation I continue to have is diet variety.

My diet right now is still very restricted. Every morning, I prepare one cup of dry oats by cooking them with water in my stainless-steel pot. I then add the contents of a 2mg copper pill and mix that in. Finally, I'll top my oatmeal with about ⅔ a cup of blueberries and a diced banana. Between breakfast and lunch, I will drink an Orgain all-in-one nutritional shake. My lunch is either white rice and a pork chop or another bowl of oatmeal without the copper pill. Between lunch and dinner, I will drink a second Orgain. Dinner is usually the same white rice and a pork chop.

It is strange to think that almost every breakfast and half of my lunches for the past 4 years of my life I have eaten the same 3 foods. I try to cope with that using humor. I'd like to believe there is somebody keeping track of the oatmeal bought from the Trader Joe's east of Cleveland who was very confused in 2022 when I first moved to the area. Sometimes I hope that in the afterlife they will give out arbitrary awards and I will proudly walk up and claim the award for most oatmeal eaten in the 21st century. I'm at least hoping to be in the top five of all time over the course of human history.

Jokes aside, it is unfortunate that I am stuck eating the same foods almost every day. The Orgain supplements have a good amount of vitamins and minerals, so that helps prevent most deficiencies I would get from my restricted diet. Every week I try adding in other foods, but all of my attempts are usually met with moderate to severe GI symptoms. This limited diet means that I have to pack my own lunches the three days I go into the office for work and cannot rely on the cafeteria for food. I work from home the other two days of the week, which allows me to prepare lunch at home. I also am unable to partake in any of the food at the in-person meetings we have twice yearly. Despite these things I am very satisfied with my ability to work as a dietitian, and I hope I continue to be able to take good care of my patients.

Chapter 14 (Autobiography) Practice Resilience and Never Give Up the Goal of Becoming a Registered Dietitian

By Susan K Greener, BSN, DTR

Susan standing with her cane.

I was the youngest of five children, raised by both of my parents in a rural town in northwest Ohio during the 1960s. My mother grew up in Toledo, Ohio during the Great Depression, where her family faced food insecurity. They often relied on food banks, breadlines, and soup kitchens for meals, which led to a lack of essential nutrients and caused my mother to lose all of her teeth at a young age. On the other hand, my dad grew up in a small rural town, living with multiple generations in one house. When he was young, he suffered a terrible loss when he lost his father and grandfather within a week. After a couple of years, his mother remarried, and they moved from the family home. With the remarriage, the family's financial situation improved, and they were able to have gardens, fruit trees, and preserve food by canning. Seeing old photos of my father as a child he was always the chubby kid. My parents met and married after World War II. As the war ended, the economy improved, and their access to food also got better. During the 1950s and 1960s, they expanded their family with five children in seven years. My father, a truck driver, was often away for weeks at a time due to his job. And when he was home he ate and drank alcohol. He was an alcoholic; his highest weight was around 350 pounds. Our family ate in shifts because the kitchen table couldn't fit everyone at once. My mother diligently ensured that there was plenty of food. Since my mother didn't drive, we relied on companies that delivered staples like bread, milk, and eggs. Our meals mainly consisted of high-fat meats, limited fruits and vegetables, and desserts as regular components. We never went hungry, and there were always three meals a day.

When magazines started featuring recipes with more convenient foods, like many other moms, my mother began using them too. She was a self-taught baker known for her wide variety of Christmas cookies that she made each year. She would always save a couple of your favorite ones for when you came over. I used to joke with her that my problem was that they were all my favorite. She continued to make cookies diligently into her 80s, until her hands were no longer functional due to arthritis.

When we were young adults, all of my siblings were considered to be of normal weight. I noticed that their body types all took after my mother, her average weight was never over 160 pounds while I took after my overweight father. His average weight was always around 300 pounds. I was considered chubby but never obese. My three older brothers used to tease me, calling me names like "Shamu" and "the whale" to make fun of my weight. Despite this, they would also encourage me to participate in eating contests to see how much I could eat at once. Although I was younger, I often won these contests. My sister and I were encouraged to start cooking; however, I was very messy and was called "disaster in the kitchen." The first time I became conscious of my weight and eating habits was when I started liking boys. In the 1970s, being thin, no matter how you achieved it, was the standard. I started resorting to extreme measures to lose weight, such as limiting my food intake and excessive exercising. I was even influenced by a male high school teacher who, upon noticing my weight loss, told me that it wasn't enough after looking me up and down.

When I was 14, I met my future husband and we started dating. We continued our relationship throughout high school. During my senior year, at 17, I became pregnant. Since my husband was already working at a good job in an auto factory after graduating a year ahead of me, my mom insisted that I couldn't raise a baby at home. My mother always taught me that being a mother and homemaker was all you should want to be. So, before graduation, we got married with the consent of my parents. My husband became my legal guardian for 6 months until I turned 18. After getting married, my mother-in-law explained to me that our roles were to be split like a 1950s husband and wife. He would work, and I would take care of household responsibilities like budgeting, grocery shopping, cooking, cleaning, and raising our children. I struggled with these tasks because I only took one semester of home economics in school, but never had a nutrition course.

Even though I loved my husband and wanted to get married, my life was turned upside down. He worked a second shift job. I hadn't even graduated from high school and I didn't have a driver's license. I had to fight the school to include my married name at the graduation ceremony. Neither of my parents, spouse, or siblings came to the graduation ceremony, leaving me feeling alone and abandoned by family and friends. I think this is when my depression really started. Comforting myself with food and using pregnancy as an excuse, I found myself eating anything I wanted. By the time I delivered my daughter, I had weighed the most I ever had — 201 pounds, gaining 60 pounds. My daughter's birth weight was over 10 pounds.

Within a year after giving birth, I was able to get back to my original weight of 140 pounds. In 1980, the bottom fell out of the auto industry, and as a result, my husband wasn't working, so we had to rely on government programs for food and rent. Two years later, during my second pregnancy, I gained 70 pounds. Despite being on the Women, Infants and Children (or WIC) Program, I never received any nutrition education for myself, only for the children. Over the next couple of years, most doctors informed me that studies showed women who have big babies were at risk of developing diabetes. When my husband returned to work after four years, I continued to struggle to lose the weight. My husband sat me down and told me I was overweight and needed to lose weight for our marriage to continue. That got me motivated. To be honest, it made me so mad, it lit a fire in me. I started by walking and cutting back on sweets. Without any intervention, I lost over 100 pounds in one year.

As I aspired to lead a healthier lifestyle, I took the initiative to cook healthier meals and prioritize fitness. However, my lack of knowledge about nutrition made it challenging for me to provide healthy, nutritious meals for my family. Joining a health spa exposed me to inquiries about nutrition, which led me to immerse myself in reading various resources such as books and magazines on nutrition and teaching aerobic classes. When I came across an advertisement in Fitness magazine for the American Dietetic Association, I realized my desire to pursue a career in dietetics. I pursued a career as a dietitian due to my profound affinity for food, culinary arts, and the promotion of healthy lifestyles. I had acquired foundational knowledge in food and culinary practices from my mother and grandmothers, who served as influential and independent role models. Their influence, be it good or bad, profoundly shaped my values, traditions, and eating behaviors that have structured my life.

By this time, my children were in grade school. After years of contemplation, I finally gathered the courage to enroll in nutrition classes. The first class I attended was a free session offered by a vitamin company, which turned out to be a pivotal moment for me as it revealed my potential to empower individuals to transform their lives through good nutritional practices. With some research, I found a local community college teaching dietetics. However, I realized that it had been 10 years since I was in high school, and when I took my entrance testing, I found out that I had forgotten a lot of basic math and English. I had to take several classes just to qualify for the program. Technology had advanced significantly since the days when I used a manual typewriter, so I had to learn how to use a computer. It was very challenging because, like everything else, I had no support and I was on my own. My mother never understood the reason why I aspired to have an education and a career. She used to ask me, "Why are you doing this? You were never very good in school." Due to the length of time it was taking me to complete my education, most of my family and friends thought it was just something I was doing for fun or to find a new spouse. I still had to do all the household chores my mother-in-law had assigned me so many years before. I continued my education to become a dietetic technician for a couple of years.

I had a lot of stress to deal with, as my father's lifestyle caught up with him. Even though he stopped drinking many years before, he was battling colon cancer while I was in my clinical rotation just two semesters away from graduating. After his last surgery, a diagnosis of terminal cancer was given and he was placed on total parenteral nutrition (or TPN). After several months in the hospital/skilled unit on TPN, the only way he could be released was for someone to administer TPN to him. I agreed and was educated by a home health nurse. For nine months, I drove to my parents' house twice a day to provide his TPN. At the same time, I was studying parental nutrition and tube feeding at school. Balancing all of this while maintaining a marriage, household, exercise and school, and raising two children was very tough, and I ended up giving up exercise, which was probably the thing I needed most. The semester my father passed away, I failed one class by 1.7 points, which caused me to be out of the program. My professor believed that it would be best for me to take a class on death and dying, thinking that I did not handle my father's passing appropriately. This also cost me an extra $1,000.

In order to accomplish my dream, I had to overcome my depression and start taking medication for it. During this time, I had to retake a class and re-enter the clinical portion of the program. I eventually graduated from Owen's Community College with an associate degree in dietetics in 1999. The journey to graduation felt never-ending, and my mother did not attend that ceremony either. When I took my exam for the Dietetic Technician, Registered (or DTR) credentials, I failed. However, the second time I passed the exam and earned my DTR credentials. I settled for the title of DTR thinking I might go back to school at a later date to become a registered dietitian (or RD). I needed time to grieve from the loss of my father. Drawing from my personal experiences, I believed I could offer comfort and understanding to improve nutritional support. However, it was much more challenging than I anticipated to find a job in this field.

I took my first job as a manager in a long-term care facility. I worked for about six months and quit without giving any notice. The facility had problems recruiting employees to work in the kitchen, and they never had enough staff to run the food line. Part of my job was to fill in if they didn't have enough staff. I gave it all I had, but that wasn't for me. This experience taught me that I am more of a people person and that I needed to interact with the patients.

One of the most valuable experiences that significantly contributed to my career was my ten-year tenure as a DTR at a prominent hospital in my area. During this time, I honed my skills in patient assessment, recommending supplemental feedings, creating specialized menus, and providing personalized diet education. Additionally, I was responsible for preparing tube feedings for the entire hospital and fortifying breast milk for the Neonatal Intensive Care Unit. It was during this period that I confided in one of the dietitians, Sue Lincoln, that I wanted to be a dietitian but never thought I could do it. Sue became my mentor. She embodied the qualities of an exemplary mentor with dedication to the profession, profound knowledge, resilience, and unwavering support. I worked late, and she worked late, and we would have long conversations during those hours. Despite initially brushing off her suggestions, she persistently encouraged me to pursue further education to become an RD. We would discuss scenarios for new trauma patients, and Sue would have me tell her what tube feeding product to start the patient on and why. I had very low self-esteem, and she had a way to make me see the value in myself. That was something I had never had before I met her.

Approximately six months after meeting Sue, she received a diagnosis of breast cancer, which had metastasized to her bones and liver. As a result of her condition, she began using a walker due to a hip fracture. This marked my first interaction with a disabled individual who was employed as a dietitian. Despite the absence of light-duty assignments, Sue was subjected to a physical assessment by management, who doubted her ability to continue in her role. However, she defied expectations and successfully passed the scrutiny. Witnessing her adversity was profoundly challenging, yet she persisted in her work until her passing. Sue succumbed to terminal breast cancer in September 2009, at the hospital where she had worked for 29 years.

Her funeral was held in the hospital chapel.

For many years, I witnessed co-workers with disabilities in the department struggling with management. We had no light duty jobs and if you couldn't come back to work, you were fired after two years and no longer received medical insurance. The hospital had hired me as a part-time diet technician for 16 hours a week but I ended up working full-time hours for 32 hours a week. I had already begun experiencing health issues of my own with severe bleeding which caused me to have a hysterectomy, and 3 weeks later I had rectal surgery. Upon returning to work, I was scheduled for 11 days straight so another co-worker could go on vacation. Their rule was I was only hired part time so I would only get part time disability checks. I went to the union and they couldn't do anything. Every time I would question my status, the management would cut my hours. In the spring of 2011, I decided to enroll in just one class, and I excelled. I encountered management struggles when my manager told me that it was great that I had gotten a B in my class, but if I had wanted to continue, she would not work around my class schedule. I thought this was so unfair because I always picked up any extra hours. Truly my experience, was not favorable. The company rule was no light duty jobs. So, if you couldn't do the work and went on sick leave for up to two years, then you were terminated. I started to get written up for little things like putting the wrong sticker on a formula or miscalculating a formula by 21 calories. Co-workers told me that they all laughed at the minuscule amount. But rules are rules and I was written up for not having someone check my math. I was devastated because I loved my job.

With my spouse's support, in May 2011, I made the tough decision to give my two-week notice for my job at the hospital. The day I left was filled with emotions. My good luck party was at lunch and I was doing my job so they had it without me. However, two of my colleagues managed to acquire some of Sue's school notebooks and gifted them to me. I was deeply touched and cried for about an hour. I carried that notebook to many of my nutrition classes hoping it would give me that emotional support I longed for. I missed co-workers and friends but none of them called me. Still not having that label of being disabled, there was no going back only forward. It was at this time I started to reapply for the dietetics program to become an RD.

I had already been undergoing medical treatment for thyroid nodules and a problem with my big toe, and that's where it all began. I had to schedule my surgeries around my coursework. I found myself working until the night before surgery to complete everything and submit it to the professor. This actually helped me relax and heal because the semester was finally over. I had half of my thyroid removed in August 2011. The foot turned out to be more serious than I thought and I had surgery during my winter semester break. No walking for four months. This limited my activity to the point that I had to rent a scooter. It was very difficult hopping on one foot to the back of a vehicle and getting a scooter out when standing on one leg only. I became very depressed and sat around and ate whatever, mostly chocolate, which caused me to start gaining weight.

Prior to my thyroid surgery, the pre-op CT scan revealed gallstones. At that time, I opted against having them removed because I wasn't experiencing any issues and wanted to focus on completing my studies. In September 2012, I had a fall that injured my back. I started visiting a pain clinic, where I received steroid injections and nerve ablations. I usually scheduled my injections around my classes and returned to school and sat for hours. This continued for over a year, with no apparent improvement. No magnetic resonance imaging (or MRI) or other tests were ever requested. People began suggesting I use a cane, but I resisted as I felt it would be giving up. I already felt disadvantaged being in my 50s. It was challenging because handicapped parking was not conveniently located near any of the campus buildings. In early 2013, I woke up with stomach pain and realized it was likely due to the gallstones. I went through the necessary steps to see a surgeon, scheduled a surgery date, and completed my preop testing. On the day of my testing, I felt extremely dizzy, but dismissed it, attributing it to my long-term symptoms. However, the night before the scheduled surgery, the doctor called to inform me that he couldn't proceed with the surgery because my liver enzymes were over 20 times higher than normal. His plan was to admit me and conduct further tests. As I lay there in the hospital I remember crying because I was in so much pain with my back. After all the test results, I had my gallbladder removed the next morning. From there, I had to see my primary care physician for my liver. He thought we should watch my liver enzymes to see if they would improve after some medication changes. Well, after 18 months, there were no changes in the liver enzymes. So, he referred me to a Gastroenterologist. After monitoring me for months, I had a liver biopsy. The diagnosis was stage 2 fatty liver disease. I had every emotion, sad, mad, and trying to understand why because I had never drunk alcohol. I was told that if I did nothing, I would have eight to ten years before I would need a new liver.

I wasn't going to sit around and do nothing. My weight had reached its highest point at 287 pounds. Some of the doctors suggested I have weight loss surgery. Being in the nutrition field, I heard a lot of different opinions, both good and bad. I really didn't need their opinions. It was never to help me it was just what they thought. I had gastric bypass surgery in December 2015. After the surgery, the doctor told me I would never have lost weight because my liver was too large. The next semester was tough, with a challenging 50-minute commute to campus. There were times when I had to pull over and vomit, or run out of class to the bathroom due to dumping syndrome. This is common after stomach surgery because food in the stomach moves too quickly to the small intestine. Symptoms include nausea, diarrhea, abdominal cramps, and dizziness. Despite these difficulties, I managed to lose 116 pounds. One of my professors asked me to speak in a nutrition class about my experience. Most of the students had very little knowledge and just couldn't understand why I couldn't lose weight on my own.

I was trying to stay active after losing a lot of weight, but I started experiencing frequent falls. For three years, I consulted with many doctors who all insisted that the issue was with my back, despite my insistence that the problem was with my hips. None of them seemed to listen. Despite the intense pain I was in, none of my doctors ordered an MRI. But I felt like my prayers were finally answered when I found Dr. E. I initially saw him for pain in my right leg, and he was the first to order an MRI. However, the insurance company did not approve the MRI, so I was back to square one. I started to doubt myself and wondered if the pain was all in my head, because nobody seemed to take it seriously. The pain was so unbearable that most days it was all about which I could think. I also had been having vertigo which is a sensation of dizziness or spinning that can occur due to problems in the inner ear, brain, or sensory pathways that help with balance. They did allow an MRI of my brain. The results said I had a small stroke at an undetermined time.

I could barely make it through the semester. It seemed like writing papers was the worst. While struggling physically to do my undergraduate coursework, I networked with colleagues in the profession, at events of the Academy of Nutrition and Dietetics (or Academy), and with Academy groups. I volunteered with the underprivileged through Ohio State University Extension. I helped children in the Summer Garden Study by providing knowledge of picking and growing vegetables. I used my creativity working with Ohio Snap-education classes providing nutrition classes, cooking meals and setting up grocery store tours. Most of these were great experiences, and I made some lifelong friends.

I graduated with a Bachelor of Science degree in dietetics from Bowling Green University in 2017. That was the first time I heard someone say anything about my walking. An acquaintance texted me to congratulate me on graduating. Before I could reply to inquire how he saw me out of so many people, he shared that he recognized me because of my walk. That really hurt because I had been to so many doctors, and not one of them ordered an MRI of my hips despite the amount of pain I was experiencing. After graduation, I tried to maintain a normal life and get out of bed. My spouse kept telling me to use a cane, but for over a year, I refused. During one of our outings, in 2017 I fell again and was in so much pain that I had to be taken to the car by a shuttle. I didn't tell anyone because I was embarrassed about falling again. This time, the pain was on my left hip instead of my right hip. After a week, I returned to Dr. E and he asked why I hadn't come back. I explained that it was due to insurance reasons. He left the room to call insurance, and finally, I got an MRI of my left hip. The next day, I saw the doctor, and was told that I had a torn gluteus maximus muscle. As the largest muscle in your buttocks, the gluteus maximus muscle performs a major role in many physical activities that require strength and power in the lower body. I was scheduled for surgery the following day and had three torn tendons repaired on my left hip and was discharged home on crutches. However, after the pain medication was discontinued, the pain was still present in the right hip. There was a waiting period of one year after surgery to enable the leg to bear body weight without re-injury. During the waiting period, I continued to get steroid injections every couple of months for pain control.

My grade point average was not the greatest and being in so much pain I had never applied for the graduate program. I was looking at taking a year off. Despite this, I began taking prerequisite courses for the graduate program. I had only applied for one graduate program. I told myself if I didn't get in I would just go back and work as a DTR. When I opened my computer, it said my application was accepted. I made my husband come and read it just so he could see the same thing as me. Throughout this time, I continued to experience persistent pain in my right hip and faced challenges obtaining approval from my insurance provider for the necessary treatment. Eventually, after going back and forth with the insurance company again and waiting what seemed to be forever I got an MRI. Despite these challenges, I proceeded with the orientation for the graduate program. In 2018, a week before classes began I had surgery for my right hip, which revealed multiple tendon tears requiring an extensive recovery period with a cumbersome brace (Figure 1), rendering me immobile for four months. The brace keeps the hip in socket while the tendons heal. I had other restrictions including not bending over a 90-degree angle which meant laying down was more comfortable. With the help of a home health aide, I learned how to get in the shower, get up and down and dress without bending. During this recovery phase, my physician emphasized the importance of a nutrient-rich diet for optimal healing. I was in a cycle of being inactive and gaining weight again.

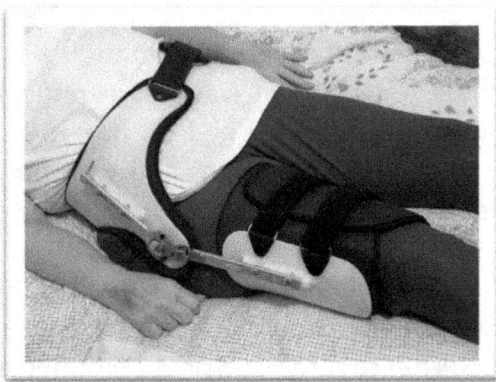

Figure 1. Susan laying down and wearing the cumbersome brace.

I chose a distance graduate program so that I could pick my own schedule. The remote program required that students must be at least 50 miles away from the school itself. I had to find my own preceptors for required competencies in clinical, management, foodservice, and community practice. None of the preceptors I worked with knew me before, and I would inform them if I anticipated any difficulties due to my disabilities. Most of them were accommodating to my disabilities, but one was not. On the first day, this preceptor asked if I would be able to manage the stairs in the unit where I would be working, making comments like "it's only two floors." The situation worsened as I was humiliated in front of other nurses and doctors on the units regarding my work, with everyone laughing at me. There were also concerns about what water I drank, the food I ate, my workout schedule, and even the time of day I worked out. While doing my work on the computer, this preceptor would stand behind me and watch every word I wrote, and correct me before I could hit the spell check. I agreed to do a presentation for the diabetes educator; during the presentation, I paused so the audience could ask questions and was written up for pausing. I tried not to give excuses for my performance so I didn't tell him about the stroke. I cried all the way home every day. But it was the first time I worked as an intern since my stroke. It took me an hour to drive one way to each facility, so I did not eat because I was afraid I wouldn't be able to find a bathroom for my dumping syndrome. From not eating most days, I experienced low blood sugars, low potassium, and low-calorie intake. I just wanted to finish my 16 weeks of rotations. Halfway through my long-term care rotation the pandemic hit and everything stopped. No interns could enter facilities. All rotation work had to be completed via case studies online. That was just as difficult for me because I learn from hands-on teaching. I had no one to ask questions or encourage me. I had to email questions and wait for a reply. That was difficult for me because I would lose my thought process. For me it was like being self-taught.

On my days without rotations, I helped my mom with all of her doctors' appointments and set up her pills for the week. The week before one of my hip surgeries, I took her to three doctor appointments. She was getting dementia and every time she saw me she would ask, "What's wrong with your walking?" I got tired of explaining and would just reply, "Mom, this is how I walk, remember?" After a 14-year battle with heart disease my mom passed away from complications associated with the disease.

I had gone so long with compensating to walk that I developed a Trendelenburg gait. This is an abnormal walking pattern indicating weakness in the abductor muscles of the hip. When a step is taken, the pelvis drops on the opposite side of the stance leg, and the trunk may lean toward the stance leg to maintain balance. The causes include various conditions that affect the hip abductors. Diagnosis is based on physical examination and observation of a person's walking pattern. Treatment includes physical therapy, strengthening exercises, use of assistive devices, or surgery depending on the underlying cause. I had gone to physical therapy so many times that insurance stopped me because I depleted my benefits yet had no results. Therefore, friends and family that saw me asked "what is wrong with your walking," "oh you have gained weight," "why are you still going to school; just go on disability." Even the physical therapist said I walked like a duck. I found it so hurtful that all these people would comment. I never heard any words of encouragement. What they didn't understand was that if I knew why I walked like this I would fix it.

My last step was to take the exam to be an RD. While studying for the RD exam, my daughter called to tell me that my grandson was being tested for Attention Deficit Disorder (or ADD). She paused and said, "Mom, I think you have it, too." I thought about all my years of struggling when I had to do course work. I followed up with a doctor's appointment and an evaluation, received the ADD diagnosis, and was put on medication. After starting the medication for the first time, I was able to concentrate on a task. I studied for months to take the RD exam. I was told that you can request accommodations to take the exam but was not informed of the mountain of paperwork required to do so. I did not ask for any disability accommodations because of the paperwork required and the time and expense to obtain it. In today's world, one has to pay to get doctors to do paperwork and have the time to go to the required appointments and pay for the appointments. To me it was just one more hoop to jump through to complete my career goal. I took the RD exam but did not pass. The time frame was not my problem. I believe it was just nerves. In the time since I failed, I have gotten multiple kidney infections and kidney stones.

With all my medical problems, I struggle with the idea of someone hiring me. I was told by an employment lawyer years ago that you don't have to disclose anything. I have never put anything down on past applications. I can hide some of my disabilities but I cannot hide others like the walking. I sit and think about whether I should just go on disability. My advice on the decision to disclose any disability to an employer is yes. In some jobs you will have to pass a physical and you don't want to lie. Some people don't like to disclose disabilities for fear of not getting hired or losing a job. An idea I have is to let me shadow the job and demonstrate that I can do it. I encourage dietetic practitioners without disabilities to realize that just because a person doesn't have a visible disability doesn't mean they don't have one or more disabilities. Some people with disabilities work harder to do a good job. Employees with disabilities typically stay in the position for longer than employees without disabilities; this is important because employers spend a lot of money on training new employees.

In conclusion, I would never change the journey I have been on. I believe all experiences good or bad made me stronger. I have learned that my story is one of resilience to keep going when life knocks me down. There was a time after my second hip surgery when I could tell you that this really kicked my butt. If I could go back in time and change anything about the graduate program I would tell more preceptors that I needed accommodations. When I think back on the amount of pain I was in, I wouldn't try to be the hero; I would have withdrawn from the program and reapplied. Honestly, some things I don't remember due to the pain I was in. I still have to pass the RD exam and I am getting ready to schedule it.

I recently learned that each US state has a vocational rehabilitation (or VR) program for people with disabilities who want to work to achieve their career goals. I plan to contact the VR program in Ohio and request their support for taking the RD exam, mobility devices, being hired for an RD job, and obtaining necessary accommodations for an RD job.

At age 62, my disabilities limit my walking. It's exhausting when I try and walk with or without a cane. Some days are better than others. Sometimes when shopping I use the motorized cart. My stroke caused processing challenges such as inability to recall how to spell some words in a timely manner. I have dumping syndrome so I never know when I am going to have to use the bathroom. Therefore, when I first enter a place such as a store, I locate the bathroom and I take a change of clothes just in case. Most times I stay home because of it. I still struggle to keep my blood sugars and potassium within normal ranges. But I can report that six years after my weight loss surgery, I have lost 45 pounds. With the help of a therapist, I am learning how to be proud of myself.

    I still have personal accomplishments to complete beyond my career goal of becoming and working as an RD. As a young child my grandmother had us come over and help her in the canning processes. I tried canning tomatoes once when my children were little but found it very messy. I used to say I had more on the floor than in the jars. During the pandemic I tried canning again and I did a great job at it. I took what my grandmother taught me about canning, and I placed first and second place at my county fair. A little piece of me knew that she was proud of me. My next personal accomplishment to complete is to make a cookbook with all of the canning recipes that my mom and grandmother used.

Editors: Suzanne Domel Baxter and Cheryl Iny Harris

Chapter 15 (Autobiography) Chronically Fascinating

By Jordan Griffing, MS, RD, LD

Jordan with her husband and two dogs

I've just recently passed my ninth anniversary since becoming a registered dietitian (or RD), so the nostalgia is flowing and I've pondered a lot lately about how I ended up here. As I write this in my office at a dialysis facility, a place I literally swore as an undergraduate student I'd never be, I'm reminded of so many pit stops along my journey. I am in awe of how it all led me here. I hope that maybe it will help others reading this as well. Millions and millions of people can say their life and journey within the medical system started at birth, and a large majority of those only have a few encounters outside of that; but for many, me included, the journey becomes such a significant part of daily life it is almost as if we have become professional patients. In addition to the other parts of life, we also must fit in hundreds, if not thousands, of healthcare encounters that never seem to end. I came into this world with orthopedic birth defects and to date have undergone 12 orthopedic surgeries and innumerable procedures. For the first 21 years of life, I was told I likely had a type of muscular dystrophy, but despite dozens of tests and years of opinions I never quite fit any of the diagnostic criteria for a subtype. I was diagnosed with Charcot Marie Tooth Type II as a "best we can do" diagnosis and just went from there. I did what I could to learn the most about the likely condition I had. My family and I got involved with the Muscular Dystrophy Association; we would follow along each year with the telethon to see how much money was being raised for research and continued praying for treatments/cures. I found solace in the community of others that were similarly afflicted and tried to continue living life the best I knew how.

Still, at present, I mostly remain a medical anomaly, often finding myself searching for answers that may never come. In 2013, I went to the Mayo Clinic in search of answers. It was confirmed that I did not have muscular dystrophy, but some similar condition (still without a name — much less a treatment or a cure). In addition to the visible disability of my neuromuscular and orthopedic issues I also have invisible disabilities like fibromyalgia, Inappropriate Sinus Tachycardia and others that affect my autonomic system like Postural Orthostatic Tachycardia Syndrome and Mast Cell Activation Syndrome. Throughout my childhood I had to wear the ugliest orthotic shoes with uncomfortable braces in an effort to walk "normally." By the age of 18, I was using a wheelchair as needed especially when standing was required for more than a few minutes or navigating situations that required a lot of walking, such as an airport or mall. As my conditions have progressed over the years, my mobility device arsenal grew in response – now involving a shower chair, grab bars in the bathroom, elevated toilet seats, a walker/rollator and adaptive driving pedals just to name a few.

Going to doctors' offices, being in the hospital, and undergoing testing has been such a normal part of my life that it always felt natural when the time came to choose a career to stay within my comfortable healthcare bubble. There were times when the area of specialty changed — whether it was research, being a physician, or some other role but it wasn't until my sophomore year at Baylor University that I stumbled upon dietetics. I didn't want to put in the commitment of medical school if I didn't have a definitive end goal, so I entrusted the help of the career counselors. I took a test that was sort of like an aptitude test had a baby with the Myers-Briggs personality test and it produced a list of the most popular jobs for my personality type — and as it turns out, dietetics was at the top of the list! Because I started as a pre-med/biology major, many of my freshman courses would transfer, it was a career with clinical indications, and a subject relevant to literally every human on the planet, so I signed up for my first course and never looked back.

Another excellent resource Baylor University offered was an Office of Access and Learning Accommodations, which allowed me several options that made my college and graduate school life easier. Many college students are encouraged to walk or bike to classes, neither of which was a feasible option for me. There were only a handful of accessible spots spread around campus and Baylor security were big fans of handing out parking tickets. After many discussions with staff, my personal patient advocate (my mom) suggested the eventual resolution which didn't cost anyone anything, and I ended up getting parking "immunity" that prevented security from giving me a parking ticket for parking closer to the doors in a maintenance or other "reserved" type spot when accessible spots weren't available. I have dexterity issues with my hands and was allowed to take my laptop to classes, even if the professor didn't allow them as it's easier for me to type than write. I had the option to have someone assigned to my classes to take notes for me, but having my laptop was enough at the time. Also, if I had an exam that required a lot of writing, I was able to take that exam at the accommodation office so that I could use a computer and type instead.

Due to my conditions travel is difficult for me, which made deciding where to apply for my internship very nerve wracking. I ended up applying for and getting into a distance internship through Iowa State University, which allowed me to complete my rotations at the facilities of my choice. This allowed me to stay in Waco, TX where I already had clinical roots down, and a reasonable commute each day. Within each rotation I had a sit-down meeting with my overseer to discuss any specific accommodations that would need to be made and to set expectations for the things I struggled with. For the most part, I didn't need much accommodation during the internship, other than having basic wheelchair access when needed and not having multiple facilities to visit on the same day.

Navigating disability in the workplace is difficult to say the least, and I can say that even being nine years in, I don't have it figured out. There are Americans with Disabilities Act laws and certain things that are theoretically off limits for employers, but unfortunately in my experience there are many ways for them to sidestep these or find a loophole. It's hard to know how much to disclose and when, so for me that has been situational just depending on how the interview is going and the vibe I'm getting from whoever is in the room. Most of the time it comes up in some capacity as people can see my wheelchair. In response to questions, I speak to my ability to get on the same level as the patients because I've been one my whole life, but I don't know that I've ever spoken about specific accommodations until after I have an official offer. You'd think especially in the medical field accommodations would be simple and straightforward, as this group of people tends to have heavier exposure to individuals with disabilities — but in all honesty, in my experience, it's no better and, in some cases, has been worse than other fields. If I had to sum it up in one statement: your supervisor/manager will make all the difference. I've had terrible bosses who did not honor my reasonable accommodations because it was "unfair" to the rest of the team, or it required them to do something a tad different from how they've dealt with any other employee. I've also had an employer voluntarily spend over $10,000 for my clinic to have automatic doors so I don't have to fight their heaviness every day. As far as workplace accommodations go these days, it's fairly similar to my internship days — I use my wheelchair at work so wherever I go must have enough space to accommodate that. I have an ergonomic keyboard and vertical mouse which allow me to use my hands for longer periods of time, though usually items like this I have to purchase myself. The biggest accommodation I find helpful, which also protects my job, is intermittent use of the Family and Medical Leave Act (or FMLA). The unfortunate part is you must be with a company for a year before you're eligible, but it's so worth it to push through as much as you can to try to make it to that landmark. Intermittent FMLA gives me the ability to miss a few days a month if needed due to flare ups and can also be used to provide protected times for doctor's appointments as well — which comes in handy when you have over five physicians on your team, most of which are not even in the same city and require travel. I also get the peace of mind that my job is protected, even when my body is unreliable. A secondary accommodation that I've gotten for most of my positions is the ability to work remotely when feasible.

When I was in undergraduate courses and thinking about my future, the physical feasibility of a long-term career wasn't quite as heavy as it is now, almost a decade in but thankfully dietetics is flexible enough that it continues to be an option for me. One of the best parts of dietetics is how vast the opportunities are and there is a place for almost everyone. I've spent much of my career thus far in a clinical setting — primarily in hospitals. Starting out in a hospital is a great way to begin getting experience. You see so many different conditions and medical units all within the same place that you quickly learn your own style of working with patients. From this you can narrow down if there is a specialty you want to aim for. Hospitals are often fast-paced and a fairly easy place to work logistically if you use a wheelchair or other mobility aid as most hospitals are built with that in mind. Whether it was working with adults or children, I found overall that hospital work is predictable, which works out well for me. My schedule day to day was very consistent and I often would know exactly what I would be doing each day and had a set routine. Whereas my experiences working in the outpatient setting, both remotely and in person, are not quite as consistent day to day, but overall have less pressure than the inpatient world. With the world of dietetics there's something for everyone! There's also sports, private practice, grocery stores, community-based jobs, teaching, and so many others that are potential options as well. Another bonus with the world of dietetics is you can float between them at any point. For example, I don't really want to teach right now, but that's something I can always fall back on later down the road if/when I decide that might be physically easier to do, but I can still be working in my field of choice and find value there.

I knew from very early on in my nutrition studies that the Neonatal Intensive Care Unit (or NICU) was where I wanted to end up, and after five years of waiting, studying, and hoping, my opportunity came. Being in a level IV NICU is by far the highlight of my career and where all my love and passion for nutrition is. Nutrition support (i.e., having to be fed through a variety of different tubes, or having nutrition intravenously — also known as peripheral or total parenteral nutrition (TPN/PPN)) has always been my favorite part of nutrition, and most of the tiny humans need some type of nutrition support. Being able to see the tiniest 400-gram baby right in front of you is something that is hard to forget, and such an incredible experience to literally watch them grow before your eyes. It's also one of the hardest jobs I've ever had because when you lose a patient, it seems so much more unfair when it's a tiny human versus an older adult who has had a chance to have a life. I loved being in a teaching hospital that not only fostered my own learning but allowed me to teach others about my little love nuggets and how to best care for them. Every morning I'd round on every single one of my babies to assess their growth from the previous day, and decide what changes needed to be made to their diets/labs. Several hours of the day were spent in rounds discussing these things with the other members of the multidisciplinary teams. My afternoons were mostly spent educating parents on how to mix fortified formula or breastmilk before discharge, teaching residents and interns about neonatal nutrition, and charting my notes. Unfortunately, this is my prime example of how a manager can make or break a position, because mine was ultimately the reason I had to leave what otherwise was my dream job. My physical health from all the stress and lack of support became too much for me to bear, and I had to find something that wasn't slowly draining everything I had to offer.

Long story short — the pause in my NICU story has led to my current position in a dialysis facility. Even though my job title is "clinical dietitian" for both, the actual day to day and knowledge sets could not be more different. I swore no one could ever pay me enough to work with dialysis patients, but turns out this was false! While I do not have the passion and burning fire of desire to learn all the things about dialysis, this has been the best job I've ever had and is absolutely what I needed for this stage of my life, even if it's not necessarily what I want forever. Dialysis as a whole has always tended to pay better than inpatient dietetic positions, and being in the outpatient world is a significant decrease in the daily stress level, which for me is directly tied to my symptoms. My manager here is EVERYTHING. I have never felt my manager had my back or would fight for me until now. She sees me first as a capable, hard-working employee and my health issues are secondary. She has shown a genuine interest in learning how she can help me be my most successful self and has been a light of hope and confidence in a sea of darkness, wondering if any manager would see value above my illness. She treats me just as wonderfully as she does any other dietitian on her team, and that is something money cannot buy. My days now consist of educating, caring for, and monitoring labs for dialysis patients. I cover multiple clinics, some of which require the patients to come in the center for treatment but one of my clinics is for patients who do dialysis at home. Much of my job is to help educate patients on nutrition education to help maximize their dialysis by eating low phosphorous/potassium/sodium foods. This job also crosses into pharmacy territory a bit as I educate patients on phosphorous binders that they must take with meals to help absorb additional phosphorous since the kidney can't get rid of it all anymore and help them decide which binder might be most appropriate. One major difference between inpatient and outpatient is that specifically with dialysis, you really get to know your patients and become part of their lives. The in-center patients are having to come for at least 12 hours every week so you get the opportunity to really know them on a personal basis and make a personalized and significant impact on their healthcare. They definitely aren't as cute as my NICU babies, but I have found meaning here just the same. I would love to think a return to the NICU might still be possible, but for now this is where my path is leading me.

    Getting to watch the creation of the Disabilities in Nutrition and Dietetics Member Interest Group (or simply Disabilities MIG) has been a really neat experience and one that I wish had started so many years ago! Neva and Suzi presented a session at the Food and Nutrition Conference and Expo when I had the opportunity to go in 2018 and our partnership has continued since. The Dietitians with Disabilities Facebook group has also been a really great way to meet other dietetics professionals who experience some of the same things I do, and it's a safe space for us to help each other out and feel less alone. It's also been a space to openly be able to talk about the hardships of employment with disabilities, and we all learn from each other in addition to being another support system, which can never be overstated.

As a society we definitely still have a long way to go in terms of inclusivity and diversity, but I think positive progress is being made. Within the past couple of years, subjects like mental health and emotions have become less taboo, we're learning different words to identify people and how to be inclusive of all types. During the COVID pandemic the world saw that so many occupations can be done remotely, curbside orders became a viable option at so many stores and I believe the world of accessibility grew enormously as a result. Companies like OXO exist that cater to easier-to-handle kitchen items and cooking, grocery stores like H-E-B are making more fresh, ready to cook meals that take out all the prep work, and there are more pre-cut fruit and veggie options now as well. Even as I write this there are high hopes and optimistic whispers about airline travel in your own wheelchair being a possibility soon! The changes are slow – but they're coming.

Navigating the world is difficult, and often made much more difficult when disabilities are also thrown in the mix. My advice for future RDs and those with disabilities regardless of occupation is to not give up. I would like to think that with projects like this book, we're increasing awareness/education that makes it easier for incoming generations to follow, and maybe one day accessibility won't be something to fight for anymore and will instead be the norm. There are days when I love being able to have the opportunity to participate in projects like this one and helping educate the world on disability etiquette and showing that we have inherent worth as much as any able-bodied human. But then there are days when I am mad at the world, ashamed of my limitations and frustrated that this is my lot in life. I've learned that alongside disability comes the fluidity of the grief cycle, and am trying to learn that no matter what, each day has its purpose regardless of my level of functionality that day. It seems such a prevalent attitude that those with disabilities are faking their illness, when in reality we are so often faking wellness. If you work with or know someone with a disability, visible or invisible, my biggest piece of advice is to believe them. Even better, research their condition if they have felt safe enough to share it with you. Ask questions and learn how to best help that person without overstepping. If you yourself have a disability, know that you are not alone —– you are seen and you are heard. Whether you decide dietetics is for you or not, I hope that you find the path that brings you a sense of worth and purpose. For me, that has been nutrition. Despite my physical limitations I have still found a way to contribute to society, support my family, feel like my life has meaning, and hopefully have helped a few patients and co-workers along the way.

Editors: Suzanne Domel Baxter and Cheryl Iny Harris

Chapter 16 (Autobiography) Nourishing Resilience: The Story of a Gastrointestinal (or GI) Dietitian

By Cheryl Iny Harris, MPH, RD

1.
2.

1. *Cheryl at 16 years old. She went from one knee brace to two because her knees kept dislocating. She still often needs to use knee braces.*
2. *Cheryl sitting on a stool and working with a tall plant in her garden.*

I've always wanted to pursue a career in nutrition. Well, maybe not always. There was a period of time where I wanted to be a butterfly, a firefighter, a chocolate taster, a lawyer, a veterinarian — and then I found out pets die. But from the time I was a teen, food was fascinating. My family is Middle eastern, food is the center of culture, and you feed *everyone*. Then when I started running track, I realized how much food affected my performance and I was hooked. I never looked back.

Initially, my interests were around sports nutrition, public health, then eating disorders, but I was really interested in almost all kinds of nutrition. I did my undergrad work in nutritional sciences at Cornell and my master's in public health nutrition at the University of

California Berkeley (or UC Berkley). My dietetic internship was through a combined MPH/internship program at UC Berkeley as well.

Despite having a handful of mild symptoms as a teen, I was fortunate to be a reasonably healthy kid. More sprains, torn ligaments and joints that popped than expected, but nothing major. There were signs that all was not well during undergrad. I started having vision difficulties in biology lab classes. I couldn't see clearly through a microscope, and I asked what I could do. Could I get it displayed on a wall instead? No. I could copy answers from someone else. I didn't know what disability accommodations were, and I certainly had no idea that this would apply to me. This was 1996 or so, and awareness of disabilities, or at least, my awareness of disabilities was very different. So, I did nothing. I missed out on learning and did poorly in that class.

I started having significant symptoms around the age of 21, during my combined MPH/dietetics internship — dizziness, elevated heart rate, chest pains, palpitations, profoundly overwhelming fatigue, and more. Now, I would hope this would be caught pretty quickly as Postural Orthostatic Tachycardia Syndrome (or POTS), but in 2001, I was told I was anxious, and a medication change was helpful. A kind professor gave me an extension on a paper, but I didn't know I could get any other support. I still fondly remember Dr. Zak Sabry and his kindness. It's amazing how even decades later we carry the people who go out of their way to help.

I was incredibly lucky that I worked at a wellness center when I was at UC Berkeley. I had a boss named Kathy who was disabled. She was born with hands, but without arms. Kathy was an incredibly competent woman who modeled living a full life and actively leading a team. She drove a car with adaptive steering equipment, typed, and did everything she needed to. I don't know if Kathy and I ever discussed her disabilities explicitly, but I always had the sense that Kathy's disabilities were a part of her, but did not limit or define her. I have no doubt that Kathy's example served as a role model for me, clearly demonstrating that I could do or be what I chose. I am endlessly grateful that I was so fortunate to have this sort of mentoring as a formative experience. I wish I remembered her full name so I could find her and thank her!

When I graduated, I moved from California to Virginia and I worked for Virginia Cooperative extension while I studied for the registered dietitian (or RD) exam. I loved teaching nutrition classes although it was really physically draining. I did have a sense, even then, that there was something going on medically, because I remember being sure to have a job that kept me on an insurance plan. I passed the RD exam on the first try and didn't require accommodations. I took a job soon after in 2003 with the Women, Infants, and Children (or WIC) State agency in the District of Columbia (or DC).

My job at DC WIC State agency was initially a great fit. I was writing grants, teaching classes, supervising and more. After about a year, I started having increasing muscle and joint pains, overwhelming fatigue, frighteningly rapid weight loss, gastrointestinal issues, and a laundry list of seemingly unrelated issues. I went to easily a hundred doctors in the next two decades before I finally got a diagnosis of Ehlers-Danlos Syndrome (or EDS).

Everything at this job, everything felt like a battle. Initially I could not stand or walk so I was rolling around in an assistive device. The doors were too heavy for me so I literally had difficulty getting out of the office and using the bathroom — I had one dislocated and one subluxed (mildly dislocated) shoulder. This was my "normal," but when I could no longer stand, I couldn't do things I had formerly taken for granted, like open doors. And did I mention I was having gastrointestinal (or GI) problems? Back in the early 2000s, Virginia disability tags were not recognized in DC when I worked there, so I had to get separate tags, and I amassed a parking ticket collection in the interim. I could not get approval to work remotely, although there was very little about my job that required being there physically. While my supervisor was tremendously supportive, I had some co-workers who made comments based on my disability that were entirely inappropriate. Although it did not make sense financially or in terms of benefits, I decided to leave and go into private practice in 2007. It's one of the best decisions I've ever made.

I always thought I would be spending my career working with underserved populations. Once I developed GI issues — and boy, do I mean humbling GI issues — I realized what an underserved population it was. And so, I started my practice in 2007 working with people with digestive problems, autoimmune disorders, and problems like mine — joint pain, including people with EDS, although despite my efforts, my own diagnosis came years later.

I still have my practice, Harris Whole Health, which is about to turn 18 years old. I'm now practicing online because of the complications of EDS affecting my ability to see, and therefore drive. Specifically, I have a condition called convergence insufficiency, which affects how my eyes coordinate, and my eyes get tired very easily. I'm still working to find solutions. I use a range of assistive equipment, from screen readers to magnifiers to special glasses to special apps on my phone. I used to use a cane for walking and balance; I don't anymore. I still use a wheelchair sometimes when I'm going to medical appointments or need to go a longer distance.

Another resource I use is one that I know I'm lucky to have — my husband. Because of my vision, I'm not driving, and my husband drives me to medical appointments. I'm self-employed, so I can't access benefits like the Family and Medical Leave Act (or FMLA). But *he* can access his FMLA through his employer, which covers taking care of a spouse. We didn't realize that initially, so he was taking vacation time for the first few years. Now he is using FMLA to help me get to medical appointments and also *ahem* advocating for me at appointments.

In terms of self-care resources, I've found that stress management and really good boundaries are absolutely essential. I tend to want to take on too much, and get very enthusiastic about too many projects. I want to over-deliver to my clients, and often have people calling about urgent needs. But the reality is that when I try to take on too much, I get burnt out pretty quickly. There are very distinct warning signs that I get, first that I should slow down, then that things are going to get ugly very soon, and if I still don't listen, I go into post-exertional malaise. Once that hits, it takes weeks or sometimes months to recover.

But in a larger sense, when I haven't set boundaries, taken enough time off, taken adequate breaks, or taken the time I need for medical appointments, I can't do my job as well and I start getting resentful. That's a yellow flag for me that I'm not getting what I need. I think that's the case for everyone, but particularly for people juggling medical needs and work obligations. For me, with my disabilities, that means that sleep is medicine, regular meals and fluid are an absolute non-negotiable; if I'm doing something stressful, I have to take time off later, and I have to plan in time for regular physical therapy and meditation. I've also found it really helpful to practice self-compassion. It's often hard, and sometimes harder than it should be to get everyday things done. Part of being in private practice is doing new things and making a lot of mistakes, so it's necessary. Figuring out how to be gentle with myself wasn't always my habit, so it's still a work in progress.

For those reading or listening who aren't familiar with the daily tasks of a dietitian in private practice, that means communicating with new clients, scheduling appointments, counseling clients, providing handouts and educational materials I've developed, taking notes, and sending the notes afterwards, and sometimes sending notes to the doctors, and billing or filing insurance claims, and sending superbills. Finding an online practice software platform that was screen reader friendly was challenging, and I've found transitioning quite tricky and draining, but I'm getting there. Sometimes I also teach classes online or write papers as well.

I don't know how my disabilities affect my capacity as a practitioner, except I would say that it makes me passionate about understanding complex issues — not just mine, of course. I'd like to think it gives me an extra layer of compassion, empathy, and understanding for other people. And as I've read in some of these other wonderful chapters, I do think people with disabilities are absolutely more resilient and learn to be good at problem solving because we know the world isn't going to show up ready for us.

There is also the disconnect between how I experience myself and how others experience me. Over a dozen years ago, I was working in a chronic pain clinic and they held an open house. Someone asked what I did, and I said I was a dietitian. The man very transparently assessed my body (yuck) and said, of course. Your body is your calling card. I glared at him, not quite knowing what to say. His words stuck in my head. I don't feel like my appearance reflects my skills, but I can't control anyone else's views. Some of my disabilities are visible some of the time, and I don't know how other people view my disabilities. I find it a bit tricky to be in a profession where people sometimes equate eating well with control over health. It's a constant balancing act, and one that I haven't quite made my peace with yet knowing that when I do, things will change again.

My disabilities do limit me in a range of other more logistical ways. Between challenges with walking, vision, proprioception, and balance, at this point, I cannot attend events in person and I can only interact with colleagues online. I feel lucky that there are so many forums to network with peers, but it still isn't the same.

Food...ah, food. Food can be so tricky. I order groceries online, and I have for years. I can't say how much I miss farmer's markets, and I do garden as much of my own food as possible. I do have a limited diet, and for better and worse, dietary changes have helped me manage my symptoms better, even if they do have a quality-of-life cost. My digestive issues have been well managed for at least the last 15 years, and I'm more grateful for that than words can express. Through the process of my diagnostic and medical odyssey, many practitioners insisted on restrictive diets. I hated them. It's always so easy to restrict, and so hard to get off a diet, because it's so difficult to figure out what foods are problematic. I think it's really shaped my philosophy against restrictive diets unless they are necessary, and trying to emphasize reintroduction as quickly as possible. I've been able to reintroduce many foods, although not as many as I'd like. It's still a process, and I celebrate every win. Some dairy products, like small amounts of butter, are recently back in my life, and I could *not* be happier! I think it helps me understand my clients better and relate to the very real struggles and anxieties many people have around food.

I do also make many adaptations in the kitchen. I always kneel on a stool to chop or cook. I have all sorts of gadgets — food processors of different sizes, a Vitamix, etc. Chopping is generally just too much of a struggle. When I can't get what I want pre-cut, my husband is my designated chopper. I think that's his preference because I'm not sure he trusts me around a knife, because boy, people with EDS generally don't have good proprioception and I am definitely a good example of that. And when there's something I really want to make but it's just too complex to do all at once, I break down the meal prep into stages, with each stage in manageable portions. So, I'm in the middle of making a fun cake, and I've got two kinds of frosting already made in the freezer because there is no way I have the strength or energy to do all the baking and decoration at once. Once upon a time, I worked in a bakery, and that's something I really enjoyed.

I try to be conscious about what I disclose, and how. I don't generally tell clients about my disabilities because I don't think it's necessary or helpful. My story is convoluted, and I don't want to get down a rabbit hole. I always try to internally ask the question why I'm disclosing something. Is it because I want to be seen and known? That's a totally understandable human need, but it's a need that needs to be met outside of client sessions. If I'm clear that I'm disclosing some part of my disability story because I think it will provide the client useful insight, sometimes I do share. I have to be honest, I have come to terms with my disabilities, but the process of diagnosis was difficult. Like many people with EDS, it was more than two decades of hearing my problems were psychological and not getting the help I needed.

I try to give back and volunteer my time in a range of ways. I'm the Inclusion, Diversity, Equity and Access (or IDEA) Liaison for the Disabilities in Nutrition and Dietetics Member Interest Group. I have been an author for five peer-reviewed articles on EDS, POTS, Mast Cell Disease and disability access. I've spoken for webinars and podcasts on EDS and POTS. I also run a mindfulness group for people with trauma. And, of course, I'm volunteering on this book. A lot of this is in the hopes that people have a different, and better, experience than I did.

So, what would I do differently? Well, I sure wish I had gotten a diagnosis a couple of decades earlier, but time travel isn't a thing. I also wish I had known about the access opportunities for people with disabilities earlier, but I didn't know. I also didn't identify as disabled until around 2005. I think before then, I had medical problems and difficulties, but I always viewed them as temporary, and I always had the mindset that because someone else had it worse, I didn't need help. I've learned that someone else always will have it worse, and that's irrelevant. If I (or anyone else) would benefit from support, or a mobility aid, or whatever, I should get it if possible. No one benefits from my suffering or your suffering if you're reading this and wondering.

Also, and this is a public service announcement for the able-bodied folks reading this — disability access isn't a special need. Making sure that co-workers, students, or interns have access to a bathroom or food isn't "special," it's literally just the bare minimum requirement, and something that everyone should have. There's nothing special about it.

Editors: Suzanne Domel Baxter and Cheryl Iny Harris

Chapter 17 (Autobiography)
How Disability Pride Catalyzed My Path to Dietetics

By Alena Iris Basa Morales, RD/RDN

Alena Iris Basa Morales

      I want you to read my story and understand my disability to be a core informant of my internal relationship. My disability encapsulates a complicated but loving communication between myself and my body, a story describing the interconnectedness of personhood and feeling. When my identity is understood, truly understood by others, I find community. When it isn't, I experience ableism, isolation, and invalidation. I'm human, so I sometimes internalize this. The multitude of feelings surrounding my chronic illnesses and my disability identity — pride, frustration, anticipation, elation, love, and so much more — act as a council that often sings in harmony, but occasionally disagrees. At the end of the day, this journey has gifted me an awareness that simple empathy can't quite comprehend. For me, disability acts as an accountability method of loving myself, taking care of myself, and contributing to the community around me. The intentionality of self-love is crucial amidst a world that can be unkind and violent. A tangible reminder to show up for myself and others like me reaffirms my commitment to my internal joy. This is where my disability pride lies. I love being disabled and feel grateful for the way it guides me through my life.

It's funny how things manifest and fall into place. As a child, I never even considered becoming a dietitian until I became disabled, although I have wanted to work in healthcare my entire life. I grew up with wonderful disabled role models from a young age, the most meaningful being my mother, a clinical scientist, and my grandmother, a nurse. My grandma, upon acquiring her disabilities, called herself the "disabled diva" and even had a matching license plate cover on her wheelchair van to match. This role model for a positive relationship with disability started a positive trajectory towards accepting my own. I was born able bodied and even was an athlete in martial arts, but soon developed disabling symptoms such as chronic pain and tachycardia around age twelve years. This progressed into multiple systemic symptoms that doctors couldn't figure out, prompting me to go to the Mayo Clinic in Rochester Minnesota at age fourteen years. After extensive diagnostic testing, I was eventually diagnosed with Postural Orthostatic Tachycardia Syndrome (or POTS). POTS is a life-long chronic illness that can briefly be described as an autonomic nervous system disorder that causes abnormalities in involuntary body functions such as heart rate, gastrointestinal (or GI) motility, circulation, blood volume, and more. It is most distinctly exacerbated by dehydration, orthostatic changes, and temperature changes. My nutritional needs changed to require a high salt diet (4-7 grams/day) and a high fluid (~4-5 L/day) diet as an essential part of managing POTS. The recommendations vary widely, but according to my physician I have been prescribed the higher end of the recommendations!

After finding my groove, things were stable for a while until I developed a severe case of C. Diff colitis, a life-threatening bacterial infection of the colon, which lasted for almost a year. Although the C. Diff colitis eventually resolved, the aftermath of the infection caused the development of two more chronic diseases. The most dangerous, Mast Cell Disease, is a life-long systemic white blood cell condition that most roughly translates to being "allergic to life." Mast Cell Disease continues to greatly impact me to this day, but the disabling symptoms I experience (pain, flu-like symptoms, GI issues, etc.) are very dynamic. The second, gastroparesis and intestinal failure, had a severe impact on my life from ages 14-18. I continue to experience occasional gastroparesis flare-ups that impact me, but my intestinal function has significantly improved over the past decade. Both conditions had a debilitating effect on me. During the peak of my battle with gastroparesis, the inability to intake hardly any food or fluids caused my POTS to spiral out of control, and I could hardly function without experiencing almost daily episodes of multi-system anaphylaxis from a wide variety of internal and external changes (crying, throwing up, temperature changes, fragrance, etc.) as a result of the Mast Cell Disease. At one point, I required 1-4 EpiPens per day!

At this time of my life, my chronic illnesses seemed almost intelligent, causing me to hardly be able to get out of bed. We now know how closely intertwined these three diseases are, so it was no wonder I felt as if they were ganging up on me, causing complications that could fuel the progression of another, and so forth, until I was trapped in a cycle that no doctor knew how to stop. My mother and my pediatrician tirelessly navigated the medical system to provide me answers and care, but were met with insurance denials and specialists not wanting to deal with me. A major barrier that impacts my ability to receive comprehensive care has been the lack of awareness about my disabilities. POTS and Mast Cell disease in particular are very complicated, underdiagnosed, and often misunderstood.

Nowadays, I encounter more physicians who know my conditions, but this hasn't always been the case. Many hospital visits, which in themselves became progressively more frequent during my teenage years as I became progressively malnourished and dehydrated, were met with invalidation and even harm. I have also experienced dismissal of my symptoms due to factors such as my weight and age. Much of the pushback I have received seems to stem from a place of frustration that my chronic illnesses cannot be cured with a cut-and-dry intervention. Unfortunately, disabled and chronically ill people are notoriously perceived as antagonists to the curative mission of healthcare, often exposing the gaps in standardized diagnostic and palliative services. I joined an unfortunate statistic of complex patients who weren't believed, at a point in history where a medical condition was not well understood.

A positive memory I recall with a healthcare provider was with a dietitian during a difficult hospital stay that lasted a few weeks. Although I only saw her once, her validation and ability to interweave my symptoms into an accessible nutrition plan made me feel heard as a patient.

These days, I continue to feel disabled by these conditions, especially as new complications develop, but I am fortunate to have enough experience with them where I know the strategies needed to address symptoms. One notable tool that completely transformed my quality of life was my central line for intravenous fluids and medications. At 16, I received a PICC line to at least provide hydration for my POTS and thus quiet the Mast Cell Disease some, during a time when I could not intake the necessary fluid and salt requirements I needed. Despite its reduced risks compared to a central line, I was refused a feeding tube because of my weight. This resource allowed me to slowly improve my nutritional status as I continued on with intravenous fluids through a portacath. Now, over ten years later, I have reduced the amount of intravenous fluids/medications I started with as other resources have emerged, but they are still an invaluable resource in my toolbox that I continue to use.

I went to the Rochester Minnesota Mayo Clinic a second time at age 16 years so I could obtain a more sustainable treatment from physicians who had a better understanding of my conditions. I got a few more "side quest" diagnoses there (the most notable being Polycystic Ovarian Syndrome), and was put on the best regimen that was available at the time. My GI motility was slowly getting on the right track, but it took an additional approximately five years of experimental medication before my Mast Cell Disease was no longer causing daily life-threatening reactions. At age 17, I began experiencing strange neurological and musculoskeletal symptoms that progressed to the point where I could no longer walk. I wish I could reveal the answer as to what was going on, but there isn't one yet. There are abnormal test results that imply an autoimmune and musculoskeletal etiology, but nobody can pinpoint exactly what it is. To this day, almost ten years later, I continue to experience the symptoms without knowing what is going on, and I consider this to be my most disabling chronic illnesses at this point in time. I now have the luxury of more advanced medicine and physicians who understand my comorbidities a bit better, so these days, we are getting somewhere with the diagnostic process. In the meantime, all they could do for me was give me a wheelchair and some crutches to assist me with my new mobility impairments.

As I became more aware of the disabling and chronic nature of my condition, I started to factor my symptoms into my daily routine and focused on finding strategies to keep up with school. This would not have been possible were it not for an eighth-grade history teacher who saw me overworking myself to keep up with school amidst absences and flare-ups. She suggested to the guidance counselor that I needed academic accommodations such as extended test times and assignment extensions. I didn't know what this meant at first, but it completely changed my life. I now had the tools to balance my schoolwork without exacerbating my symptoms, allowing me to attend school more and understand the material better. I was silent about my accommodations at first, but classmates began to notice that I was doing things a bit differently. This prompted curious conversations that accommodations aren't an unfair advantage, but tools to help me receive the same benefits of education as everyone else. As the years went on, my classmates started to even help accommodate me by sharing notes, pushing my wheelchair, catching me up on lectures I missed, and more. I'd like to think this was the very beginning of realizing how changes in my environment can improve my health and well-being.

With my body being the drama queen it is, I knew going to college and using my brain was the key to a future where I could be independent. Enduring my tumultuous nutrition journey, and inspired by the empathy shown to me by that one dietitian, I decided to pursue a dietetics career myself. I attended the University of California, Berkeley for several reasons, one of them being its reputation as being the "birthplace" of the disability rights movement. College was good for me because it forced me to navigate independent living and get out of my self-pity. It was rough at first as my illnesses were still unstable, but with my new regimen, I was slowly getting there. The mental refreshment of getting out of the environment where I almost died seemed to reset me, giving me some space to think about how I can fit this new body into the world I wanted. Until medicine could catch up to my needs and properly diagnose/treat me, I knew I needed to get creative with the way I navigated the world so I could continue to pursue life with the abilities I had. In other words, I had no choice but to transition my life to a disability framework for survival.

I definitely identified as a "baby crip" at the beginning of my time at Berkeley. My mobility disabilities were still fresh, not even a year old, so I desperately needed a community to help me figure out the "hows" and sometimes even the "whys." Being lucky enough to go to college in the Bay Area of California, a hub of disability justice and culture, I met countless wonderful disabled people who taught me how to feel empowered as a disabled person, identify ableism, and advocate for what I deserved. On the institutional level, I received new services that changed the game for me including a scribe to assist in exams, alternative media software named Kurzweil that turned PDFs into audiobooks, wheelchair accessible lab benches, triple time for exams, note-taking services, and more. In my dorm, I had access to features that maximized my independent living, including but not limited to automatic doors, a roll-in shower, and an adjustable desk. I initially went to Berkeley with my former service dog, whom I had from ages 12–21 years, and she even had access to drinking stations around campus. Although there were undoubtedly access barriers and ableism around the university, my time at Berkeley allowed me to live independently in ways I could only dream of, and I met people who provided invaluable advice for my personal and professional success.

A particularly life-changing resource shared to me by a dear friend of mine was the California Department of Rehabilitation (or DOR). This resource helps people with disabilities work towards accessible employment goals through services such as paying for tuition, hosting professional workshops, providing a transportation stipend, providing textbooks/school supplies, holding mock interviews, providing equipment for trades/careers, and much more. After providing medical documentation of my disability and meeting with a counselor, I underwent several months of workshops to determine my exact needs in the context of my professional goals before finalizing my case. I received full academic funding for both my dietetics degree and my dietetics internship. I am forever grateful for DOR which allowed me to sustainably pursue my goals.

With more resources in my toolbox to meet my basic needs, I had more capacity to do the labor needed to embrace my identities as a queer, disabled, Mexican Filipina woman. I eagerly sought out and immersed myself in intersectional culture. In the disability realm, I experienced disabled art within disabled spaces, made by and for disabled people. Slowly, I began to reimagine my body as my home. Sometimes it's a bit messy and a bit unique, but it's mine, and I became increasingly prouder of it. My life became more joyful and whole *because* of my disability. I began mentoring other "baby crips" like I once was, and advocated to make Berkeley and the larger Bay Area more accessible. I pursued a minor in Disability Studies and used my knowledge to educate the community about disability justice. I conducted research on food access and disability with the University of California, San Francisco, throughout my undergraduate and internship years. My advocacy gained traction both on and off campus, and I played an integral role in many important initiatives. My proudest advocacy achievement was co-founding a Disability Cultural Center at UC Berkeley, one of the few of its kind in the country. I even worked in the UC Berkeley Disability Access and Compliance (or DAC) office as a student employee. A sister office to the Disabled Students Program office that provided classroom accommodations, the DAC office provided non-academic campus accommodations such as accessibility for extracurriculars, addressing buildings/physical access, auditing electronic access, training staff/faculty on accessibility, and addressing grievances.

Had it not been the disability community to uplift me through these pivotal points in my life, I would not be as independent or assured of myself as I am today. It was clear that the medical malpractice and access gaps I experienced (and continue to experience) were structurally designed to exclude me and harm me. But disability culture taught me to assert my needs, to get creative and turn my world into a place that works for me. I learned that the onus isn't on me to assimilate into the world, but rather the onus is on the world to restructure itself to celebrate people like me. In dietetics spaces, I found students who thought similarly to me, and we fostered important conversations about accessibility in dietetics. The loving interdependence between my disabled friends and I materialized in group shopping trips, cooking nights, appliance swapping (my favorite accessible appliance? An air fryer!), offering snacks and drinks in our backpacks to each other, and so much more. I learned from my friend who also had a dynamic mobility disability how to use a rolling walker around the kitchen to navigate long recipes. I learned from my blind friend how to efficiently shop for and save food by using an app that converts items in my fridge into accessible recipes. (I use "My Fridge Food," but there are many different ones.) I learned from my friend with mental health disabilities how to keep a stockpile of non-perishable liquids and salty snacks so my POTS can be managed in case of a natural disaster. I learned from my mother, a badass disabled woman herself, the importance of prepping and freezing meals for days when I don't have the energy to cook. I am able to feed myself and hold cups, but I often struggle with dropping cups and spilling on myself, so I learned from my friend with cerebral palsy the importance of using a straw and cups with a lid. Although these adaptations aren't medical interventions, I believe they played a role in improving my health by allowing me to sustain the nutrition and self-care interventions I need in an accessible way.

I had an extremely solid grasp of my disability identity until about three years into my college experience. One day, while rolling in my wheelchair along a designated crosswalk, I was violently hit by a car driving 30 miles an hour. It was determined that the car did not even slow or use its brakes despite other pedestrians and cars signaling for them to stop. To this day I still don't know the reason why. Were it not for my wheelchair taking the brunt of the impact, I was told I would be dead. I sustained some neck and tailbone injuries that still impact me and have caused complications such as central spinal stenosis (narrowing of the spinal canal), but the most notable impact was a severe case of Post-Concussion Syndrome that manifested into a chronic brain injury. Not only did I have to figure out how to incorporate my new physical disabilities into my existing ones, but I had to navigate my new brain. I was fortunate enough to have a mild albeit lifelong case in the grand scheme of traumatic brain injuries, but to me, the adjustment was life changing. Some of my more acute symptoms have lessened as time has gone on, but I continue to experience disabilities such as motion sickness, migraines, learning disabilities, and social difficulties. I continue to have mixed feelings about what this experience brought me, and I still struggle to incorporate it into my disability identity. I started identifying myself as neurodivergent about two years ago as a way to better encapsulate my new perspective, and it has felt healing. Now almost five years after the accident, it remains a daily process to relearn myself and share this part of my story. Re-engaging in disability justice in this new context of my life reminded me to give myself grace, to take my time and write a crisp new map of my identity rather than grappling with the old one that no longer applies to me.

As I got closer to finishing my Didactic Program in Dietetics (or DPD), I learned from disabled elders the importance of carrying my accommodations beyond college and into other stages of my life, including my dietetics internship and my RD exam. As a dietetics intern, I knew what I needed to accommodate my mobility disabilities and chronic illnesses, but I was unsure of what accommodations I needed for my brain injury for my internship. I had learned a few tricks to navigate the increased difficulty with reading comprehension to finish my dietetics degree, including frequent breaks and asynchronous lectures, but these were only feasible because of the online platform my school had transitioned to during the COVID-19 pandemic. An entire year of in-person clinical internship rotations felt daunting to me. Due to these new needs, I chose to apply to the Berkeley Individualized Supervised Practice Program in Dietetics, the same university as my DPD. I chose this program because the program director was already familiar with my needs and I was able to cover its tuition through my existing case with the DOR. Due to the fact that I was no longer affiliated with the university as a student nor an employee, but as an intern was regarded as a "visiting scholar" with no assigned accommodations office, it was definitely a learning process.

Most of the program went smoothly, and I actually excelled with the one-on-one learning style of having a preceptor. I received high marks for my bedside manner and unique interventions, which I credit to my many years of navigating the medical system and identifying its gaps with my fellow community members. The biggest problem I encountered in my dietetics internship was during my longest rotation which was in critical care. I was informed by the hospital that I could not attend rounds due to my wheelchair being "in the way," despite almost everyone at rounds having a bulky rolling desk that was larger than my wheelchair. I had to call into rounds but was only allowed to call into the patients I was assigned to, causing me to miss out on many learning opportunities. I became frustrated and less confident in my knowledge. This was perceived as me not succeeding in the rotation, causing my preceptors to ask me harder questions and make me work longer hours than the other interns. With the support of the other interns who felt I was being treated unfairly, I reported my preceptors to my program director, who had no idea this was happening. I was put on a different rotation taught by a preceptor who believed in me and knew how I learned, and I soon excelled again. Looking back, there were undoubtedly things I could have done differently, such as studying more efficiently and speaking up sooner, but my spirit was slowly being drained, and I just went into survival mode. The way my rotation was re-designed due to ableism set me up for failure. I thought my director was aware of the situation and even played a part in it, causing me to hesitate in sharing my needs, but she was not aware due to the different systems between the university and the contracted hospital. If I have any advice for any prospective dietetics interns with disabilities based on this experience, it's to choose an internship that has a strong communication line between the university and the rotation sites. A university with an on-site hospital that has the same accommodations office as the university may be ideal, but if this is not feasible, ensure that your director is given consistent updates with how the rotation is fulfilling your accommodations. I wish that I had spoken up sooner and given constructive feedback on the sites when I had the opportunity so they could learn how to accommodate interns with disabilities in the future. I encourage interns with disabilities to be confident in expressing their needs, and recognize the assets you are bringing to the table due to having a disability! As someone who now precepts interns at a hospital, I keep this experience in the back of my mind and try to open a dialogue of communication between myself and my interns to ensure that they are accommodated and empowered as healthcare workers.

    In preparation for the RD exam, I applied for accommodations similar to those I received in college. I'd encourage anyone with disabilities applying for RD exam accommodations to apply several months to a year in advance of the time you plan on taking it. The accommodation process is very strict because the Commission on Dietetic Registration requires it to be complete and finalized (including accommodation revisions) prior to even scheduling your exam date. Although I provided my university letters of accommodation, extensive medical documentation was also required. If you require disability equipment during your exam, make sure to ask for an accommodation regarding every single piece of that equipment rather than a lumped in set. For example, I received approval for extra time, specialized pencils, a distraction-free testing area, and usage of my intravenous fluids. I did not, however, think I needed to ask for an accommodation for the backpack that holds my intravenous fluids, but I was denied the ability to use the backpack even after offering it to the proctor to inspect. Despite this, I passed my RD exam on my first attempt and proudly became a Registered Dietitian in 2022.

    Moving back to my hometown in San Diego county after my time in the Bay Area provided me with a fresh perspective of the community I grew up in. I now feel more prepared to share my knowledge and engage with my community in an empowering way, a stark difference from the beginnings of my disability identity. I enjoy finding new outlets of disability joy as I rebuild roots. I moved back into my multi-generational household for disability and Filipino culture reasons, causing me to adjust my independent living strategies learned in Berkeley to a larger household. Many members in my household have varying disabilities, so interdependence is essential as we all use our unique abilities to contribute to cooking and cleaning. I am the main grocery shopper of my household because I am knowledgeable of prices and can lean on the shopping cart for stability while I look around. I also often find myself in the kitchen with my sitting stool and air fryer, cooking in large batches to create low-effort microwaveable portions to use later.

    A few of my accommodations have stuck with me through my career as a clinical dietitian at Palomar Medical Center, a small healthcare group in San Diego that consists of two hospitals and one long-term care facility. I still encounter access barriers (most notably, parking) and ableism from distant colleagues who do not know how to talk about disability in a non-medical manner, but I am fortunate that my fellow clinical dietitians are supportive and accommodating. I explore new accessibility devices (most notably, crutches) with curiosity to how they would benefit me, instead of shame. More importantly, I infuse my knowledge of disability culture to connect with my patients with disabilities and provide more accessible care. Three months into my current position, I received an award from the hospital for my bedside manner and compassionate care, which I directly attribute to these skills. My experiences as a disability advocate have transitioned more directly in the dietetics realm, and I often find others in the field like me through mutual projects, speaking at conferences, speaking for webinars, and more.

After reading the extremely abridged highlights of my story, you may be thinking why would I have disability pride after all I've been through? Disability pride is an internal narrative that must be nurtured and allowed space to thrive. For me, it is a survival mechanism, a form of advocacy, a key to break free from the chains of internalized ableism. The only reason why disability pride tends to be doubted is because society attributes the disability experience to be inherently negative, thus leading people to believe that people with disabilities cannot be happy and joyful. I have often encountered other people who have told me "thank goodness I don't have what you have" or when referring to their own experience with disability, "thank goodness my disability was temporary." Yes, my disability experience has led to many changes in my life, and the unanswered aspects of my diagnoses can be frustrating. However, these things have much less weight when I make the daily choice to lean into disability pride. Disability makes me feel more, love deeper, and understand others better. I know how to embrace my self-worth more by both recognizing the ways my disabilities have uniquely benefitted the world around me, and understanding that disability itself is an inevitable part of the human experience that I should not feel ashamed about.

Although not everyone may identify with disability as a cultural identity, all humans have preferred ways of getting around, navigating the world, and providing/receiving help. In my case, I didn't truly benefit from the modern innovations of healthcare until I paired my medical treatments alongside accommodations and access tools.

Working and socializing in the disability community, I also know that my story is not as unique as it seems, and this type of comprehensive care is urgently needed. I believe shifting our society to this mindset poses an incredible opportunity to reduce stigma in healthcare by providing care off the basis that there is no real definition of a "normal" body, but rather bodies that need varying levels of curative, palliative, and social support. My career as a dietitian is just beginning, but my storied experiences as a disabled person pose a perspective that I believe is underrepresented, undervalued, and non-negotiable for this field to grow.

Editors: Suzanne Domel Baxter and Cheryl Iny Harris

Chapter 18 (Autobiography) Nourished by Trust: A Blind Dietitian and her Loyal Guide Dog

By Danielle Sykora, BS, MS, RDN

Danielle Sykora

Background and Education

My undergraduate education was completed at Delaware Valley University, a small agricultural school in Pennsylvania. Here I studied environmental science with a specialization in sustainable agriculture. While I always held interest in environmental protection and the natural world, I struggled with which aspect of such a broad field would be the most rewarding to focus on.

Around the same time, an intriguing phenomenon was brought to my attention. Several of my pets experienced a variety of chronic health conditions. In an effort to alleviate their discomfort, I began researching the fundamentals of canine nutrition. With a simple change in diet, all of my animals displayed a complete resolution or drastic reduction in the symptoms of their chronic health conditions. This led me to ask the question that changed the course of my career: if a simple change in diet could have such a significant impact on the health of animals, why would the same not be true for humans? While I continue to maintain a passion for animal nutrition, this revolution led me to study human nutrition in graduate school. After all, I already received a thorough education on how food is produced along with its impact on the environment. It made sense to come full circle and understand the impact of nutrition on health, and in turn how food choices also influence agriculture and the environment.

My graduate education was completed in my home state of New Jersey at Montclair State University where I completed a master's in nutrition and food science. As I learned more about nutrition, I concluded that I must obtain the Registered Dietitian credential to truly be an expert in the field. Because my undergraduate degree was not in nutrition, I also completed a certificate program along with my MS that allowed me to obtain all necessary coursework dictated by the Academy of Nutrition and Dietetics (or Academy).

Technology, Orientation, and Mobility

To further emphasize my somewhat nontraditional background, I have been totally blind nearly all of my life due to a rare pediatric cancer known as retinoblastoma. I use a variety of adaptive techniques to navigate this society, which was created for nondisabled people. To use a computer and smart phone, I utilize software called a screen reader. Several types of screen readers exist that vary in cost and the devices they are designed to integrate with; however, all work in fundamentally the same way. Text on the screen is converted into speech, and the screen can be navigated using keyboard commands instead of a mouse. Screen readers can be used to access everything from websites to electronic medical records (or EMRs) to word processing applications. However, some limitations do exist. Screen readers cannot be used to access images, handwritten text, or software not designed to integrate with screen reader technology. Over the past year or two, exciting advancements in artificial intelligence (or AI) have begun to bridge the gap, allowing some access to materials that screen readers cannot interpret. For example, providing a description of an image is an intriguing function of apps utilizing AI; however, AI is still a very new development that is not always 100% reliable.

When it comes to accessing food and obtaining nutrition information, screen readers, AI, and other types of technology can be very important tools. A screen reader can be used to look up the ingredient list or nutrition facts on a computer or smart phone if a blind person knows the name of a food but is unable to read the writing on the packaging. Apps that scan bar codes and present nutrition information may be useful as well, though it may be difficult for someone with little to no vision to locate the bar code. AI (in apps like Be My Eyes or Seeing AI) can be used in combination with a screen reader on a smart phone to take a picture of a product, in order to determine what the product is, and nutrition information contained on the packaging. Magnifiers, such as those found in accessibility settings on smart phones, may be an option for reading labels for those with enough vision to read large print. Smart phone apps also exist which connect a visually impaired person with a sighted volunteer (Be My Eyes) or employee (Aira) who can describe visual information seen through a smart phone camera on a one-way video call, which is another option to access nutrition information on product packaging that may be difficult to access through other means. Be My Eyes or Aira may also be a reasonable accommodation to allow a dietitian to perform certain job duties. Clients who have limited proficiency with technology may have some success using a device like Amazon Alexa or Google Home to look up recipes or nutrition facts.

Along with a screen reader, I use a refreshable Braille display. A Braille display works alongside a screen reader to convert text into Braille. I find using a combination of speech and Braille is the most effective technique for me personally, while some screen reader users don't use a Braille display at all. I was provided a laptop, Braille display, and screen reader as well as partial tuition reimbursement throughout my years of school by my state's department of rehabilitation, specifically the New Jersey Commission for the Blind and Visually Impaired (or CBVI).

Along with screen readers, mobility tools are one of the most important accommodations I utilize. I learned to travel using a cane in childhood from an Orientation and Mobility Instructor provided by

CBVI. Orientation and mobility training teaches the effective use of a long white cane along with nonvisual techniques for travel, such as crossing streets by listening to traffic and using auditory and tactile landmarks to orient oneself in the environment. Subsequently, I began working a service dog, guide dog to be specific, just prior to my senior year of high school. I received both my first and second guide dogs from the Guide Dog Foundation, one of many service dog training programs throughout the country. Service dogs are dogs individually trained to perform tasks that mitigate their handler's disability; guide dogs are simply a subtype of service dog trained to perform tasks that mitigate blindness. My service dog performs tasks such as alerting me to changes in elevation, avoiding obstacles, and finding designated objects and locations that allow me to safely navigate the environment. In situations where it may not be possible or desirable to work my service dog, I utilize a cane. A cane and a guide dog are both effective tools to travel safely with their own unique advantages and disadvantages; however, for me a guide dog is by far the more efficient and preferable option.

There are many other techniques I employ to adapt visual content and activities to more accessible forms. These generally rely on turning visual content into tactile or auditory forms of information. Though this does not apply to my level of vision personally, people who have more residual vision may also prefer using high contrast colors to make visual content more obvious. A variety of tactile markers can be used to improve accessibility. For example, tactile markers can be placed on kitchen appliances. Tactile diagrams can be constructed to relay information contained in graphs or diagrams. Products like measuring cups and spoons can be purchased containing Braille or large print, as well as in high contrast colors. Talking scales can be used to weigh food, and talking thermometers can be used to take temperatures. High contrast cutting boards are available to make it easier to see food while cutting, though cutting food can also be accomplished completely nonvisually. High contrast plates can be used to make it easier for people to see the food on their plate, such as using a black plate for white food. Serving meals on a cafeteria tray is another option that can be beneficial. It makes it easy for the person to find everything (plate, utensils, drink), provides some contrast, and is easier to carry when one hand is occupied with a mobility tool like a cane or guide dog.

Adaptive Techniques and Alternative Tools for Cooking, Eating, and Grocery Shopping

Grocery shopping with a visual impairment also often requires some alternative techniques. One option is to shop with a friend or family member who can assist with finding products. Another popular option is to ask customer service if an employee can provide assistance finding products, generally considered a reasonable accommodation under the Americans with Disabilities Act. Some people may prefer to use online shopping, which requires only that the products be picked up or may even be delivered, but this likely has an additional cost. If an individual has a lot of remaining vision or is shopping in a familiar store in search of just a few products, they may be able to shop independently. Service dogs can even be taught to find specific areas in a store like registers, or types of food like the case containing bananas.

Academic Accommodations

Throughout my years in school, I consistently utilized several accommodations while other accommodations were very specific to individual courses. For all classes, I contacted professors several weeks prior to the semester via email to introduce myself and request accommodations. Mainly, I would ask that all materials (handouts, assignments, exams, etc.) be provided in an accessible electronic format. In addition, I requested copies of PowerPoint slides that would be presented along with lectures prior to the class where they be used, assuming they were not already available via an online platform. Beyond this, I worked with each individual professor to identify any unique barriers in the particular course in order to determine if any additional accommodations were needed. For example, a lab assistant in a particularly visual lab, alternative exam questions in place of those based on images, a reader to describe critical images or navigate inaccessible software, etc. In addition, each university has a disability services office that can advocate for students and provide professors with a letter stating each student's approved accommodations. While I certainly did utilize some of these services from time to time, I strongly preferred to communicate directly with professors whenever possible. I provided an accommodation letter only if a professor requested it as proof of disability. However, because the accommodations I requested for the most part would not have actually provided a competitive advantage to a nondisabled student, most professors did not require an accommodation letter. While I believe accommodation letters work quite well for common, straightforward accommodations like extended time on exams, I do not think they effectively convey more complex accommodations like screen reader accessibility on their own. Accommodation letters are also often provided on the first day of class; whereas I needed to contact professors prior to the beginning of the semester to ensure I already had accommodations in place for the first day. In addition, I found some professors simply assumed an accommodation letter simply meant extended time was needed and therefore did not carefully read the letter. However, they were more likely to read an email and ask questions or engage in a productive conversation on the first day of class.

Completing the Dietetics Internship

I completed my dietetics internship at Montclair State University. In many ways, reasonable accommodations were quite similar to those obtained during college. The classroom portion of the internship, like any other college class, primarily required requesting material in an accessible electronic format. I requested to be placed at facilities accessible via public transportation or virtual rotations. For each facility, I contacted my preceptor ahead of time to arrange for any accommodations that might be needed.

For my internship clinical rotations, accommodations primarily involved inquiring about the type of EMR used. One facility used a cloud based EMR (Point Click Care) that is accessible with the screen reader I use on my personal computer (VoiceOver); therefore, I was able to access the EMR using my own screen reader and laptop. The second facility used an EMR (Epic) that is only accessible with one particular type of screen reader (JAWS for Windows), purchased by the facility, and required additional steps to set up. Unfortunately, it was not clear that additional software and configuration were needed, resulting in me not having access to the EMR for four of my nine weeks at this facility. The third facility utilizing an EMR was a short rotation where it was not worth exploring options for screen reader access for the brief amount of time interns typically used the EMR. In the situations in which I did not have access to the EMR, my preceptor would copy relevant information from the EMR and send it to me via email without patient identifying information. I would then write my note and email it back to the preceptor for review. An inaccessible EMR is an inconvenience in an internship setting; however, an inaccessible EMR can be a significant barrier to employment. Unfortunately, it is often impossible to know if an EMR is truly screen reader accessible without attempting to use it. Companies vary greatly in their knowledge of accessibility, and rarely have ever had someone actually test the product using a screen reader. Also, companies tend to place more emphasis on accessibility of only the client facing side of the EMR, perhaps falsely believing practitioners cannot be visually impaired.

In addition, for my foodservice rotation, I arranged for my service dog to be left in a particular office when I needed to enter the kitchen—one of the few places service dogs are not permitted. Another rotation was completed at a facility that had poor access to WIFI. Because I am not able to simply use any desktop computer available due to the need for a screen reader, this rotation was made hybrid so that I could complete assignments at home with WIFI access.

Credentialing Exam

Like any other dietetics student, the completion of my dietetics internship meant it was time to take the registration exam for dietitians. In order to obtain accommodations, I completed the accommodation request process through Pearson Vue which administers the exam. Unfortunately, the Commission on Dietetic Registration (or CDR) had failed to make the registration exam screen reader accessible. Therefore, my only option to complete the exam was to request a reader and scribe, to read exam questions and record my responses. While this accommodation is satisfactory to complete the exam, it does not provide the same level of autonomy as the ability to complete an exam independently using a screen reader. In addition, it left me with no option for using the equivalent of scratch paper to perform calculations.

Professional organizations like CDR can demonstrate a commitment to diversity and inclusion by ensuring exams such as those for registered dietitian nutritionists (or RDNs) and dietetics technicians, registered (or DTRs) are screen reader accessible and allowing screen readers to be used as an accommodation to take these exams. Typically, Pearson Vue will provide the test taker with a computer that has screen reader technology installed to take the exam.

Disability Disclosure and Arranging Reasonable Accommodations for Employment

When it comes to employment, I prefer to disclose my disability after receiving a job offer, which is possible for me when interviews are conducted over the phone or video conferencing. While it is nearly always assumed blindness is a visible disability, this is not true for me in situations such as virtual environments where I am not using a mobility tool. If the interview is in person, I simply allow the presence of my cane or service dog to alert the interviewer that I have a disability. I generally don't discuss my disability or accommodations until receiving a job offer unless it comes up in conversation. Upon successful completion of the registration exam, I was hired by a company which contracts with long term care facilities to provide dietitians. The job duties were quite similar to any dietitian role in long term care. Complete nutrition assessments on all newly admitted patients, quarterly assessments on all residents, and monthly assessments on high-risk residents. Obtain food preferences from all residents, and recommend therapeutic diets and nutrition supplements as needed. Gather weights on all residents at least monthly, with significant weight losses requiring a full nutrition assessment. Ensure coordination of care when needed such as reporting significant weight losses to physicians, monthly weight loss meetings with nursing, and discussing nutritional status for residents on dialysis with dialysis RDNs. Complete malnutrition screenings and

Minimum Data Sets. Work with the food service company to ensure meals are appropriate and appealing. After signing my offer letter, I contacted human resources to request accommodations that I knew would be required.

Like my education and internship experience, for my job, I used a screen reader to access the EMR which fortunately I knew was screen reader accessible from use during my internship. I also notified my employer that I use a service dog. While in most cases handlers are not required to provide advanced notice that they will be accompanied by a service dog, employment requires that the use of a service dog be requested as an accommodation.

The need for some accommodations may not be known until experiencing the facility firsthand. Fortunately, once on site I realized that while rooms did not have Braille numbers, room signs did have numbers in raised print; this allowed me to find patient rooms independently with no accommodations. In contrast, I found three different processes that relied on handwritten material that would not be accessible to me. A solution for one of these processes was to switch from a handwritten to a typed form. For the other two processes, the other practitioners involved were unwilling or unable to switch to a more accessible alternative. The accommodation provided involved me taking a picture of the handwritten material and sending it to a regional dietitian within the company to be entered into the appropriate location. In addition, meal rounds/tray audits required accommodations as I am not able to see food on trays. I presented several options for accommodations including using one of a number of video-based apps that would allow a sighted person to check the tray via my phone camera. Another alternative could have been using video conferencing to allow another dietitian within the company to view the trays again using my phone camera. This would allow me to record whether trays were compliant and follow up with the kitchen if changes needed to be made immediately. My employer ultimately decided on having a regional dietitian come to the facility once a week to conduct a tray audit. However, the company ultimately abruptly terminated my employment due to the increased cost of having another dietitian on site, without discussion of alternative accommodations that would be less expensive.

Establishing a Private Practice

Upon termination of employment, I continued to search and apply for jobs in a variety of practice areas. Eventually, I was hired for a very similar role at another long-term care/subacute rehab facility. I approached the accommodation process the same way. In addition, I have begun to explore the process of establishing a private practice. While I would prefer to gain more experience before working in private practice full time, self-employment does greatly reduce the amount of accessibility barriers and employment discrimination while providing much more flexibility. Fortunately, all of the prerequisite steps to establishing a private practice can be completed online from creating a business to credentialing with insurance to setting up a website, EMR, and patient forms. I found most processes to be accessible, though a few steps needed for insurance credentialing were not entirely screen reader accessible. I utilized the one-month free trial offered by many EMRs to test screen reader accessibility. Simple Practice and Kalix both appear to be largely screen reader accessible. While Simple Practice appears to be more accessible out of the box, the customer service team at Kalix has been the most willing to quickly and effectively resolve accessibility concerns brought to their attention of any company I have ever worked with. Ultimately, I chose Kalix as my EMR and submit insurance claims through Availity.

Barriers to Employment and Participation in Professional Organizations

The field of dietetics can unfortunately present many barriers for people with disabilities, a contributing factor as to why disability diversity is lacking within this profession. Taking my own experience of seeking employment as an example, there are many barriers and considerations I must face when looking and applying for a job that a nondisabled person likely will not need to consider. Is the job location accessible with public transportation or ride share? Will the company require me to cover another facility not listed in the job description that is not accessible with public transportation or ride share? What EMR does the company use? Is it accessible with a screen reader? Do patient rooms have room numbers in Braille or raised print? Will disclosing my disability or use of a service dog in an interview prevent me from receiving a job offer? Will referring to my experiences as a disabled practitioner and patient or advocacy efforts support my claim of commitment to promoting diversity and inclusion, or cause the interviewer to believe my disability makes me a liability or inferior practitioner? Did I not receive an offer of employment because I was truly not the best candidate for the position, or because the company simply would rather not hire a disabled practitioner if they can avoid it? Does the company outright state applicants cannot have a certain type of disability in the job description?

In addition to barriers to employment, professional organizations currently often do not take into consideration that dietetics professionals, patients, clients, or anyone in the general public for that matter with an interest in accessing nutrition content may have a disability.

The Disabilities in Nutrition and Dietetics Member Interest Group (or Disabilities MIG) seeks to improve accessibility in and inclusivity for people with disabilities in dietetics through its education and advocacy efforts. The Disabilities MIG advocates for accessibility and inclusivity within professional organizations such as CDR and the Academy by bringing accessibility challenges to the attention of leadership, providing relevant resources, and promoting awareness of reasonable accommodations. Likewise, this group also encourages inclusion of and consideration for people with disabilities in nutrition policy and research. The Disabilities MIG also serves as a resource to gather likeminded individuals to share knowledge and experiences as well as educate those interested in learning more about diversity and inclusion.

How to Support Disabled Practitioners and Clients

Dietetics practitioners without disabilities can support their disabled colleagues and patients in a number of ways. First and foremost, recognize that people with disabilities are people too, and are no more or less likely to be successful than anyone else. In addition, a disability can affect anyone at any time; disabilities are not limited to older adults or people who fail to adhere to healthy lifestyle habits. It is critical to understand that not all people, even if they have the same disability, will require the same accommodations or any accommodations at all. For example, an 80-year-old long term care resident with cognitive decline and recent vision loss will require completely different accommodations than a 40-year-old client working full time seeking outpatient nutrition services who has been legally blind for 20 years, who will in turn require different accommodations compared to a dietitian who has been totally blind since birth.

Dietetics practitioners who fairly consider disabled practitioners for jobs they are qualified for and who make a genuine effort to provide reasonable accommodations are perhaps the single most important allies. There are many barriers for disabled dietitians; one barrier that simply should not exist is the bias of hiring managers assuming disabled people are inherently inferior practitioners or a liability. Many disabled employees exhibit lower turnover rates compared to their nondisabled counterparts. Due to varying life experiences, disabled employees often display heightened problem-solving abilities, innovation, and creativity. It is second nature for many people with disabilities to seek solutions to problems and improve processes. Employees with disabilities also can assist facilities to better meet the needs of patients with disabilities, and by extension improve patient care overall. In addition, recognize that reasonable accommodations exist in order to level the playing field, providing alternatives that allow disabled employees to complete essential job functions; reasonable accommodations are not privileges or special treatment. According to the Job Accommodation Network, most reasonable accommodations also in fact are low cost or free. The Job Accommodation Network provides many resources concerning reasonable accommodations in the context of Title I of the Americans with Disabilities Act, which may be beneficial to both employees and employers alike.

Another way to increase accessibility for both practitioners and patients with disabilities is by making content available in accessible formats. For example, provide downloadable resources in PDF format only if the PDFs are tagged; otherwise, provide downloadable resources in HTML or as password-protected Word documents. Ensure that websites meet the Web Content Accessibility Guidelines. Providing image and video descriptions as well as video captions on social media, blogs, or website content makes information much more widely available. Including image descriptions as alt text also provides the added benefit of improving search engine optimization. Making handouts or patient forms available in alternative and accessible formats upon request, such as large print or electronically, can allow visually impaired patients to access information relevant to their health. In cases where a person's ability to obtain or prepare food may be impacted by their disability, engage in an open discussion of potential alternative techniques rather than simply assuming the patient cannot independently improve nutritional status. Don't assume all disabled patients have a caregiver; assess their support network and access to resources just like any other patient. Practitioners should encourage patients to seek alternative techniques and assistive devices that may contribute to improving nutritional quality when appropriate. Coordination of care may also be appropriate in cases where clients or patients may benefit from learning alternative techniques for nutrition related life skills such as cooking.

Service Dogs Vs. Therapy Dogs

Nondisabled dietetics practitioners can support handlers of service dogs by educating themselves on how service dogs differ from therapy dogs, emotional support dogs, and pets. Emotional support dogs are dogs who benefit individuals with disabilities through their presence alone, providing comfort, relief from isolation, and a sense of purpose merely by existing. While emotional support dogs are permitted in non-pet-friendly housing and may in some cases be considered a reasonable accommodation in an employment setting, handlers of emotional support dogs have no legal protection to take their dogs into public places. Therapy dogs, common in clinical settings, are dogs with basic obedience training and stable temperaments who are brought by volunteers to interact with patients and staff during visits scheduled in advance with the facility. It is completely voluntary when and where a facility allows therapy dogs, and if they choose to permit them at all. In contrast, service dogs are considered medical equipment, trained to perform tasks to mitigate their handler's disability in addition to having excellent behavior in public. Handlers are legally permitted to be accompanied by their service dog almost anywhere the general public is allowed. While therapy dogs are often certified by one of a number of therapy dog organizations, there is no legally recognized registration or certification for service dogs. If a facility requires therapy dogs or visiting pets to meet certain criteria for access such as providing vaccination records or needing to provide advanced notice to the facility, these restrictions cannot be applied to service dogs. Service dogs should be ignored while they are working, because petting, speaking to, or offering food may distract them from their work and put their handler's safety at risk. While it is important to avoid asking intrusive questions about a person's disability and focusing valuable time discussing their service dog that should instead be spent on nutrition related conversation, it is appropriate to discuss the service dog if it is relevant to the individual's nutrition status. For example, a diabetic alert dog trained to alert to dangerously high or low blood glucose is an integral piece of blood glucose management for some people with Type 1 Diabetes. An allergen detection dog trained to alert to allergens for people with severe food allergies, or even gluten for people with Celiac Disease, also may be relevant to a person's treatment plan. People with many types of disabilities may be more willing or able to exercise or independently complete errands when accompanied by a service dog trained to perform tasks that increase safety, reduce energy expenditure, and/or limit/prevent symptoms. For those interested in learning more about service dogs relating to the dietetics profession, I have coauthored an article in the *Journal of the Academy of Nutrition and Dietetics* titled "Valuing Diversity in Dietetics: Considerations for Service Dogs in School, Internships, and the Workplace" (published in September 2022, volume 122, issue 9, pages 1595-1599).

Conclusion

Overall, having a disability does not preclude an individual from being a competent dietetics practitioner specifically or functioning member of society in general. There are a variety of adaptive techniques, assistive technologies, medical equipment, and reasonable accommodations utilized by disabled people to accomplish daily tasks. Diversity among dietetics practitioners can only lead to an improved ability to better understand, represent, and serve a diverse patient population. By making nutrition content accessible for everyone, dietetics practitioners can fully realize their goal to improve nutrition status for their patients. The purpose, vision, mission, and goals of the Disabilities in Nutrition and Dietetics Member Interest Group of the Academy directly address these needs.

Editors: Suzanne Domel Baxter and Cheryl Iny Harris

Chapter 19 (Autobiography) My Journey into Dietetics as a Disabled, Chronically Ill Dietitian

By Juliana Tamayo, MS, RD, LDN, CNSC

Juliana Tamayo

I have not been sick my whole life, or maybe I have but I was not aware of it. And that is the beauty of disability, that it is dynamic and ever-changing. Anyone can become disabled in a split second. For me, it happened gradually. By the time I was in 11th grade, I knew something was off. I had struggled with health issues since I was 11 years old. High blood pressure, concerns for lupus, kidney biopsies, migraines that resulted in disabling vertigo episodes, tinnitus, and more. However, when I turned 17, I noticed I could not keep food down, and I became very intolerant to foods around me. People praised me for weight loss initially, but then it turned into concern for eating disorders, and soon, I was simply another teenager riddled with body image issues.

I was born and raised in Bogotá, Colombia. I always knew I wanted to come to the United States for college, and I did just that at age 18. At the time, I moved to Washington, DC, a place I now call home. During my college years, I continued to experience odd symptoms, unable to keep my weight up, periods of nausea and vomiting, fatigue, and body aches. However, I carried that eating disorder diagnosis with me, and fully believed this was all caused by my mind. It was not until my last year of undergraduate that I started losing weight rapidly and even my safe foods became dangerous. At some point, I could not even keep down water.

By 2015 and with the help of my partner, I set on to find a real diagnosis. As many with chronic illnesses and disabilities know, getting a diagnosis can be just as difficult as having the illness itself. For years we could not figure it out. I kept losing weight and wasting away. But at the same time, I completed some milestones in my life. I graduated college with a BA in English Creative Writing Journalism and Mass Communications. My experience as a college student was a pretty traditional one on the surface level, but deep inside, it was not. I struggled with a body that was not working properly, not tolerating food, many gastrointestinal symptoms, fatigue, hair loss, and more importantly, the uncertainty of why it was happening to me. It was not until I graduated from undergraduate that I decided to find real answers to my problems.

After college, I worked in radio and communications as a digital media manager. It was an exciting time for me; I got to travel to conferences, interview Latinx artists, and even meet President Obama! But at the same time, my health kept deteriorating. I could barely keep my weight up, my face and eyes became sullen, and I was very, very tired all the time. The journey to get diagnosed was not easy. I started with umbrella terms, like acid reflux, stress, and a hiatal hernia. Eventually, the diagnoses became more specific.

Soon enough, I had several diagnoses. From gastroparesis, Median Arcuate Ligament Syndrome (or MALS), Eosinophilic Esophagitis, lupus, and Crohn's disease. My journey has been long and thorough. I have undergone more surgeries than I can count on both hands. I have had endless hospital visits and stays. I am one hundred percent dependent on my feeding tube for nutrition. I wish I could say my journey has been smooth sailing, but it has not.

My first go with nutrition support started with total parenteral nutrition (or TPN). This is a method of nutrition that skips the gastrointestinal (or GI) tract and instead uses a vein for nutrition, in this case a vein that deposits in the superior vena cava. TPN can provide enough nutrition for many individuals with absorption issues and those unable to use their GI tract. TPN saved my life and brought me back from the darkest times. It gave me a reason to go on and truly inspired me to help others like me. I went from withering away into a skeleton to regaining energy and strength, and learning that being different does not mean the end. Soon enough, trips to the Mayo Clinic and now the Cleveland Clinic have shown me that there is more to me than my diagnoses.

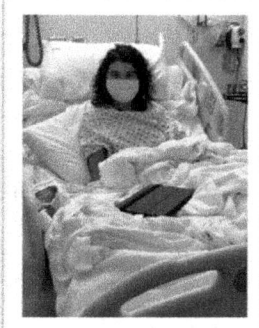 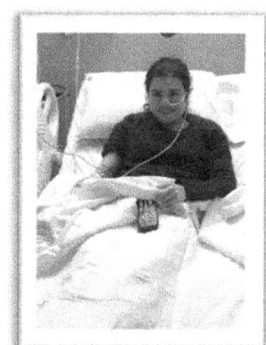 

Three photos of Juliana after several of her surgeries.

After a while on TPN, my doctors at the Mayo Clinic decided to help me transition to jejunal tube feeds. Also known as enteral nutrition, tube feeds are a better option to TPN because they use the GI tract, though they might skip a part of it. Some people utilize a G tube to feed directly into the stomach, but in my case, doctors wanted to try feeding into the second portion of my intestine, the jejunum, using a jejunostomy (or J) tube.

During this time, I finally started to feel my life come back to me. I went from being a walking corpse with no energy, to slowly rebuilding my body back. I wish I could say feeding tubes are easy. They are not. I initially had a gastro-jejunostomy (or GJ) tube; this one went in through my stomach but had a longer tube attached that reached the second portion of my intestine for feeding. The "G" or gastric port could be used for medications or "venting" if I ever had nausea. However, this tube quickly flipped from my jejunum into my mouth multiple times, so I had to have both tubes surgically separated. Soon after, my team decided to pull my G tube, and leave me with a simple direct jejunostomy, or direct tube to the jejunum. Still, the issues with my J tube were never-ending. I suffer from fistulizing Crohn's, which means my Crohn's likes to create pockets of inflammation in areas of the intestine that then lead to unusual and unnatural connections between organs that should not exist. In my case, often between my intestinal wall and my skin, which means I have a high risk for infection.

Because of my fistulizing Crohn's, I have had multiple abscesses around my J tube site that turn into fistulas and result in me losing my site. When an abscess forms for me, it usually leads to a small or big fistula creating, which can require surgery, and means that tube site is now unusable. So far, this current tube site has been healthy for over six months, and I will take that win!

Through it all, though, the team of dietitians that guided me through TPN and enteral nutrition had my back. The team of dietitians managing my parenteral and enteral nutrition would always check in on me, call me every day, explain my lab results, guide me through symptoms management, and take the time to work out plans with me for weight gain. They truly made the day-to-day much more manageable. These dietitians were the inspiration behind me pursuing a second career, and deciding to get a Master's degree in Nutrition and Dietetics. The journey would not be easy though. I started to casually look at my options in early 2017. By the end of the year, I began taking only the prerequisites needed to enter any Didactic Program in Dietetics (or DPD) and Master's of Science. While it probably would have been more affordable to go to community college, I had trouble leaving the house most days. I relied heavily on the little energy I did muster, and most days, I had to use any physical amount of energy I had to dog walk and dog sit to help provide for myself and my studies. I was lucky that by the time I started seeking my second career, online schooling was more affordable, accessible, and respected.

In 2018, I got into two schools in Washington, DC, where I live. I was ready to commit to one school, but something in the back of my mind made me rethink my choices. Many readers with disabilities will relate to this, that when you are disabled, you develop a "sixth sense" about issues that might arise from situations. This was one of those moments for me. One of my many diagnoses is Postural Orthostatic Tachycardia Syndrome (or POTS), which causes blood to pool in my legs when I stand up or change positions quickly, making my heart rate increase, causing me to faint at times. While I now have it more under control, in 2018, I used to faint multiple times a day, which made driving hard, if not impossible, and limited my ability to be independent. When faced with the admissions and enrollment process, I also had many problems and complications related to financial aid, scheduling classes, and even understanding curricula. Because I got little to no support from staff, I quickly realized this would be the norm throughout my schooling and decided to choose another school.

I do not think I need to explain to many who have chronic illnesses or disabilities how difficult it is to find spaces that work *for* and *with* us and not against us. After a lot of searching, I decided the best answer for me would be to pursue my degree online through Kansas State University (or K-State). Pretty quickly, I realized this was the best decision I could have made because there was a flexible schedule, classmates from all sorts of backgrounds, and mentors who understood where I was coming from. More importantly, my Master's advisor and mentor throughout my journey helped me see that my own story made my career in dietetics that much more important and impactful. Because I went to an online Master's degree, I did not have to ask for accommodations, but there were times when I wished I had. During my time at K-State, I had to have surgeries and hospitalizations that pushed me to my limit. Luckily, I never missed the mark, but I could not have done this had I been attending a traditional degree.

My master's thesis was based on the quality of life of people living on enteral and parenteral nutrition, a project that became very close to my heart and that I am still very passionate about for personal reasons. K-State gave me the voice and platform to pursue a passion project and turn it into a thesis on which I could base my post-graduate career. It was truly a positive experience for me, but getting there took a lot of mental and physical work on my part, searching and digging for a school that would support me and my specific needs as a disabled student.

During my time at K-State, I also prepared myself for the internship matching process. A process that is often terrifying for everyone, but more so for disabled individuals. For me, it was a matter of distance and safety. Would I be able to live at home with my long-time partner? Would I need to drive long distances every day? *Could* I drive long distances every day? I live in Washington, DC, where there are a finite number of programs and they are very competitive. I was eventually matched to the Sodexo Dietetics Internship, which in itself is very accommodating and often has individuals from all walks of life. The Sodexo Dietetics Internship is a distance internship, and it allows students to work for only 32 hours a week, unlike traditional internships that require 40 hours. It also helps you find all your sites except for community, which saves you time and effort. The DC location is mostly focused in Washington, DC, Maryland, and Virginia, which was very beneficial to me in terms of travel and accommodations.

Juliana and her partner

At my internship, I had similar struggles. Long hours, long distances to cover. I even had to take time to have major abdominal surgery. However, because my program was a distance one, my internship director helped me work around my schedule so I could fit some of my hours online and finish my internship on time. I did have to find hotel rooms in Baltimore and stay away from my partner and home for a few weeks because I was recovering from surgery and could not drive an hour and a half each way. I created these accommodations for myself because I knew they were needed for my body and mind to heal properly. I could have been a bit more forward with my internship director of my needs, but the truth is, at this time I had already had to relocate my foodservice rotation and change my schedule around twice. I was scared that asking for more would be detrimental to my relationship with the internship program, so I decided to commit to the schedule.

I completed my internship in May 2022, but I already had signed a job offer at a hospital in Washington, DC. During my internship, my love for clinical nutrition was reinforced. I love clinical and always will. I have spent months at a time in hospitals, but more so, I am passionate about parenteral nutrition and enteral nutrition. I am alive thanks to nutrition support after all. Before graduating, I had a job as a staff dietitian in a trauma 1-level hospital in Washington, DC. I was able to get this job thanks to my connections during my internship and my personal story. Sometimes your disability can become your superpower if you make it so.

Before I started my job at the beginning of July 2022, I wanted to take the registered dietitian (or RD) exam. I knew that I needed to focus on studying and could not work and study at the same time. Unlike my abled-bodied peers, my energy is limited, I come home exhausted after a long day at work and usually need a nap at a minimum. I took two weeks to study full-time, it was very difficult, but I made it my only job. I decided against pursuing accommodations during my RD exam. I qualify for them. For one, I have a feeding tube and need access to a bathroom often due to my Crohn's disease. I also need snacks, and water, and get hypoglycemic and lightheaded. However, getting approval for some accommodations for the RD exam required massive documentation which can take weeks at a time, and I did not have that luxury. Instead, I once again created my accommodations by doing things that were not necessarily safe, but that I knew would get me through the exam.

Since I knew I could not use the bathroom, I barely had anything to eat that day, I focused on drinking Gatorade, and I took some candy for my blood sugars. My jejunostomy tends to leak sometimes, as is normal with J tubes, but since I could not look at my tube without getting suspicious looks from test proctors, I put a lot of gauze and a sanitary pad on my tube site. Needless to say, I was not *relaxed*, but I could at least focus on the task at hand. I finished my exam, and passed! It was a relief. I did have snacks and hydration afterward. While I do not recommend putting yourself through situations where your health might suffer, as I did, I knew that this was my choice to make simply because advocating and fighting for accommodations would have caused more stress and anxiety for me at a time when I was already having physical illness from the stress.

After I passed my exam, I pretty much started my job right away. I have been working at this hospital for two years. I am now in a more advanced position with much more responsibility. However, my initial position was not an easy one. While my boss knows my story and so do my colleagues, I did not request many accommodations. There are some reasons why I chose this job though, over the other offer I had. First, the team is larger, which means when someone is out, it is not up to me to cover the *whole* hospital. Second, my boss met me through my personal story first and approached me as an asset to the hospital because of my story, which means she also understands my disabilities and what they entail. Third, I had a long conversation regarding my medical needs, including emergent surgeries, hospitalizations, sick days, etc. The policy here is always, health first. While I work very hard, sometimes harder than I should, I know that my coworkers and my boss have my back. I can always take the time I need to have surgery or be in the hospital when I need it. I already had two surgeries while at this job, and I am preparing to have a third one shortly. Finally, my commute is short and I can take public transportation, something that I could not do during my internship or for the other job offer.

Choosing a job because you plan on missing days or because you have to think about not having to drive is not something that able-bodied people have to think about. However, as many disabled people know, this is at the forefront of our minds when we choose where to go and where we work. For me, it was an easy decision, as I have to prioritize being close to home, but also having flexibility. One last selling point for this job is that after COVID-19, we can work from home a bit. For the most part, clinical jobs are known for being demanding and in-person all the time. In this case, the job is demanding, but I can start work from home, finish at home, and leave early on specific occasions, such as illness, doctor's appointments, travel, or family matters, etc. A luxury that for us disabled people is unique and appreciated, particularly on sick days or days when I need to go to the doctor, which is multiple times a month. I will clarify, though, that this luxury is given to everyone, not just me, so it is not an accommodation, just a selling point for a job that usually does not afford this situation.

The start of this job was chaotic. It came right after COVID, but still in the middle of it when the staff were going through a lot of changes. I immediately got thrown into the midst of it and began covering a cardiovascular surgical intensive care unit (or CVICU) with over 24 beds, along with another four floors. With this amount of responsibility, I had to hit the ground running. At the same time, I met a good friend of mine who was also new, and through good dark humor, we both endured hard times. I wish I had set more boundaries back then, as my boss expects this pace of work from me even now when we are fully staffed and not struggling anymore. But I will admit that I feel like it made me a better dietitian and gave me the confidence to become a better professional rather quickly.

Within my first year, I went from being a staff dietitian to a heart transplant and heart failure dietitian, covering the CVICU, doing selection rounds, multi-disciplinary rounds, family meetings to define patient plans of care, and more. I also began a TPN mentorship at my hospital for dietitians to be able to prescribe and order TPN fully on their own. Because it is such a large hospital (~900+ beds), we often have over 20+ patients on TPN and require dietitians to complete a mentorship before being able to see TPN patients. For the most part, the process takes months, but I completed the mentorship program within 4-6 weeks. Part of it was my passion for nutrition support, but the other part was the fact that during this time, I also transitioned from heart transplant RD to trauma/general surgery RD, which meant seeing patients who needed TPN on a daily basis.

I currently still cover these areas. I'm in charge of a surgical intensive care unit, where I primarily see surgery and trauma patients. I also cover the step-down floor for these patients, where patients that do not require intensive level of care anymore go to recover. My last floor is a medicine/behavioral health one. In my day-to-day, I screen patients, see them, and provide recommendations. This means I spend time going through the clinical criteria my hospital has defined to decide whether a patient needs to be seen, I add them to my list for the day, I visit them, write an initial or follow up note, diagnose them with a nutrition diagnosis, and provide a plan of care, which includes interventions related to nutrition issues.

However, I have more responsibilities during the week outside my regular duties. I do multi-disciplinary rounds on Tuesdays and cover all trauma and surgery patients for the hospital, providing a round-up of nutrition issues/concerns for these patients. I'm also secondary coverage for the TPN dietitian, which means I cover the whole nutrition support team when the RDs in charge are off. These duties include seeing new TPN patients, making sure orders are in, ordering and managing labs, changing orders as needed, contacting providers, troubleshooting issues, daily rounds with the TPN pharmacists, and more.

When I see my patients, I do not immediately disclose my disabilities. My case is somewhat different, after all, I have a J tube, and I have been on TPN before. I can often relate to many of the issues my patients have. I have had multiple fistula repair surgeries and even a temporary ostomy, which is a bag in my intestine connecting my intestine with my abdominal wall in an attempt to heal the fistula, or hole that had been created. However, I only share my story when I feel the patient is disheartened at their current situation and needs encouragement. Disclosing your story can be tricky when it comes to patients, so I always do it in such a way that it is respectful and relates to their own needs and journey.

I became a dietitian to help patients like me, and through my current role, I get to do that more often than not. I am not sure my body will allow me to work full-time and in person forever. There are days when I come home and I can barely keep my eyes open. I have a Crohn's flare often and malabsorb my tube feeds, which means I am unable to meet my energy needs, so I have to make do with what little intake I can take orally, which is limited to a very few safe foods that do not cause any GI distress, such as oatmeal, potatoes, yogurt, or certain types of fish. As with any chronic illness, tolerance also depends on how my day is going and how the food is prepared.

Still, I have accomplished a lot in these past two years. I also sat for the board-certified nutrition support specialist exam in October 2023 and passed on my first try. This has been a goal of mine since I knew what it stood for and what nutrition support jobs required. Doing it within two years of experience under my belt was an accomplishment and allowed me to grow at work, too. I am now a Clinical Dietitian I and will likely be promoted to Clinical Dietitian II soon.

I am not sure what my future holds. I know that I enjoy advocating for nutrition support and access to quality of life. I will be a moderator for Malnutrition Awareness Week 2024 in a panel titled "Nutrition Support Access: Breaking Down Barriers" for the American Society for Parenteral and Enteral Nutrition. I was nominated by my boss thanks to my story and my own experience as a nutrition support user. I also just received an award for excellent patient service, which I think is simply a reflection of my passion for my job and mission in life. I am not sure if I will ever move into a more hybrid workplace. My dream job is a nutrition support job from home, where I can save my energy and do what I love. But I have learned with time that being sick also means being flexible with your expectations, and this means, I take my life day by day and I am grateful for what is to come.

Will I take sick days in the near future? Probably. Will I need surgery and time off? Most likely soon. Do I think that I would do anything differently because of my illnesses? Not really. The one thing I would tell my younger self is to not be afraid to ask for help and to be different. While the world is not designed for disabled individuals, I have always found a way to make accommodations happen for myself. Is it fair? Not really, I wish it was not like that, and I will fight for better access every day. But I do not regret my decisions because they brought me to where I am today and I could not be prouder of myself.

For those students, especially those second-career students, who like me might be second-guessing their decisions, I say, trust your gut and fight for your place. You deserve a spot at the table, every time. Access for me has not been difficult only because I am disabled, it is often difficult to be the only Latinx member in a room. When I first got my job, I was the only person of color in the office. It is nice to see that things are changing, but access is only sometimes, and oftentimes, you have to find your allies and make your path.

If you need to take online classes instead of in-person, do it. If you need extra time for the exam, ask for it. If you have to take a day off for your mental or physical health, school or work can wait. If you need support, seek it, someone out there will understand and help you. Most likely, others around you are going through similar situations. When I share my story, I attract compassionate and empathetic friends and colleagues who have shared life experiences that make them understand me and my needs. The mentors I have found throughout my journey have been essential in leading me to where I need to be.

At the end of the day, my journey has not been easy or linear. I still have days where I think about quitting and staying home again. But the sacrifices and the effort have paid off. I'm happy to say that I love what I do, and every day, I see a patient or two who relates to me and I seem to make their day better, and everything makes sense.

I will continue to be disabled for the rest of my life. I'm currently undergoing a treatment change for my Crohn's disease, as it seems to not be responding well to my biologic treatment. I'm also preparing to have major hip surgery because I have a torn ligament in my hip and the pain is getting more and more unbearable, something I did not expect to need at 31 years old, but that comes with having many joint disease issues and other possible chronic illnesses that I'm yet to be diagnosed with. I travel to Cleveland Clinic every six months to get my tube changed and have my appointments. I see my specialists at least every three months. I get immunoglobulin intravenous therapy infusions monthly. While all these treatments are somewhat helpful, I will likely need more abdominal surgeries in the future, and I'm also exploring other potential diagnoses that may lead me toward a better quality of life. I already have more scars on my belly than most humans could ever imagine. However, none of this defines my path and none of your disabilities should define yours. If anything, all of these things make me a better dietitian, who understands the struggle for health care, access, and empathy in the healthcare system. So, if you are a student or simply thinking about pursuing a career in dietetics, know that it is possible. Is it easy? No, but many along the way are willing to lend you an ally hand and support your dreams, me included.

Chapter 20 (Autobiography) Breaking through the Silence: My Journey to Becoming a Registered Dietitian as a deaf Individual

By Wendy Wittenbrook, MA, RD, CSP, LD, FAND

1. 2. 3.
1. Wendy around age three years when speech therapy started.
2. Wendy in second grade when she began wearing a hearing aid in one ear.
3. Wendy on day one of kindergarten, the year they learned she was deaf.

I was deaf when I was born. My parents were 18 and 21 years old when I was born, and at that time there was no newborn hearing screening. I started in outpatient speech therapy when I was three years old because I was not talking very much, and it was difficult for others to understand me. Initially, it was attributed to me being an only child and spending most of my time around adults. My mother was always able to understand what I was trying to say and give me what I needed.

I was not diagnosed as deaf until I was in kindergarten. That year, my teacher told my parents that I did not acknowledge her unless she was looking at me when she spoke, and she suggested that my parents get my hearing tested.

People who are deaf may have speech that is difficult to understand; it is related to the inability to hear their own voice in addition to other speech sounds. Lowercase deaf is used to refer to the audiological condition of not hearing. This is a person who is deaf but who does not identify as part of the Deaf community. They live in a hearing world, attend public and private mainstream schools, use technology to hear, and typically deal with their hearing loss in medical terms. Uppercase Deaf refers to a group of deaf people who identify themselves as culturally Deaf and have a strong identity as a member of the Deaf community. They share a language, such as American Sign Language (or ASL), and a culture, including attending schools and programs for the Deaf. I identify as deaf because I do not speak ASL. I read lips and use technology to function in a hearing world.

Mild hearing loss can result in a child missing 50% of what is spoken in a classroom. You hear with your brain, not with your ears. It takes significant brain processing power to listen. This can result in auditory fatigue. Individuals can have trouble remembering verbal information or learning new words. This can be mistaken for a learning disability.

My first audiogram was when I was six years old in kindergarten. The test showed right ear moderate high-frequency sensorineural loss and left ear moderate mixed loss through 2000 Hz and severe sensorineural loss >2000 Hz. I was also diagnosed with a left fixed stapes (one of the small bones in the middle ear). For context, high frequency loss above 2000 Hz is birds chirping, women and children's voices, words that start or end with s, h, f, th. An individual can hear but not understand what is being said. Sensorineural hearing loss is damage to the inner ear or auditory nerve. This is permanent, and affects loudness, clarity and range of sounds. Conductive hearing loss affects the movement of sound through the external or middle ear, and the inner ear does not get the full sound. So, in layman's terms: my left ear had two types of hearing loss (sensorineural and conductive), and my right ear had sensorineural loss. I was diagnosed as moderately deaf. My physician recommended a hearing aid consultation to use in educational settings. Although I was involved in the Texas Day School Program for the Deaf, I attended the local public school.

During elementary school, I had multiple ear surgeries. The first two surgeries were myringotomies to place ear tubes and drain fluid from my ears to remove any conductive barriers to hearing. I also had two tympanoplasties on my left ear. A tympanoplasty is surgical repair of a perforated eardrum with or without repair of the ossicles. The ossicles are the small bones of the middle ear that transmit sound wave vibrations from the eardrum to the middle ear. We found out that I had a fixed stapes in my left ear, which was the cause of the conductive hearing loss in that ear. In second grade, my audiologist recommended a hearing aid due to "Wendy's demanding listening needs," especially in educational settings. I began to use a hearing aid in my left ear in 1978 to amplify frequencies I had difficulty hearing.

I attended public school in a small Texas town of 2,000 residents. The only other d/Deaf person I knew was my elderly grandmother. Despite being deaf, I participated in competitive events that required listening, such as storytelling (you listen to a story then retell it to the judges using your interpretation, including acting) and spelling. To this day, I do not know why or how I even placed in these events without being able to hear. I was labeled a bookworm, and reading and math were my favorite subjects in school. Despite consistently achieving top grades and graduating from high school as Salutatorian, I struggled until well into adulthood to internalize a sense of intelligence due to my deafness. The only accommodation while in public school from kindergarten to 12th grade was to sit in the front of the class. I wore my hearing aid only to school. The school district provided speech therapy for a couple of years, and our sessions were relegated to the book storeroom. In fifth grade, I joined band and played percussion based on the recommendation of my otolaryngologist to protect my grafted eardrum. I took dance classes, twirling classes, played tee ball, volleyball, and basketball through my formative years. My parents did not stop me from doing anything except getting my ears pierced. I finally got my ears pierced when I was 27, a few months before I got married.

During high school, I worked part time at the local nursing home in the kitchen. I got to know all of the residents in addition to their food preferences and dislikes. I met the Registered Dietitian who came to do assessments and plan the menus. Later in high school, I thought that would be something I would be interested in studying in college. The only college I applied to was the University of Texas at Austin (or UT). I applied to the Dietetics program. UT politely responded that I would have to apply to the Coordinated Program in Dietetics at the end of my sophomore year in order to obtain my Bachelor of Science in Nutrition and become eligible to take the registration exam for dietitians. I started UT as a Nutrition major in the Fall of 1989.

The Americans with Disabilities Act (or ADA) was signed into law in 1990 and became effective in 1992 while I was in college. Before I started college, I had an audiological evaluation. The recommendation was to "assess potential for successful use of binaural amplification." I did not qualify to receive disability services from the state or university. I only wore my hearing aid to classes. I did not wear it after class or on weekends. I applied to and was accepted to the Coordinated Program in Dietetics. During my Coordinated Program, I had rotations in clinical, community and foodservice settings. Foodservice was the noisiest of all the settings due to all of the kitchen activities. Working in clinical settings could also be difficult due to difficulty hearing voices. During this time, I was unable to wear my hearing aid during one of my classes because the microphones in my hearing aid kept picking up sounds from the heating, ventilation, and air conditioning system. So, I took an entire class without the benefit of a hearing aid. I talked to the Ombudsman's office at the time, and there was nothing that could be done; this was around the time the ADA had been signed but was not yet in effect. I continued to finish my bachelor's degree in Dietetics, passed my Registration exam, and completed a Master of Arts in Nutritional Sciences. When I took my registration exam in the fall of 1993, the exam was a pencil and paper exam with Scantron sheets. I had no accommodations for the exam (as the exam itself did not require hearing), with the exception of the instructions provided by the proctor. Looking back, I am amazed that I completed two degrees and a dietetics internship without any accommodations for my disability.

For the first five years of my dietetics career, I worked with adults who had HIV/AIDS in both a small community-based organization in San Antonio and later at Cook County Hospital in Chicago, IL. I developed programs to provide nutrition services, including nutrition assessment and evaluation, and nutrition education for people with HIV/AIDS in community-based organizations and healthcare facilities, including a large urban outpatient clinic. In both of these positions, I provided medical nutrition therapy as part of a multidisciplinary team and worked with many disciplines, including psychology, substance abuse treatment counseling, and massage therapy. In both of these roles, I also worked with industry representatives to stock samples of oral nutritional supplements for clients.

I did not have any accommodations at either of these jobs. Eight years after the recommendation to get a hearing aid in the right ear for binaural amplification, I finally got a hearing aid for my right ear. This made a big difference because the hearing aids amplified the sounds. I had no clue that toilets were so loud when you flushed them! In Chicago, live interpreters were provided for language interpretation to all staff and were not considered a disability accommodation.

After we moved back to Texas, I began to work in pediatrics at a hospital that provided specialized care for children with developmental disabilities and special health care needs. This was very different than working with adults. When you work with adults, you typically meet with just the patient. However, when you work with children, there are more people — such as parents, siblings, nurses, and other family members —in the exam room. This results in a noisier environment. My hearing began to worsen, and it became more difficult and exhausting to listen, hear, focus, and understand all day. I became a lot more self-conscious of my speech, especially if a parent would say something like "I thought you might be deaf because of the way you talk."

In this position, I assessed the nutritional status and needs of medically complex patients, developed and implemented an individualized Medical Nutrition Therapy plan of care, recommended and implemented effective interventions, and monitored/evaluated nutrition care outcomes. I developed protocols for parenteral nutrition, served on the hospital-wide patient education committee, and developed patient education materials. I was able to participate in orthopedic research projects by collecting and analyzing nutrition data for patients enrolled in the studies. We precepted dietetics interns throughout the year.

After 2003, my speech discrimination (or ability to identify words) worsened from 88% to 52% in my right ear and from 76% to 0-4% in my left ear. I was diagnosed profoundly deaf (mixed type) in my left ear and severely deaf in the right. When I was 42, I developed tinnitus in both ears. My audiologist made adjustments to my hearing aids to try and "drown out" the tinnitus by saturating my auditory nerve with sound. I started to wear my hearing aids all day from morning until bedtime, instead of only wearing them for work. My neurotologist began to suggest that I might benefit from a cochlear implant.

My health insurance began to cover hearing aids after The Affordable Care Act was passed. I was eligible to get new hearing aids every three years to ensure I had the most up to date technology. The technology advanced so that when I obtained an updated set of hearing aids, there was a streamer that I could wear around my neck. I was able to connect my desk phone and my iPhone to the streamer and could stream conversations and music into both ears. It was amazing to hear in stereo for the first time. The Texas Department of Assistive and Rehabilitative Services did cover the cost for the streamer, since it was not a covered benefit with my health insurance plan.

In 2018, I began to advocate for accommodations at my workplace. I shared an office with multiple dietitians. Hearing and understanding families and coworkers became more difficult, especially with background noise, such as other people in an exam room, overhead announcements, and background office chatter. We also had interns for most of the year, which meant we usually had several people in the office. This added more ambient sound along with the usual background noises. My physician gave me a letter to submit to Occupational Health and Human Resources at work stating that a quieter environment would help me focus on my work. Initially, a white noise machine was installed with very limited benefit. I provided the audiogram from my audiologist so that the machine could be programmed to help provide some background white noise to drown out the tinnitus to no avail. After an 18-to-24-month process involving multiple departments, our office was remodeled. Carpet and sound-absorbing ceiling tiles and cubicles were installed. I tried a closed-captioned phone, which did not work very well with my hearing aids.

My audiologist helped me find a solution for talking on the phone, which was to forward my desk phone to my cell phone. Cell phone technology quickly advanced, and then I did not even need the external streamer to stream all of my calls, music and video directly to my hearing aids. On a personal note, I began to use the closed captioning devices at the movie theater. They look like a 1980s gooseneck lamp and provide captions in green dot matrix font. For those of you born after the laser printer era, dot matrix font refers to the type of printers that were used in the past. Closed caption technology needs an upgrade so that users can use their cell phones with an app to read the subtitles, or provide universal closed captions for all movies.

In March of 2020, the governor of Texas shut the state of Texas down for six weeks due to the COVID-19 pandemic. I did not realize how much I had relied on lip reading for communication until everyone wore masks and I was unable to see lips to read them. The masks also muffled sounds and made it even more difficult to hear and understand speech. There are masks available with a clear window around the mouth to make the lips visible for lip reading. These masks are also very helpful for children to see smiles that are normally hidden behind a mask. Social distancing also made it more difficult to hear other people talking. However, the masks are still very hot due to the plastic material and tend to fog up. One benefit during COVID-19 was that patient visits were limited to one parent/guardian in the room. I became more reliant on technology than ever before, just like the rest of the world at that time. I used telephone translators instead of live translators. I streamed audio to my hearing aids as much as possible, and I used closed captioning on Teams (at that time not all of the online meeting platforms had live captions available). Other technology options that were available (but not used by me) were loop systems, speech to text apps, and instant messaging apps. Our electronic medical record allowed us to securely email families while remaining HIPAA compliant, which ensured I would "hear" 100% of what my patient's families were telling me.

After many years of denying that I would benefit from a cochlear implant (or CI) in my left ear, in February of 2020 I decided to proceed with a CI in my left ear. The COVID-19 pandemic started a month later, and solidified my decision to proceed with surgery. My insurance deductible and out of pocket maximum had been met, so I had a left CI placed on 12/31/2020 and rolled out of the operating room in the early evening before midnight struck and a new year started and my private insurance deductible and out of pocket maximum were reset for the year.

A CI uses a sound processor and microphone that are worn behind the ear. The transmitter sends sound signals to a receiver and a stimulator implanted under the skin, which stimulate the auditory nerve with electrodes that have been threaded into the cochlea. Sound is converted into electrical impulses, and the electrode array collects the impulses and sends them to the auditory nerve to be interpreted into sound. A CI does not provide or restore full or natural hearing. A hearing aid takes sound and amplifies it to transmit through the ear, while a CI bypasses the damaged part of the ear (in my case, the fixed stapes in my middle ear and neural damage of the cochlea). It then sends the signal directly to the auditory nerve. Simply put, a hearing aid makes sound louder, and a CI increases the volume and helps you distinguish the different sounds and pitches.

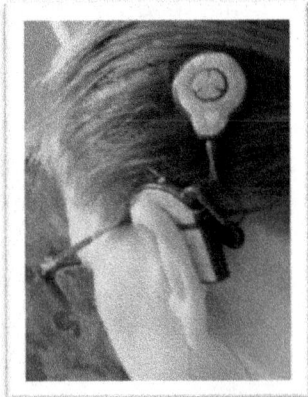

Wendy, with a cochlear implant in her left ear decorated for a holiday.

Over the years, I have seen how patients benefited from technology in all aspects of their lives, including ventilators, power wheelchairs, and dynavox speech devices. This helped me make my decision to get a CI. At the time I had the CI surgery, I had two coworkers who also had CIs — one had bilateral CI and the other had a right sided

CI with a left hearing aid. We all had the same surgeon and formed an informal support group while I was at home recuperating and doing hearing rehabilitation prior to returning to work. I felt like the three of us being open about our hearing devices helped to increase awareness of disabilities and importance of inclusion, in addition to demonstrating the ability to have a successful career with a disability.

The CI is typically not activated until a couple of weeks after surgery. On activation day, I was very excited and fortunate to be able to hear sounds and voices immediately, even though everyone sounded like Mickey Mouse. During my Family and Medical Leave Act (or FMLA), I did hearing rehabilitation at home to train my brain to hear and recognize sounds. FMLA is job-protected leave for specified family and medical reasons with continuation of group health insurance coverage for up to 12 work weeks. I read out loud and watched documentaries; I had used closed captioning for years, but documentaries were recommended specifically due to the intonation and pacing of speech. Every day, there was a new sound that I had never heard before that most people probably take for granted. Some of these sounds include the sound of the dog tags jingling as my dog walks around the house, the crinkle of the snack packages that my family gets out of the pantry or refrigerator, and the sound of running water, which I fortunately figured out what it was before the sink overflowed! I can now hear the fire alarm and kitchen timers chirping. For me, being deaf does not require accommodation for shopping or cooking, because with my CI and hearing aid I can finally hear water boiling and the kitchen timers. Prior to my CI, I would always have to keep an eye on the timer while cooking or baking, because I could never hear it, or my children would tell me the timer was beeping. When I went shopping or out to eat, I was frequently unable to hear and understand overhead announcements and other people. I would either ask them to repeat themselves several times (much to their great frustration) or ask a family member/friend to repeat what was said.

I identify as a deaf bimodal listener; I use a hearing aid in one ear and a CI in the other. At home, I use a TV streamer to stream the sound directly into my devices. Another neat feature I just learned about a year ago was that I can completely shut off the microphones so that I only hear the streaming audio — no more barking dogs during my

TV shows! Eating out in restaurants is still hard for me with all of the background noise, so we continue to make adjustments to my programming so I can focus on talking and listening to my group. Prior to my CI, I did not realize how much I used to "check out" in social settings because I could not hear and was exhausted from all of the work trying to hear. I participate a lot more in social settings now!

At work, I forward my desk phone to my cell phone. We also have Vocera, which is a hands-free communication device that allows staff to call and text on a wireless network. I had great difficulty using this device, because there was not a way to stream it to my hearing devices. I worked for several months with the IT department at work, and they were able to enable a feature that allows me to forward any Vocera calls to the Vocera app on my cell phone. This means I can hear in stereo! I can also use the app to make phone calls instead of using my desk phone. I tried several types of headphones, and none of them were comfortable or had sufficient volume to meet my needs. The IT department at your work can also be a great resource for trouble shooting. In my case, it was a great learning process for them. I also recently found out there is another coworker who wears bilateral hearing devices and has trouble using Vocera, so I recommended she contact IT for assistance. We use Microsoft Teams and Zoom for video calls and meetings, and I always use live captions to read the transcript of the call/meeting. If my surroundings get too loud and I am feeling overwhelmed with sensory input, I shut off my external microphones for a bit and listen to some music so that I can focus on my work.

A couple of years ago, I realized I was no longer able to hear my alarm clock in the morning. I now use an alarm clock with a bed shaker that I place underneath my pillow at night. I am also unable to hear smoke alarms in the house when I am not wearing my devices. Several years ago, we purchased a smoke alarm for our bedroom that has a strobe light, and it does wake me up at night if any of the alarms in the house go off while I am sleeping.

Research shows a link between deafness and depression. Using technology to function in a hearing world has significantly improved my mental health. It is still very difficult for me to understand strong accents until I have talked to the person for a bit and my brain has become more familiar with their speech pattern and accent.

Future practitioners should stay up to date with audiograms and follow-up visits. I went eight years without an audiogram — essentially elementary school to senior year of high school. Contact the rehabilitation program in your state; they may be able to assist with the cost of hearing aids and CIs if not covered by insurance. I qualified for the state of Texas Department of Assistive and Rehabilitative Services to cover the cost of my first hearing aid streamer after my audiologist completed the paperwork. Since the Affordable Care Act was passed, my insurance has covered most of the cost of the hearing aids after I paid my deductible and coinsurance. Familiarize yourself with your insurance benefits and know what your insurance will cover and what you are responsible for. Hearing aids, CI equipment, batteries, accessories and surgeries are expensive!

If I were born today instead of in 1970, I would have been identified as deaf with newborn hearing testing, referred to an audiologist, worn hearing devices at a very early age, and likely also learned ASL. The critical time period for language development is birth to age five. In school, I would have had a 504 plan in place for educational accommodations that would include regular sessions of speech therapy provided by the school district. I would have had hearing devices in both ears at a much earlier age and proceeded with CI surgery sooner. I would have had a mini microphone for teachers to wear so that their voices streamed directly into my hearing devices. When I started college, I would have taken my 504 plan to the office for students with disabilities to help me secure disability accommodations for my classes. Now, there is so much more awareness of inclusion for individuals with disabilities.

I am sad that I went so long without much help, but at the same time, I am also amazed at how much I have accomplished and done without the full benefit of hearing. When my right ear qualifies for a CI, I will not hesitate to move forward with the surgery. There is a risk of losing all of your hearing with the surgery, but most people tend to have a bit of residual hearing left after the surgery.

My CI has made a significant improvement not only in my hearing, but in my quality of life. In a quiet environment, I went from 7%-word recognition pre-CI surgery to 93%-word recognition at six months post-CI surgery with a hearing aid. In a noisy environment, I went from 0%-word recognition pre-CI surgery to 76% at six months post-CI surgery with a hearing aid. Now, I have 100%-word recognition in a quiet environment and 95% in a noisy environment while using both my CI and hearing aid!

I do not discuss my disability with everyone. I disclose as much or as little as I need to based on the situation. However, I am more likely to disclose if I am having a particularly hard time hearing and understanding based on noise in the environment, or if I am unable to understand what others are saying and have to ask them to repeat themselves a few times and they appear frustrated with me.

Throughout my nearly three-decade career as a dietetics practitioner, I have volunteered in several different positions at local and national levels. I am the current Chair-Elect for the Disabilities in Nutrition and Dietetics Member Interest Group and received the 2017 Behavioral Health Nutrition Dietetic Practice Group Award for Excellence in Practice for Intellectual and Developmental Disabilities. In 2022, I had the privilege of presenting at the Academy of Nutrition and Dietetics annual Food and Nutrition Conference and Expo about my personal journey with my disability and discussed the importance of effective communication in healthcare settings. My research unveiled alarming statistics — poor communication can lead to reduced provider-patient trust, medical errors, and only 30% of the English language is readable on the lips without sound. Moreover, individuals who are d/Deaf face a higher risk of depression, underscoring the urgent need for improved accessibility and support systems. Access to a completely accessible language has a distinct impact on brain development, and recent neuroimaging research has shown differences in adult neurostructure among deaf individuals, influenced by the timing and quality of language access during early childhood (Hall, 2017).

While navigating the challenges of living in a world designed primarily for the hearing, I have found my voice and purpose as a dietitian and advocate for people with disabilities to help create a more inclusive society. I hope my experience as a clinical dietitian will inspire others to work towards their dreams, regardless of their disability. The extensive use of technology along with my CI and hearing aid have enabled me to bridge the gap for me to function between the deaf and hearing world. It has truly been a remarkable journey.

In conclusion, I would like to offer the following suggestions for effectively interacting with individuals who are d/Deaf in medical settings, drawing from both my experience as a provider and as a deaf consumer.

- Provide important information on clearly displayed signs.
- Provide access for scheduling appointments and contacting staff/providers outside of appointments via email, text, video chat, telehealth, electronic medical record access.
- Note in the medical chart when a patient is d/Deaf in addition to their communication preference (ASL, lip reading, writing notes) and whether they use hearing aids or have a CI.
- Increase staff awareness. If a patient uses hearing aids/CI, they may have a microphone that can be used to speak into and stream directly into their devices to allow for binaural hearing. Voice to text apps can also be used. Schedule and plan for ASL interpretation services when needed, including allowing adequate time for the appointment.
- During appointments, make eye contact and be sure to look at the patient you are speaking to, even if an interpreter is being used.
- Speak clearly at a normal volume with normal lip movements and a moderate pace.
- Use visual information and written materials.
- Utilize teach back methods to determine that the information presented has been understood.
- If you utilize videos, YouTube, telehealth, and other platforms, provide close captioning.
- Ensure that the exam room and/or office are well lit.
- Reduce background noises/distractions in the exam room and/or office.
- Ensure privacy for conversations so that personal health information is protected.
- Use clear masks or clear face shields when masks are required.

References:

Hall WC, Levin LL, and Anderson ML. Language deprivation syndrome: a possible neurodevelopmental disorder with sociocultural origins. *Soc Psychiatry Psychiatr Epidemiol.* 2017;52:761–776. doi: 10.1007/s00127-017-1351-7

Chapter 21
Disability Resources

By Suzanne Domel Baxter, PhD, RD, LD, FADA, FAND

Introduction

This chapter briefly summarizes various disability resources organized by category (i.e., federal, national, college/university, professional, financial aid and scholarships, books, miscellaneous) and in alphabetical order within category. Awareness of these resources is beneficial for people with and without disabilities. Please refer to Chapter 3 which concerns the Disabilities in Nutrition and Dietetics Member Interest Group of the Academy of Nutrition and Dietetics, and to Chapter 5 which concerns state Vocational Rehabilitation programs and Centers for Independent Living.

Federal

Campaign for Disability Employment

The Campaign for Disability Employment (or CDE) repeats the following two messages: 1) every day, people with disabilities can and do make important contributions to America's businesses, and 2) people with disabilities have the drive to succeed in employment along with the skills and talent to deliver results and value for their employers. The CDE is a highly collaborative effort among several disability and business organizations to showcase supportive, inclusive workplaces for all workers. CDE's multi-faceted campaign called "What Can YOU Do?" features a series of five public service announcements (or PSAs) and coordinating media products, all designed to promote positive employment outcomes for people with disabilities. The CDE's five PSAs are titled "I Can," "Because," "Who I Am," "Working Works" and "Mental Health at Work: What Can I Do?" These five PSAs are aired on television and radio stations nationwide in donated airtime. All five PSAs can be downloaded from the CDE website, along with other tools and tangible ideas for supporting the CDE goals. The CDE is funded by the US Department of Labor's Office of Disability Employment Policy. Visit CDE's website at www.whatcanyoudocampaign.org.

Center for Advancing Policy on Employment for Youth

More than 1.3 million young people between the ages of 16 and 24 have a disability. The Center for Advancing Policy on Employment for Youth (or CAPE-Youth) addresses barriers that youth with disabilities face in transitioning successfully from youth systems into adulthood; these barriers result in lower employment outcomes, educational attainment, and community participation than their peers. CAPE-Youth is a collaboration between the Council of State Governments and the K Lisa Yang and Hock E Tan Institute on Employment and Disability at Cornell University. CAPE-Youth helps states build capacity in their youth service delivery and workforce systems to improve employment outcomes for youth and young adults with disabilities by conducting research, developing partnerships, and sharing best practices. Also, CAPE-Youth helps states identify new opportunities to expand career pathways, work-based learning, strategic partnerships, systems coordination and professional development for practitioners. The US Department of Labor's Office of Disability Employment Policy funds CAPE-Youth. Visit the CAPE-Youth website at capeyouth.org.

Employer Assistance and Resource Network on Disability Inclusion

The Employer Assistance and Resource Network on Disability Inclusion (or EARN) provides information and resources to help employers recruit, hire, retain, and advance qualified individuals with disabilities; build inclusive workplace cultures; and achieve diversity, equity, inclusion, and accessibility goals. EARN's Learning Center offers a variety of training resources including self-paced online courses. EARN's services are primarily for employers. The resources include webinars, self-paced trainings on creating disability-inclusive workplaces, disability etiquette/awareness training, COVID-19 resources to understand and navigate the intersection between the pandemic and disability policies and practices, laws for federal government contractors, neurodiversity resources, a small business toolkit, a mental health toolkit, and a toolkit to build equitable pathways to good jobs and help disabled workers get ahead. Although EARN is not a resource for job seekers with disabilities, it has a webpage with information about resources for job seekers and a webpage for employers looking to identify candidates with disabilities. EARN is funded by the US Department of Labor's Office of Disability Employment Policy. Visit EARN's website at askearn.org.

Job Accommodation Network

The Job Accommodation Network (or JAN) is the leading source of free, expert, and confidential guidance on workplace accommodations and disability employment issues. Job accommodations perform a key role in creating inclusive workplaces, advancing the goals of the Americans with Disabilities Act (or ADA), and increasing employment opportunities for people with disabilities. JAN benefits employers and people with health conditions and disabilities by providing trusted guidance on the ADA and practical accommodation solutions which helps everyone recognize the value that qualified workers with disabilities add to the workforce. JAN has served customers nationwide and worldwide for 40 years. JAN offers free one-on-one practical guidance and technical assistance concerning job accommodation solutions, Title 1 of the ADA and related legislation, and self-employment and entrepreneurship options for people with disabilities. Individualized consultations by JAN assist the following three group: 1) employers seeking guidance on job accommodation solutions and compliance with Title I of the ADA; 2) people with health conditions and disabilities seeking information about job accommodation solutions, employment rights under the ADA, and self-employment and entrepreneurship opportunities; and 3) family members and professionals in rehabilitation, medical, and education as they strive to support successful employment outcomes for people with health conditions and disabilities. JAN consultants are highly qualified and experienced innovators and thought leaders on disability employment issues. JAN is a service of the US Department of Labor's Office of Disability Employment Policy. Visit JAN's website at askjan.org.

National Center on Leadership for the Employment and Economic Advancement of People with Disabilities

The National Center on Leadership for the Employment and Economic Advancement of People with Disabilities (or LEAD Center) is a Workforce Innovation and Opportunity Act (or WIOA) policy development center. The LEAD Center delivers policy research and recommendations, technical assistance, and demonstration projects to promote inclusion and equity, and to facilitate the adoption and integration of inclusive WIOA programs, policies, and practices. The *Workforce Development* section on the LEAD Center website provides links to information about meeting WIOA requirements, strategies to reduce challenges and broaden access, state-by-state data on outcomes, and successful initiatives that can serve as models. Each US state sets a course to make sure that workplace systems provide equal opportunity and full participation for people with disabilities. The *Workforce Development* section has a link to *State Specific Policies and Data* which opens a webpage with a map of the US states; you can click on each state to learn about its policies and initiatives and find links to labor, health, vocational rehabilitation, and other agencies for each state along with relevant policies, initiatives, and services. The LEAD Center's webpage for *Financial Empowerment* provides links to information about WIOA requirements and resources for financial empowerment along with tools to promote economic advancement as an individual's work income grows. The LEAD Center's webpage for *Employment Strategies* provides links to creative approaches to promote customized employment, get information on career pathways, and learn about available technical assistance and training. The LEAD WIOA Policy Department Center is led by the National Disability Institute and is fully funded by the US Department of Labor's Office of

Disability Employment Policy. Visit the LEAD Center website at leadcenter.org.

National Council on Disability

The National Council on Disability (or simply Council in this paragraph) is an independent federal agency that provides advice to the US President, Congress, and executive branch agencies to advance policy that promotes the goals of the ADA. Most Council members are people with disabilities and members are appointed to represent people with disabilities, national disability organizations, disability services providers and administrators, researchers involved in scientific or medical research regarding disabilities, business concerns, and labor organizations. The Council meets several times each year to discuss agency priorities, policy trends, and other agency business. Most meetings are virtual on Zoom and open to the public; registration is not required but appreciated. Attending Council meetings is an excellent opportunity to learn what is happening concerning disabilities. The Council is funded through appropriations and does not provide direct legal or advocacy support to people with disabilities. The Resources page in the *Policy Advice* section of the Council's website provides links to a wealth of information concerning civil rights, education, employment, financial assistance and incentives, health care, housing, independent living, internal, legal assistance, technology, and transportation. Visit the National Council on Disability's website at www.ncd.gov.

National Disability Employment Awareness Month

The US recognizes National Disability Employment Awareness Month (or NDEAM) each October to commemorate the many contributions of people with disabilities to America's workplaces and economy. The purpose of NDEAM is to confirm the commitment to ensuring that workers with disabilities have access to good jobs every month of every year. The theme changes annually. The theme for NDEAM 2024 is *Access to Good Jobs for All*. Each NDEAM has an animated video, video descriptive transcript, press release, poster, and customizable poster. Spanish versions are available for the animated video and posters. Specific ideas to observe and celebrate NDEAM are provided for different types of organizations including employers and employees; educators and youth service professionals; state governors, legislators, and other policymakers; associations and unions; disability-related organizations; and federal agencies. There is a different suggestion to celebrate NDEAM for each of the 31 days in October. Activities for NDEAM don't have to occur only in October, so NDEAM also offers 10 year-round strategies for employers to foster disability inclusion and promote a disability-friendly workplace. NDEAM provides numerous spotlights with ready-to-use social media content that individuals and organizations can use to highlight the many leaders past and present who have worked to increase access and equity for disabled people in the workplace. NDEAM is funded by the US Department of Labor's Office of Disability Employment Policy. Visit NDEAM's website at www.dol.gov/agencies/odep/initiatives/ndeam.

Partnership on Employment & Accessible Technology

The mission of the Partnership on Employment & Accessible Technology (or PEAT) is to foster collaborations in the technology space that build inclusive workplaces for people with disabilities. PEAT's vision is a future in which new and emerging technologies are designed to be accessible to the workforce. PEAT creates resources for employers, employees, technology leaders, and others for their journey toward inclusion. The US Department of Labor's Office of Disability Employment Policy funds PEAT. Visit PEAT's website at www.peatworks.org.

National Consortium for Constituents with Disabilities

The Consortium for Constituents with Disabilities (or CCD) is the largest coalition of national organizations working together to advocate for federal public policy that ensures the self-determination, independence, empowerment, integration, and inclusion of children and adults with disabilities in all aspects of society. It has a Board of Directors, several committees and task forces, and approximately 100 member organizations. The CCD does the following:

- Identifies and researches public policy issues, develops testimony and policy recommendations, and encourages innovative solutions to public policy concerns.
- Educates members of Congress to improve public policies and programs that foster independence, productivity, integration and inclusion of people with disabilities.
- Encourages people with disabilities and their families to advocate for themselves, and coordinates grass roots efforts to support these advocacy efforts.

Visit CCD's website often at https://www.c-c-d.org/ to stay informed on national issues and events affecting the disability community.

Core Competencies on Disability for Health Care Education

The Alliance for Disability in Health Care Education partnered with the Ohio Disability and Health Program to develop a national consensus on disability competencies required for health care providers to provide quality care to patients with disabilities. A total of 152 disabled people, disability advocates, family members of disabled people, disability and health professionals, and inter-disciplinary health educators systematically evaluated and provided feedback on a draft set of disability competencies. Based on two waves of feedback, competencies were iteratively refined. Six competencies, 49 sub-competencies, and 10 principles and values emerged that are interdisciplinary and cross-disability and address topics including respect, person-centered care, and awareness of physical, attitudinal, and communication health care barriers. The disability competencies must be integrated into health education curricula so the health care workforce is prepared to deliver quality health care that is accessible and patient-centered to all patients with disabilities. Dietetics practitioners are members of the health care workforce; thus, dietetics programs need to integrate the disability competencies into their curricula. A 2021 article by Havercamp and colleagues in the *Disability and Health Journal* describes the process used to obtain national consensus on the disability competencies. The disability competencies are available online along with a form for organizations, institutions, boards, and councils to endorse the competencies as necessary standards for health care education at https://nisonger.osu.edu/education-training/ohio-disability-health-program/corecompetenciesondisability/.

The Alliance for Disability in Health Care Education is a not-for-profit organization of medical school faculty, nursing school faculty, and other health care educators who are collaborating to integrate disability-related content and experiences into health care education and training programs. The Ohio Disability and Health Program is one of 23 projects funded by the Centers for Disease Control and Prevention to improve the health of people with disabilities through physical activity, nutrition intervention, tobacco cessation, and training and education initiatives.

Disability Health Equity Research Network

The Disability Health Equity Research Network (or DHERN) supports disability health equity research, connects researchers and trainees, and fosters the inclusion of disabled people in these efforts. Activities include meetings, conferences, seminars, a monthly newsletter, the DHERN Disability Health Equity Paper Awards, and a Disability Data Equity Research Working Group. The Working Group meets monthly and engages in cooperative research on disability data equity, and promotes the participation and leadership of disabled researchers in its endeavors. High-quality data is essential to identify, understand, and address the disparities experienced by disabled people. Yet national vital statistics, surveys, and many other data collection mechanisms do not consistently include disability data or, when they do, use measurements that are not inclusive of all disabled people. The Working Group engages in conceptual and empirical research focused on making disability measurement more inclusive and equitable, and fosters understanding that disability is a demographic rather than an outcome. DHERN is funded by Johns Hopkins Disability Health Research Center and three entities at Syracuse University — the Center for Aging and Policy Studies, the Aging Studies Institute, and the Maxwell Tenth Decade Project. Visit the DHERN website at https://asi.syr.edu/disability-health-equity-research-network-dhern/.

Disability in Medicine Mutual Mentorship Program

The Disability in Medicine Mutual Mentorship Program (or DM3P) is a grassroots organization that supports disabled medical professionals and trainees as they navigate the field of medicine. The DM3P welcomes persons with disability and their allies from across all healthcare professions and all stages of training. Also, the DM3P welcomes current, future and former healthcare professionals and trainees with disabilities and chronic illness, along with allies of healthcare workers with disabilities. The DM3P exists because disabled people are underrepresented in medicine. Disabled clinicians regularly confront ableism (i.e., structural and attitudinal barriers) to their inclusion and advancement in their chosen healthcare professions. Disabled clinicians need role models, peers, and a platform for advocacy to help them challenge ableist barriers. The DM3P includes mutual mentorship which is a model of mentorship in which participants assemble in groups to support one another through problems encountered while navigating life with a shared marginalized identity. Instead of assigning formal mentor-mentee pairings, each participant serves in both the mentor and the mentee role per their lived experiences. This mutual mentorship model is ideal for the DM3P because disability can emerge at any point in the human lifespan which means a person's level of experience navigating medicine with a disability often doesn't correlate with their stage of professional training. The following bullets summarize what DM3P offers:

- Monthly Zoom meetings with guest speakers, group discussion of disability-related issues in medicine, and unstructured social time for members to build self-advocacy skills and exchange disability-specific career advice among a supportive community of healthcare workers with disabilities. Accommodations at meetings include CART captioning and auto captioning; other accommodations such as ASL interpretation are provided to participants who request this via email ahead of time.
- Private discord group for additional, asynchronous online discussions and mentorships.
- Private LinkedIn group for professional networking.
- Archive of resources from past events.
- In-person faculty development opportunities at Stanford through the Faculty Disability Forum.
- Leadership opportunities for participants who wish to take an active role organizing events for this program.

Visit the DM3P website at https://disabilitymedmentors.org/.

Disability Equity Collaborative

The Disability Equity Collaborative (or DEC) is the nation's leading organization providing evidence-based knowledge and practical solutions and tools to address the complex problems in disability access in healthcare. DEC's goal is to empower and support healthcare organizations, practitioners, and policy makers in implementing evidence-based, accessible care for their patients with disabilities, and to enact policies that ensure that patients with disabilities will receive equitable healthcare. Dr. Megan Morris and colleagues at the University of Colorado Anschutz created DEC in 2018. DEC was formalized with an Engagement Award in 2019 from the Patient-Centered Outcomes Research Institute. DEC has a free quarterly e-newsletter to keep current with its work and learn about new opportunities and resources. DEC's efforts to advance disability equity are centered in the following three main areas:

- **DEC Leaders:** The DEC Leaders group is a national collaboration of disability accessibility coordinators and people working in similar roles in healthcare organizations.

This group meets regularly through virtual meetings and an online community to share ideas and solutions to ensure equitable care for patients with disabilities.
- **Resources:** DEC has compiled and continues to update and develop a wide variety of resources that support healthcare equity initiatives, including links to training materials for staff and guides for implementing accessibility initiatives.
- **Research:** The DEC engages researchers, policy makers, funders, payers, people with disabilities, patient advocates, and healthcare organizations to identify critical research priorities and work on evidence-based interventions necessary to improve accessibility and quality of health care delivered to people with disabilities.

Visit DEC's website at https://www.disabilityequitycollaborative.org/.

Disability Rights Education and Defense Fund

The Disability Rights Education and Defense Fund (or DREDF) is a leading national civil rights law and policy center directed by individuals with disabilities and parents who have children with disabilities. The mission of DREDF is to advance the civil and human rights of people with disabilities through legal advocacy, training, education, and public policy and legislative development. The vision of DREDF is a just world where all people, with and without disabilities, live full and independent lives free of discrimination. The DREDF works with the core principles of equality of opportunity, disability accommodation, accessibility, and inclusion by employing the following three strategies:

1) **Training and Education** — The DREDF trains and educates people with disabilities and parents of children with disabilities about their rights under state and federal disability rights laws. Also, it educates lawyers, service providers, government officials, and others about disability civil rights laws and policies. The DREDF has operated a disability rights legal clinic for more than two decades in collaboration with law schools in the San Francisco Bay Area including University of California Berkeley School of Law.
2) **Legal Advocacy** — The legal advocacy work of the DREDF

encompasses a multifaceted approach to advancing disability rights and involves direct legal representation, collaboration with partners, expert legal analysis through amicus curiae briefs (or friend of the court), strategic case selection, and broader advocacy efforts aimed at fostering positive change for disabled people and families.

3) **Public Policy and Legislative Development** — The DREDF designs and employs strategies that strengthen public policy and lead to the enactment of federal and state laws protecting and advancing civil rights for people with disabilities. Examples include the Handicapped Children's Protection Act, the Civil Rights Restoration Act, the landmark 1990 Americans with Disabilities Act, and the IDEA Amendments Act. The current work of the DREDF in public policy focuses on transportation, housing, marriage equality, parents with disabilities, HIV criminalization, assisted suicide, and disability and bioethics.

Visit DREDF's website at https://dredf.org.

Disability Training for Healthcare Providers

The following two new trainings about caring for patients with disabilities are available for healthcare providers and clinic staff. These trainings are free, available for professional continuing education credit, and online at https://nisonger.osu.edu/education-training/ohio-disability-health-program/disability-training-for-health-providers/:

- **Responsive Practice: Providing Health Care & Screenings to Individuals with Disabilities** — This 40-minute training will prepare healthcare personnel to describe health disparities experienced by people with disabilities, recognize the healthcare barriers faced by people with disabilities, and use strategies to provide disability-competent, responsive care.
- **Responsive Practice: Accessible & Adaptive Communication** — This 40-minute training will prepare healthcare personnel to presume that patients with disabilities are competent to understand, communicate, and participate in their own health care; identify and use alternative methods of communication with patients with

disabilities; and improve patient-provider communication and patient-centered care for people with disabilities.

The following two virtual courses are available for free and on demand with approval for continuing education by the Centers for Disease Control and Prevention at https://nisonger.osu.edu/education-training/ohio-disability-health-program/disability-healthcare-training/:

- **Healthcare Access for People with Disabilities (WD4841)** is designed to increase knowledge and change competency of providing quality healthcare, practices, and strategies for people with physical and sensory disabilities.
- **Health Care for People with Intellectual and Developmental Disabilities (WD4739)** is designed to increase knowledge and change competency of providing quality healthcare, practices, and strategies for people with developmental disabilities.

National Center on Health, Physical Activity and Disability

The National Center on Health, Physical Activity and Disability (or NCHPAD) is the nation's premier center dedicated to advancing inclusion by promoting the health and wellness of people with disabilities via evidence-based programs, campaigns, and strategic initiatives. Headquartered in the School of Health Professions at the University of Alabama at Birmingham, NCHPAD supports people across the lifespan, organizations, and communities by:

- empowering individuals with accessible resources and providing expert support for individuals with disabilities to engage in health promotion activities,
- creating disability advocates by equipping communities with the knowledge and tools needed to create inclusive environments and champion health for all, and
- building inclusive communities by advocating for policies, programs and accessible spaces to remove barriers and promote health equity.

In 2023, NCHPAD reached more than 1.5 million people with free health and wellness content online, awarded funding for more than $440,000 to boost disability inclusion and health promotion in communities and organizations, and conducted more than 2,100 live health promotion classes and sessions. NCHPAD is committed to establishing sustainable approaches to health promotion and wellness for individuals with disabilities via initiatives and services designed to empower individuals as well as to be scalable across healthcare facilities and communities nationwide. NCHPAD's strategic priorities are inclusive advocacy and community engagement, holistic healthcare and wellness infrastructure, empowerment and accessibility initiatives, partnerships and professional development, evidence-based sustainability, and resource dissemination and support. The NCHPAD collaborates with a diverse network of more than 60 partners including nonprofits, government agencies, advocacy organizations, businesses, and schools. The NCHPAD services support individuals with disabilities; healthcare professionals; allied health professionals; families and communities; educators, school administrators and advocates; and researchers. The NCHPAD offers a YouTube channel, evidence-based programs, supportive resources, social media, funding opportunities, and campaigns. NCHPAD's range of services and expertise include collaborative partnerships, resource development, program adaptations, evaluation, internships, trainings, and tailored support to ensure the tools needed to promote health equity and advance inclusion. Visit NCHPAD's website at https://www.nchpad.org/.

National Disability Rights Network

The National Disability Rights Network (or NDRN) in Washington, DC works on behalf of the Protection and Advocacy Systems and Client Assistance Programs which are the nation's largest providers of legal advocacy services for people with disabilities. The NDRN promotes the network's capacity, provides training and technical assistance to ensure that Protection and Advocacy Systems and Client Assistance Programs remain strong and effective, and advocates for laws to protect the civil and human rights of all people with disabilities. Visit NDRN's website at www.ndrn.org to find information for your US state or territory.

State Disability Rights Offices

Each US state has its own Disability Rights Office to protect and advocate for the civil and legal rights of people with disabilities in the state. These offices are named "*Disability Rights [name of state]*" and can be found online by searching for "*Disability Rights [name of state]*." For example, in Florida, it is "*Disability Rights Florida.*"

College/University

Disability Services Offices at Colleges and Universities

Each college or university must designate a Disability Services Office to support students with disabilities by serving as their accommodations advocate. This office determines and coordinates academic adjustments, reasonable modifications, and auxiliary aids for students with disabilities while maintaining the integrity of a professional program by recommending reasonable adjustments that do not compromise academic rigor or fundamentally alter the program's nature. Also, this office helps students with disabilities as well as faculty and staff understand the rights of students with disabilities. Students with disabilities must register with this office at their college/university to receive its services. Students with disabilities may need to provide this office with a note from their doctor(s) or therapist(s) explaining the student's need(s) for accommodations. Students can update their accommodations at any time or choose not to use one or more accommodations if they are not needed for certain classes. The specific name of this office may vary from one college/university to another. This book includes several autobiographies of individuals who utilized this office or equivalent at their college/university in their journey to becoming and working as credentialed dietetic practitioners with disabilities. For example, in Chapter 7 by Ryan Branson, this office is the *Disabilities Services Department*. In Chapter 9 by Alicia Connor, this office is the *Disability Services & Programs for Students Center* at a community college and the *Disability Resource Center* at a university. In Chapter 10 by Liz Dunn, this office is the *Office of Disability Resources and Services*. In Chapter 15 by Jordan Griffing, this office is the *Office of Access and Learning Accommodations*. In Chapter 17 by Alena Morales, this office is the *Disability Access and Compliance Office*.

Docs with Disabilities Initiative

The Docs with Disabilities Initiative (or DWDI) was launched in July 2022 by Dr. Lisa Meeks and her team at the University of Michigan to increase the number of healthcare providers with disabilities, address the disability access gaps in healthcare education and practice for people with disabilities, and expand education and awareness about disability inclusion. Barriers to increasing the number of healthcare providers with disabilities include lack of mentorship, knowledge of reasonable accommodations in clinical settings, and the impact of long COVID on the healthcare workforce. The DWDI has the following four main goals:

1) **Elevate People** — Share stories of physicians, nurses, and medical professionals with disabilities, in their own words.
2) **Foster Awareness** — Increase the visibility of disabled healthcare providers.
3) **Build Community** — Create a virtual space for people to connect and support one another in their journeys.
4) **Impact Inclusion** — Conduct research and education that informs policy and best practice.

To accomplish these goals, the DWDI collaborates with several organizations, including the Association of American Medical Colleges, the Stanford Medicine Alliance for Disability Inclusion and Equity, the Association of Medical Professionals with Hearing Losses, and the Johns Hopkins Disability Health Research Center. Research of the DWDI includes projects, publications, the Disability Research in Academic Medicine Consortium and research rounds. Podcasts of the DWDI include Docs with Disabilities podcasts as well as research and resources podcasts. Programs of the DWDI include Access in Medicine, Access in Nursing, a book club, Disability in Graduate Medical Education Group, Disability Resource Professionals academy and days, an international council, and a Women with Disabilities in Medicine mentor group. Resources of the DWDI include webinars, videos, medical school terminology guide, guide to USMLE step accommodations, and technical standards toolkit. Visit DWDI's website at www.docswithdisabilities.org.

Johns Hopkins Disability Health Research Center

The Johns Hopkins Disability Health Research Center (or DHRC) is shifting the paradigm from *"living"* with a disability to *"thriving"* with a disability and maximizing the health, equity, and participation of people with disabilities. The four goals of the DHRC are to: 1) develop evidence to address disability inequities, 2) create approaches to reduce disability inequities, 3) establish policies to reduce disability inequities, and 4) train the next generation of disability health leaders. The work of the DHRC is summarized in the following three bullets:

1) **Determinants of health:** People with disabilities face many under-addressed health disparities. The DHRC's work focuses on identifying and addressing the root causes of health inequities impacting people with disabilities across the four areas of access to food, transit, housing, and healthcare. Examples of projects are the SNAP dashboard, public transit accessibility dashboard, stigma among older adults with age-related vision impairments.
2) **Disability data:** The DHRC uses a disability data justice approach to focus on developing, expanding and improving methods to collect disability data. This work is grounded in perspectives of the disability community and prioritizes accessibility and equitable access to this data and information. Examples of projects are:
    a. Article in *Disability and Health Journal* in April 2024 titled "Counting Disability in the National Health Interview Survey and its Consequence: Comparing the American Community Survey to the Washington Group Measures"
    b. Article in *JAMA Network Open* in October 2021 titled "National Prevalence of Disability and Disability Types among Adults in the US, 2019"
    c. Article in *Health Affairs* in August 2022 titled "A Need

for Disability Data Justice."
3) **STEM equity and training:** People with disabilities are too often excluded from STEM, public health, and healthcare careers which hinder opportunities for advancement across these fields. The DHRC is conducting research to understand the barriers and support the development strategies to improve opportunities for career success in these areas. Examples of projects are:
    a. Article in *Nature Human Behavior* in November 2023 titled "STEM Doctorate Recipients with Disabilities Experienced Early in Life Earn Lower Salaries and Are Underrepresented among Higher Academic Positions"
    b. Article in the *New England Journal of Medicine* in January 2022 titled "Disability Inclusion as a Key Component of Research Study Diversity"
    c. A conference at the National Academies of Sciences, Engineering, and Medicine in June 2023 titled "Disrupting Ableism and Advancing STEM: A National Leadership Summit."

The DHRC also has "Included: The Disability Equity Podcast" which delves deep into issues of disability equity such as voting and healthcare from personal, advocacy, and research perspectives. Visit the DRHC website at https://disabilityhealth.jhu.edu/.

Stanford Medicine Alliance for Disability Inclusion and Equity

The Stanford Medicine Alliance for Disability Inclusion and Equity (or SMADIE) is composed of people who have disabilities and their allies. Membership is open to everyone at Stanford Medicine, including Stanford School of Medicine, Stanford Health Care, University HealthCare Alliance, Lucile Packard Children's Hospital Stanford, Packard Children's Health Alliance, and Stanford Children's Health. The SMADIE value is belief in a world where disability is celebrated as an integral part of human diversity, inclusivity, and equity. The SMADIE vision is to endeavor to transform the culture of Stanford Medicine and beyond from one of compliance to proactive anti-ableism where patients, employees, and trainees with all abilities can thrive. The SMADIE mission is to advocate for resources, education, training, policies, accessibility, and services at Stanford Medicine and beyond, not guided solely by law and an accommodations-based approach, but by dismantling systemic discrimination through universal design. SMADIE encourages synergy and collaboration within and beyond the Stanford community in service of Justice. The six specific mission functions of SMADIE follow:

1) **Educate** for sustainable change for patients with disabilities by developing accessible and practical resources to advance healthcare, medical education, and training.
2) Accelerate the discovery of transformational human-centered **research** to advance inclusive institutional practices and significantly impact the lives of people with and without disabilities.
3) Design and support **health equity** initiatives that combat health inequities and improve access to personalized and seamless care and services for patients with disabilities.
4) Support and expand a mutual **mentorship** program with individuals from all levels of healthcare training committed to fostering initiatives that enrich life-long excellence.
5) Invest and center people and **community** to advance disability equity and visibility in medicine through educational, community-building, peer support, and networking initiatives and dialogues.
6) Leverage human driven and digitally driven institutional, governmental, and community partnerships to **advocate** for long-term sustainable disability-inclusive structures.

The Stanford Disability and Telehealth Conference was held virtually in May 2024 to foster the development of universal access and promote best practices in telehealth for individuals with disabilities. The conference featured national experts in disability telehealth, telemedicine, and technology. The conference was co-sponsored by SMADIE and the American Telemedicine Association.

Visit the numerous links and resources concerning disabilities on SMADIE's website at https://med.stanford.edu/smadie.html.

Editors: Suzanne Domel Baxter and Cheryl Iny Harris

Professional

American Association of People with Disabilities

The American Association of People with Disabilities (or AAPD) is a national disability-led and cross-disability rights organization that works to increase the political and economic power of people with disabilities. The AAPD advocates for full civil rights for over 60 million Americans with disabilities by promoting equal opportunity, economic power, independent living, political participation, and quality comprehensive affordable health care. Because the disability community is massive and incredibly diverse, the AAPD is a conveyor organization that builds relationships, trust, and unity through convening open, honest conversations. Because disability is a natural part of the human experience that influences everyone, the AAPD connects the disability community with allies, businesses, schools, and the community at large, amplifying a powerful voice for change. Like champions of justice before us have proven, seemingly small actions lead to significant transformation; thus, the AAPD is an action-oriented catalyst for change, igniting sparks that ignite extraordinary results. The AAPD advocates for policy issues that improve the lives of people with disabilities and advance the collective power of the disability rights movement. The work of the AAPD includes awards, COVID-19 and higher education, Disability Equality Index, Disability Mentoring Day, Election Engagement Hub, Fannie Lou Hamer Leadership Program, Inclusive Retail Spaces Coalition, Internship Programs, and REV UP Voting Campaign. Visit the AAPD online at https://www.aapd.com/.

Association of Medical Professionals with Hearing Losses

The Association of Medical Professionals with Hearing Losses (or AMPHL) is a 501(c)(3) non-profit organization that has served thousands of Deaf and hard-of-hearing healthcare professionals and students worldwide since 1999. The AMPHL mission is to provide information, promote advocacy and mentorship, and strive to create a diverse, robust network for individuals with hearing loss interested in or working in healthcare fields. The AMPHL vision is to promote equal opportunities in the health professions among the Deaf and hard-of-hearing. The AMPHL welcomes healthcare professionals, students, interpreters, researchers, advocates, and many more. Visit AMPHL's website at https://www.amphl.org/.

Association on Higher Education and Disability

The Association on Higher Education and Disability (or AHEAD) is the leading professional membership association for individuals committed to equity for persons with disabilities in higher education. The membership of AHEAD is diverse and includes disability resource professionals, student affairs personnel, ADA coordinators, diversity officers, AT/IT staff, faculty and other instructional personnel, and colleagues who are invested in creating welcoming higher education experiences for disabled individuals. AHEAD delivers professional development opportunities through conferences, workshops, webinars, publications, and consultation; fosters community and member networking; informs members of emerging issues relevant to disability and higher education in the legislative and regulatory spheres; and disseminates data, promotes research, and furthers evidence-based practice. AHEAD has more than 5,000 members, representing all 50 states and more than 10 countries. Also, AHEAD has formal partnerships with 37 Regional Affiliates and numerous professional organizations. AHEAD members are actively engaged in service provision, consultation and training, and policy development on their campuses; also, they promote accessibility across the field of higher education and beyond. Visit AHEAD's website at https://www.ahead.org/home.

Financial Aid and Scholarships

The OnlineSchools.org website can be filtered for disabilities to provide a financial aid and scholarship guide for students with disabilities. Despite the title "OnlineSchools," the site includes both in-person as well as online programs and each scholarship's profile indicates whether online programs at accredited colleges or universities are eligible. Note, OnlineSchools is an advertising-supported site which means the listings and results are for schools that compensate OnlineSchools; however, the compensation does not influence the site's school rankings, resource guides, or other information included. The OnlineSchools.org website has drop-down menus for K-12, higher education, states, and resources. Under "Resources," click on "Financial Aid for Students with Disabilities." Or simply use the URL https://www.onlineschools.org/financial-aid/disabilities/. When on the page for "Financial Aid for Students with Disabilities," you can filter on the level of higher education, major, and focus to explore programs. Or you can scroll through the scholarship listing, which is divided into sections for all disability types, hearing loss/deafness, visual impairments, physical/mobility impairments, health impairments, and learning disabilities and mental health. Some scholarships also include students with parents or siblings with disabilities. The Resources drop-down menu also has financial aid and scholarship categories for adults and working parents; for soldiers, veterans, and their families; and for minority students.

Be sure to read Chapter 4 to learn about scholarships available from the Academy of Nutrition and Dietetics Foundation as well as Chapter 5 to learn about financial resources that might be available from state Vocational Rehabilitation Programs and Centers for Independent Living.

Books

Disability Friendly: How to Move from Clueless to Inclusive (by John D. Kemp)

People with disabilities make up at least 15% of the population and more than 1 billion people worldwide, yet are too often overlooked. This book describes how employers can harness the untapped potential of disabled employees, make reasonable accommodations, and create cultures of dignity, respect, pride, and inclusion. The author, John D. Kemp, draws from his decades of experience helping thousands of leaders create disability-friendly organizations, identifies roadblocks to understanding and engaging people with disabilities, offers proven approaches for overcoming the initial discomfort people may have working with disabled colleagues, and demonstrates how businesses, schools, government, churches, and other organizations can open up to the contributions and talents of people with disabilities. This book explains the opportunity in hiring and accommodating the millions of Americans with disabilities. This book is essential reading for human resources, information/technology professionals, and leaders who care about diversity, equity, and inclusion, but have not yet fully incorporated people with disabilities into their strategies and practices. Diversity is creating a workforce with people of all backgrounds whereas inclusion is a measure of the culture you create that allows a diverse workforce to thrive. The author is widely respected as a leader in the disability movement for more than forty years. Kemp currently serves as president and CEO of Lakeshore Foundation, an organization providing opportunities for individuals with physical disabilities to lead healthy, active, independent lives. As co-founder of the American Association of People with Disabilities and as an international speaker and disability rights leader, Kemp serves as a catalyst for change and increasing the political and economic power of people with disabilities. This book is available at Amazon.

Autism Recipe: Using Trust and Joy to Take Control of Wellness (by Sharon Lemons)

Sharon Lemons was a young mother of three boys, ages seven, five, and one week, the day her two older children were diagnosed with autism. At a time when the diagnosis was still rare and interventions were new, expensive, and not always helpful, Sharon refused to let her children be another statistic. She was determined to see them live healthy, successful lives. Through sheer tenacity and much love, she applied herself more than 40 hours a week to researching autism and developing strategies to help her children achieve optimum wellness and move ever forward toward autonomy. She was told her oldest would never hold a pencil, yet today he is a college graduate with a Bachelor of Arts in media arts and animation. As Sharon began to realize how important nutrition was to their wellness and success, she earned first a bachelor's degree in dietetics, then a master's degree in nutrition, and became a registered dietitian nutritionist specializing in behavioral health. In this book, Sharon shares her more than 30 years of experience in helping families and caregivers of individuals with autism and other behavioral challenges prepare their loved one for the ultimate goal: living a healthy and autonomous life. Sharon draws on her personal successes with her sons and others she has counseled, and through transparent anecdotes and compassionate words, she lays out effective strategies and attainable goals based around the most integral part of the home, the dinner table. Using mealtime as the springboard to teach everything from organizational skills to better nutrition to social competences and beyond, this book offers a blueprint of help and hope for anyone searching for ways to bring variety and better nutrition to their picky or behaviorally challenged eaters. Sharon is a member of the Disabilities in Nutrition and Dietetics Member Interest Group and its inaugural Treasurer. This book is available at Amazon.

Equal Access for Students with Disabilities: The Guide for Health Science and Professional Education, 2nd Edition (Editors Lisa M. Meeks, Neera R. Jain, & Elisa P. Laird)

This book on disability inclusion in health sciences education remains the most comprehensive legally informed guidance available to health science programs. The text is written in an easy-to-read, engaging manner. This book addresses all aspects of disability including disability law, focuses on the importance of fully inclusive education for health care practitioners, and provides real-world informed case studies that demonstrate best practices. The book's editors are leaders in the field of disability inclusion and have years of practice and expertise. The following bullets provide 12 chapter titles of this book:

1. Know Your Campus Resources
2. Disability Law and the Process for Determining Whether a Student Has a Disability
3. Technical Standards
4. The Process for Determining Disability Accommodations

5. Accommodations in Didactic, Lab, and Clinical Settings
6. Requesting Accommodations on Certification, Licensing, and Board Exams: Assisting Students through the Application
7. Learning in the Digital Age: Assistive Technology and Electronic Access
8. Professionalism and Communication about Disabilities and Accommodations
9. Working through Complex Scenarios
10. Debunking Myths and Addressing Legitimate Concerns
11. Dos and Don'ts for Working with Students with Disabilities
12. Chapter Review and Points for Discussion

The editors have secured the copyright to this work, allowing them to distribute the book to more people by filling an unmet need for disability resource professionals and removing financial barriers for those who need this information. Thus, free digital download of this book is available on the Docs with Disabilities website at https://www.docswithdisabilities.org/equal-access-guide. This website also provides recorded discussions for chapters 1-11 in the *Equal Access Book Club Recordings* section.

Miscellaneous

Abilities Expos

Abilities Expos are held annually in seven North American cities — Los Angeles, New York metro, Chicago, Houston, Phoenix, Fort Lauderdale, and Dallas. These expos are free, three-day, fairs featuring products, technology, informative workshops, and adaptive activities. The website provides links to numerous disability resources, many of which offer free webinars. Visit the Abilities Expos online at https://www.abilities.com/.

Accessible Pharmacy Services

Accessible Pharmacy Services was founded by blind and sighted experts in the areas of accessibility, technology, and medicine. It is the only provider of its kind, the largest blind-owned company in the US, and a worldwide leader in medication specific health equity for people with disabilities so they have an accessible opportunity to reach optimal health regardless of disability type, preferred language, or other factors that affect access to care and health outcomes. It works closely with its patients to address patient education and support, medication management, diabetes management, clinical pharmacist consultation and access, genomic testing, extreme simplification, and cost containment. It coordinates all details with doctors and insurance providers to help keep costs as low as possible. It works with its patients to identify the best packaging and labeling solutions to maximize compliance and healthcare benefits. It provides accessible packaging, accessible labeling, and home delivery all for free. Its free accessible packaging options include bottles in various sizes with easy-open lids or child-proof lids, monthly and weekly pre-sorted disposable pill organizers, pre-sorted individual daily pill packets, and single liquid dose infant medication. Its free accessible labeling options include traditional text labels in 200 different languages; oversize font labels; contrasted color background labels; grade 1 braille labels; contracted braille labels for prescription and over-the-counter medication, eye drops, insulin, vitamins, and nutritional supplements; and audio labels via ScripTalk and QR codes. (Contracted braille is also called grade 2 braille and uses contractions which are short ways of writing braille that make reading and writing braille faster and the braille takes up less space.) Accessible Pharmacy Services hosts free webinars with closed captioning and a live ASL interpreter. It has hosted a free annual virtual Blind Health Expo since 2022. It hosted a free virtual blindness and mental health summit in 2024. Visit Accessible Pharmacy Services online at https://accessiblepharmacy.com/.

Bookshare

Bookshare is an initiative that offers customizable reading experiences to promote inclusion and literacy via an accessible online library with more than a million audiobooks, textbooks, e-books, and digital braille for people with reading barriers such as blindness/visual impairment, dyslexia, or physical disabilities that make it difficult to physically manage a book. Bookshare is free for U.S. students of all ages who have qualifying disabilities and U.S. primary, secondary, and post-secondary schools through an award from the U.S. Department of Education, Office of Special Education Programs to Beneficent Technology, Inc. Visit Bookshare and Benetech online at www.bookshare.org/ and at benetech.org/work-area/bookshare/.

Digital Accessibility

Digital accessibility is the process of making digital products accessible to everyone so all users can access the same information, regardless of their impairments or disabilities. It is a legal requirement according to the ADA and Section 504 of the Rehabilitation Act. Also, it enhances user experience, broadens audience reach, and demonstrates a commitment to inclusivity and social responsibility. People with various types of disabilities — such as visual, auditory, physical, speech, cognitive, and neurological — need digital content to be accessible. Digital accessibility applies to websites, mobile applications, software, social media, email, electronic documents (such as reports, publications, PDFs) and virtual events (such as meetings, webinars, and conferences). Digital accessibility is not a "one and done" destination but instead is a journey. As new web pages, information, and downloadable resources are added, new accessibility issues can arise and must be addressed.

Digital accessibility means adherence to the *Web Content Accessibility Guidelines* (or WCAG) which are international standards for the web developed by the Web Accessibility Initiative (or WAI) of the World Wide Web Consortium (or W3C); you can find information online about this at https://www.w3.org/WAI/standards-guidelines/wcag/. Common digital accessibility failures include poor color contrast between the text and background and lack of alternative text for images. Digital inequity can begin at any age and have lasting effects on an individual's health, educational, economic, and social outcomes. Any digital content that is distributed internally and/or externally needs to be accessible. Guidance and resources are readily available to make digital content accessible. Numerous resources and online training opportunities, some free and some for pay, provide information and training on digital accessibility. Many businesses, some for profit and some nonprofit, help companies and organizations achieve digital accessibility. Also, there are many companies that will conduct free audits to determine digital accessibility, train your employees to make your digital products accessible, or to step in and make your digital products accessible. Most of these companies hire people with disabilities to conduct manual audits to identify inaccessible aspects of digital products often not caught by automated audits. Some of these companies even offer scholarships for their training programs for people with disabilities. To identify vendors that help companies and associations achieve digital accessibility, access the vendor directory on the Accessibility.com website at https://www.accessibility.com/vendor-directory and filter on the *accessibility consulting* category.

Disability Etiquette

Disability etiquette concerns respectful communication with and about people with disabilities. Appropriate disability etiquette fosters inclusion of people with disabilities and allows all individuals to be more comfortable and productive. Disability etiquette concerns all people with disabilities whether they are employees, coworkers, candidates, customers, students, or interns. One key tip concerning disability etiquette is to always rely on common sense to guide your interactions with people with disabilities. A second key tip is to behave in the same way with people with disabilities that you would with anyone else. A third key tip is to use your best judgment and consider the personal preferences of the person with whom you are interacting. The following bullets identify disability etiquette resources:

- The Job Accommodation Network (or JAN) resource titled "A

to Z: Disability Etiquette" provides disability etiquette strategies concerning recruitment etiquette; interview etiquette; and workplace etiquette for mobility, sensory, cognitive, and psychiatric impairments.
- JAN also has a training video titled, "Disability Awareness to Increase Your Comfort, Confidence and Competence."
- The Employer Assistance and Resource Network on Disability Inclusion page titled "Working Together: Ensuring People with Disabilities Feel Welcome and Included in the Workplace" provides general guidelines and best practices to interact with people with disabilities in the workplace for various phases of employment (i.e., recruitment, hiring, retaining, and advancing) as well as for various topics such as introduce yourself, speak directly to the person, use common sense, avoid intrusive questions, focus on skills, question your assumptions, respect identity preferences, be mindful about the language you use, ask first when offering assistance, do not be afraid to talk, make accessibility a priority, and do not be afraid to make a mistake.
- Centers for Independent Living and other local disability organizations or service providers are often available to provide in-person training on disability etiquette.

Disability Scoop

Disability Scoop is the nation's largest news organization devoted to providing daily coverage of autism, intellectual disability, cerebral palsy, Down syndrome, and many other disabilities. Readers include parents, caregivers, teachers, special educators, school administrators, therapists, and other disability professionals. Experts and stories from Disability Scoop are frequently cited by the national media. Visit the Disability Scoop website at https://www.disabilityscoop.com/.

Hadley and Vision Rehabilitation

Hadley's mission is to provide both practical and social/emotional help to older adults adjusting to vision loss to empower them to adapt and thrive. Hadley offers practical help, connection and support free of charge to anyone with a visual impairment or blindness, their families, and professionals who support them on a wide variety of topics including daily living, adjusting to vision loss, recreation, technology, braille, and working. More people learn braille from Hadley than from any other organization worldwide. Hadley offers free workshops with quick, practical advice from experts; audio podcasts which are recorded audio talk shows; and discussion groups which allow attendees to listen live and chat with others who share your interests on topics including writing, crafting, books, resources, growers, technology, physical activity, travel, braille, and cooking. According to Hadley, artificial intelligence has a lot to offer people with vision loss such as describing pictures, narrating scenery, and reading menus. Visit Hadley's website at https://hadleyhelps.org/.

Hadley encourages people who are new to vision loss, their family members, and healthcare providers with patients/clients with vision loss, to explore the following four services:

1) **VisionAware/APH Connect Center:** VisionAware is a free, easy-to-use informational service for adults with low vision or blindness as well as their families, caregivers, healthcare providers, and social service professionals. It provides tips and resources about living with low vision or blindness, information on eye diseases and disorders, and a searchable, free Directory of Services. Visit VisionAware's website at https://aphconnectcenter.org/visionaware/.

2) **National Eye Institute – Vision Rehabilitation Information:** There are many different types of vision rehabilitation services that can help people with visual impairment make the most of the vision they have and improve their quality of life. Talking with your eye doctor or eye care team can help determine which types of services are best for which individuals. Examples of vision rehabilitation services include employment and job training; assistive products such as lighting and reading stands; technology such as magnifiers and screen readers; daily living and independent living skills trainings; emotional support such as counseling or support groups; and transportation and household

services. Visit the National Eye Institute's website at https://www.nei.nih.gov/ and search on *vision rehabilitation*.

3) **VA Blind and Low Vision Resources:** Veterans and active-duty service members with blindness or low vision may be able to obtain advanced vision care and rehabilitation services through the Veterans Administration (or VA) to help live independent lives. Visit the VA's website at https://www.va.gov/ and search on *blind and low vision resources*.

4) **Is Vision Rehab the Best Kept Secret:** For loss of sight, the process equivalent to physical and occupational therapy is vision rehab. Stephen Kelley, Certified Vision Rehabilitation Therapist, said it is the "best kept secret" in the Web MD article titled "Vision Rehab Helps People With Low Vision Navigate the World." Many medical professionals and patients do not know that vision rehab services exist. It does not qualify as medical and is not covered by health insurance; instead, it's considered a social service and usually funded by state agencies. The fact that vision rehab services are provided at agencies for the blind may intimidate people who are visually impaired rather than blind. The priority is to get past the obstacles and get services as soon as possible. Visit the Ophthalmic Edge at https://ophthalmicedge.org/patient/ and search on *is vision rehab the best kept secret*.

The Blind Kitchen

After Debra Erickson was diagnosed with a genetic eye disease called retinitis pigmentosa, she went to the Oregon Commission for the Blind to learn essential skills for living with vision impairment. The meal preparation classes she attended there motivated her to pursue professional culinary training at McClaskey Culinary Institute. Then she worked as an instructor teaching meal preparation for blind adults at the Oregon Commission for the Blind. When the COVID-19 pandemic hit and suspended her teaching role, she founded the Blind Kitchen which officially launched in October 2022. The Blind Kitchen offers more than 80 adaptive kitchen tools carefully selected by Debra to support vision-impaired cooks as well as any home cook with or without disabilities who want to simplify their cooking activities and optimize safety in the kitchen. Also, the Blind Kitchen is an excellent resource for tips to safely manage hot cooking and sharp tools. Its online library includes videos with audio descriptions to demonstrate how to use, wash, and store each tool along with recommendations concerning shopping, food labeling, recipes, kitchen organization, and home entertaining. Visit the Blind Kitchen's website at https://theblindkitchen.com/.

Tips for Being a Good Ally to Disabled Healthcare Workers and Trainees

According to FAQs on the Disability in Medicine Mutual Mentorship Program website, allies are individuals who actively support the rights of a minority or marginalized group without being a member of that group. Also, allies continually look within to evaluate and unlearn their own biases. Additionally, allies outwardly challenge behaviors and institutional structures that oppress marginalized groups. Allies recognize and respect that because they are not part of the minority they have committed to support, it is not in their place to speak for or over members of that minority. Allies spread the word about how best to promote inclusion and equity for these communities by promoting the ideas and preferences of its members over their own opinions. Allies combat oppressive systems using strategies and philosophies expressly endorsed by the community, rather than their own agendas or belief systems. Examples of allyship to the disabled health professional community include but are not limited to the following:

1) Educate yourself about the stereotypes and challenges people with disabilities face in and out of the clinical workplace. This includes a commitment to research these issues on your own in order to offset the burden on disabled people to educate you.
2) Listen to perspectives of disabled healthcare professionals without negating their lived experiences, should they wish to share their thoughts.

3) Evaluate yourself for and unlearning any ableist opinions you may have about people with disabilities in your personal and professional life.
4) Challenge inaccurate and pejorative comments about disabled people.
5) Act as an upstander or a supportive bystander when someone is subjected to ableist discrimination in your presence.
6) Educate your colleagues, superiors, juniors, friends, and family members about best practices for disability inclusion in healthcare and the value of instituting these practices.
7) Promote and consume the works and perspectives of disabled healthcare professionals.
8) Participate in activism at the local, state, and/or national level to advance disability inclusion in and out of healthcare.
9) Commit yourself to a career such as disability scholarship or disability law that advances the rights of people with disabilities in and out of healthcare.

Editors: Suzanne Domel Baxter and Cheryl Iny Harris

Chapter 22
Disability Statistics

By Suzanne Domel Baxter, PhD, RD, LD, FADA, FAND

This chapter summarizes disability statistics for the nation and for dietetics practitioners, and briefly explains how disabilities intersect with every demographic category.

Data Visualization – National Institute for Health Care Management Foundation

Overview of Disability

According to the National Institute for Health Care Management Foundation's "Data Visualization," 29% of US adults experience a disability. Disability prevalence by type for US adults ages 18 years and older is 14% for cognitive, 12% for mobility, 8% for independent living, 6% for hearing, 6% for vision, and 4% for self-care.

Disability Rates by Demographics

Disability rates increase as people grow older. Disability prevalence by age group is 24% for ages 18 to 44 years, 29% for ages 45 to 64 years, and 44% for ages 65+ years. Approximately 70% of adults over age 65 years develop significant long-term service and support needs before the end of their lives.

Disabilities impact people of all races, ethnicities, and genders. Disability prevalence by race and ethnicity is 18% for Asian individuals, 27% for White individuals, 31% for Black individuals, 32% for Pacific Islander individuals, 33% for Hispanic/Latinx individuals, 39% for American Indian and Alaska Native individuals, and 39% for individuals who are other/multiracial. The interaction between socioeconomic and demographic factors, such as poverty and education, contributes to these disparities.

Disability is both a cause and a consequence of poverty; people with disabilities are twice as likely to live in poverty than people without disabilities. The prevalence of people with disabilities compared to people without a self-identified disability by annual income group is:
- 17% versus 6% for less than $15,000
- 11% versus 20% for less than $25,000
- 16% versus 20% for $25,000 to less than $35,000
- 19% versus 16% for $35,000 to less than $50,000 and
- 48% versus 28% for more than $50,000.

People with disabilities experience employment and underemployment challenges. The unemployment rate for people with disabilities is about twice that of people without a self-identified disability. People with disabilities are almost twice as likely to be employed part-time than people without a self-identified disability. Also, workers with disabilities are more likely to be employed in service jobs such as foodservices and health care support, which more commonly offer part-time positions.

Health Concerns for People with Disabilities

Maintaining good health is equally important for people with and without disabilities. Many people with disabilities live healthy, active, and fulfilling lives. Disability itself is not synonymous with poor health. Yet 38% of people with disabilities have fair or poor self-reported health, compared to 8% of people without a self-identified disability.

People with disabilities experience higher rates of the following co-occurring health conditions than people without an identified disability: depression (44% versus 14%), stroke (7% versus 2%), chronic obstructive pulmonary disease (13% versus 3%), and diabetes (17% versus 8%). Chronic conditions often co-occur and can lead to disability.

Long-COVID can be defined as a disability under the ADA. People with disabilities have higher rates of long-COVID than people without a self-identified disability. Long-COVID can result in disability.

In September 2023, the National Institutes of Health designated people with disabilities as a population with health disparities. This designation aims to advance research to build evidence concerning the needs of people with disabilities, the barriers they face, and effective interventions.

Health Care Access Barriers for People with Disabilities

People with disabilities experience numerous barriers to accessing health care which can cause them to delay or forgo health care and lead to poorer health outcomes. Finances are often a barrier to health care access because people with disabilities experience financial burdens related to health care. People living with a disability are less likely to be able to see a doctor and more likely to report medical debt. Inability to see a doctor due to cost in the past 12 months is 23% for people with disabilities compared to 8% of people without a self-identified disability.

Other barriers to health care access experienced by people with disabilities are negative attitudes and discrimination. Structural ableism, which can include discrimination and implicit and explicit biases towards people with disabilities, denies people with disabilities access to social and health care resources and leads to health inequities. Stereotyping occurs when assumptions are made that people with disabilities are unhealthy, lazy, or that their quality of life is poor or not valued. Stigma and discrimination occur when disability is perceived as something that needs to be cured or assumptions are made that behaviors and actions need to conform with social expectations. These negative attitudes and discrimination impact health care in several ways. Only 41% of physicians are very confident about providing the same quality of care for people with disabilities as for people without disabilities. Thirty-two percent of adults with disabilities reported unfair treatment in health care settings compared to only 10% of adults without disabilities. Diagnostic overshadowing occurs when health conditions and symptoms are misattributed to an underlying disability and can impact the timeliness and quality of care for people with disabilities.

Additional barriers to health care access experienced by people with disabilities are transportation and physical barriers. For example, people with disabilities often face lack of access to transportation. There is often inaccessible delivery of care because medical and diagnostic equipment is not accessible. Most doctor's offices lack height-adjustable exam tables as well as weight scales and mammography chairs for people who use wheelchairs. Often architectural barriers such as steps, curbs, and narrow doorways prevent mobility into and around health care facilities. Reception areas often have countertops that are high and thus inaccessible for people who use wheelchairs.

Other barriers to health care access for people with disabilities concern communication. For example, there can be a lack of language accommodations, such as sign language interpreters, closed captioning for people with hearing disabilities, and clear face masks for people who read lips. People with blindness or vision impairments often encounter barriers such as the lack of large-print, Braille, or screen-reader accessible versions of health care materials. People with cognitive disabilities often experience barriers such as the use of technical language, long sentences, and words with many syllables by health care practitioners.

Additional barriers to health care access for people with disabilities concern policies and programs. Policy barriers include a lack of enforcement or awareness of existing laws and regulations, such as not complying with the ADA. Program barriers limit the effective delivery of health care programs, such as inconvenient scheduling and insufficient time for medical exams.

Strategies to Support Health and Well-being of People with Disabilities

People with disabilities should benefit from all of the same health, well-being, and community engagement opportunities available to people without disabilities. The following bullets summarize numerous strategies to support the health and well-being of people with disabilities:

- **Community Integration:** Make health care services available to people with disabilities in their homes and communities rather than in institutional settings. Make it possible for

people with disabilities to interact with people of their choice in the most inclusive environments possible. Ensure equal opportunities for work, socialization, and other activities within the broader community.
- **Public Health Promotion:** Utilize prevention efforts to prevent disease and support the health and wellness of people with disabilities such as tailored education and counseling programs that promote physical well-being, improve nutrition, and encourage annual screenings using plain language and accessible materials.
- **Data and Research:** Improve disability data collection by designating it as a core demographic element. Expand and enhance research of health disparities for people with disabilities to inform interventions. Partner with the disability community on research and data collection.
- **Build Capacity within the Health Care System:** Develop the workforce by training health care providers in disability awareness, inclusion, person-centeredness, and cultural competency with involvement from people with disabilities. Improve the accessibility of health care facilities by recognizing and understanding barriers for people with disabilities at every point of a health care visit to prioritize solutions, inclusion, and improve usability.
- **Improve Inclusion:** Reduce bias by ensuring nondiscrimination and eliminating the stereotype that people with disabilities are unhealthy and unworthy. Utilize policy and legislation by leveraging existing federal laws and policies to reduce barriers to health care and community and improve disability data. Utilize universal design to make health care services usable and accessible to everyone through simple and intuitive design. Provide reasonable accommodations by modifying existing health care processes and physical environments to increase access and participation of people with disabilities. Involve people with disabilities by prioritizing input from people with disabilities throughout all aspects of programming and research.

Intersectionality of Disabilities with Demographics

Disabilities are influenced by multiple, overlapping identities and intersect with every demographic category and shape experiences. Understanding the intersectionality of disabilities with demographics promotes equity and inclusivity and helps to address the specific needs that disabled people experience. The following bullets summarize key aspects of intersectionality with disabilities:

- **Race and Ethnicity:** Disabled people of color often experience unique barriers such as systemic racism and limited access to resources which can intensify the challenges of being disabled.
- **Gender and Sexual Orientation:** Disabled women may experience gender-specific issues such as greater rates of discrimination and violence and challenges concerning reproductive health care. Disabled LGBTQ+ people may experience discrimination related to being disabled and their sexual orientation which can impact their mental health and access to healthcare services.
- **Socioeconomic Status:** Disabled people of lower socioeconomic status may have decreased access to healthcare, education, and employment opportunities which intensify the challenges of living with disabilities.
- **Age:** For people with disabilities, social inclusion strategies must evolve to meet the changing needs and societal expectations with age at each stage of life. (Social inclusion is the process of improving the terms on which individuals and groups, especially those who are disadvantaged or marginalized, take part in society.) For example, for children and youth with disabilities, social inclusion focuses on education and social integration with peers. For young adults with disabilities, social inclusion emphasizes higher education, employment, and independent living. For middle-aged adults with disabilities, social inclusion focuses on workplace inclusion, economic participation, and family roles. For older adults with disabilities, social inclusion focuses on preventing isolation, addressing age-related health issues, and ensuring access to care.

- **Geography:** Living in urban versus rural areas influences access to transportation, healthcare, and community support and impacts how disabled people navigate their daily lives.

Compensation and Benefits Survey of the Dietetics Profession, 2024

The Academy of Nutrition and Dietetics (or Academy) has completed this survey every other year since 2002. The 2024 survey was conducted across a probability sample drawn from the population of domestic Academy members (n = 39,904) plus domestic nonmembers (n = 74,571) maintaining current registration as a Registered Dietitian/Registered Dietitian Nutritionist or Nutrition and Dietetics Technician, Registered/Dietetic Technician, Registered. Data was collected from March 11 through April 18, 2024. The response rate was 12% with 5,652 usable responses received from the sample of 46,646 practitioners.

The demographic profile of dietetics practitioners has been essentially unchanged since 2007. Results from the 2024 survey showed that dietetics practitioners were 7% Hispanic heritage, and 10% indicated a race other than White (5% Asian, 2% Black/African American, and 3% some other race). In other words, more than 80% of the dietetics workforce is white. This is a major problem because foods eaten and preparation methods are influenced by culture which includes race/ethnicity as well as disability.

Beginning in 2019 several disability/health-related questions were added to the survey instrument due to inquiries by the co-founders of the Disabilities MIG. The 2024 survey results showed that only a small percentage of practitioners indicated they have a long-lasting condition. Specifically, only 1% reported having a condition that substantially limits one or more basic physical activities such as walking, climbing stairs, reaching, lifting, or carrying and 1% reported having blindness, deafness, or a severe vision or hearing impairment; overall, 2% indicated at least one of these. Due to a physical, mental, or emotional condition lasting six months or more, 5% reported having had difficulty learning, remembering, or concentrating, 2% reported having had difficulty working at a job or business, and 1% reported having had difficulty going outside the home alone to shop or visit a doctor's office; overall, 6% indicated difficulty doing at least one of these.

Results from the 2024 survey are included in this chapter on disability statistics so readers are aware of the crucial need for a workforce that includes more dietetics practitioners with disabilities to counsel, educate, and treat the 29% of adults with disabilities in the US in addition to the children with disabilities in the US.

Chapter 23
Concluding Remarks

By Suzanne Domel Baxter, PhD, RD, LD, FADA, FAND

Thank you so much for taking time to read this book! Hopefully, you agree that it has earned its title of "Credentialed Dietetics Practitioners with Disabilities Get the Job Done!" If you are a person with one or more disabilities and searching for a career, will you please consider the dietetics profession? It is crucial to diversify the dietetics workforce by increasing the number of credentialed dietetics practitioners with disabilities and from different races, ethnicities, and genders.

If there is considerable interest in this book, the hope and desire is to self-publish one or more additional editions with autobiographies by different sets of credentialed dietetics practitioners with disabilities!

About the Editors

Suzanne ("Suzi") Domel Baxter, PhD, RD, LD, FADA, FAND worked as a dietitian in a residential school for children with disabilities; in a hospital clinic for adults; in school food service; for the Women, Infants, and Children Program; and in nutrition research. She acquired a mobility disability in 2010 which caused her to resign her Research Professor position late in 2016. She has presented widely on nutrition and authored many peer-reviewed publications including several on disability. She is now a disability advocate. She co-founded the Disabilities in Nutrition and Dietetics Member Interest Group within the Academy of Nutrition and Dietetics. This group launched on June 1, 2023, with her as the Inaugural Chair; she is now its Past Chair. Her illustrated children's book *"When I Grow Up, I Can Be a Dietitian!"* was published in 2024. Her disability autobiography is found in Chapter 6.

Suzi

Cheryl

Cheryl Iny Harris, MPH, RD is a private practice dietitian based in Virginia who specializes in digestive disorders. She was recognized as one of the top nutritionists in the DC metro area by the *Washingtonian* and was selected as the "Emerging Dietetics Leader of the Year" for Virginia. She has presented widely on nutrition and authored several peer-reviewed publications on Ehlers Danlos syndrome, POTS, Mast Cell Diseases and on living with disabilities. Her disability autobiography is found in Chapter 16.

www.ingramcontent.com/pod-product-compliance
Lightning Source LLC
Chambersburg PA
CBHW060454030426
42337CB00015B/1585